"Corbett's *The Art of Character* is no 'how to' book or 'writing by numbers' manual. It is an artful testament to the writer's credo—that a story is only as affecting and meaningful as the characters who tell it—that writing, essentially, *is* character. Corbett writes with the grace and authority of a seasoned professional, but offers much more than the usual inventory of method and strategy. With clarity and compassion, he gets to the very thing that lies deep within us, that longing we share to discover that one distinct and authentic voice. *The Art of Character* is itself a work of art, an indispensable resource for writers of any genre, and a pedagogical tool for teachers of writing at any level."

—Elizabeth Brundage, bestselling author of
A Stranger Like You and *The Doctor's Wife*

"David Corbett has combined his unique talents as a gifted writer and an extraordinary teacher to create a superb resource on character development. Suitable for beginners to bestselling authors, *The Art of Character* should be on every serious writer's shelf next to Strunk and White's *The Elements of Style*, Anne Lamott's *Bird by Bird*, and Stephen King's *On Writing*."

—Sheldon Siegel, *New York Times* bestselling author of
Perfect Alibi and *Incriminating Evidence*

"I once made the mistake of writing a story with David Corbett. The man smoked me. He can delineate the character and personality of an accordion in three strokes. Imagine what he can do with people. This act of generosity and wisdom from a very good writer will help anyone who is staring at a blank page, any day, any time. Highly recommended."

—Luis Alberto Urrea, Pulitzer finalist and bestselling author
of *Queen of America* and *The Hummingbird's Daughter*

"Both inspiring and practical, *The Art of Character* belongs on every writer's shelf. David Corbett brilliantly illustrates those elusive tools writers need to breathe life into their characters."

—Cara Black, bestselling author of
Murder at the Lanterne Rouge

"As thorough an examination of character and what it means as you're likely to find. This is an exploration of the phenomenon of character—in as wide a variety of fiction and drama as there is. It will help any writer create and sustain human beings who make you forget you're reading, who are alive, who are worthy of our attention and sympathy."

—Robert Bausch, prizewinning author of *Out of Season*

"Writers—pay attention! *The Art of Character* is a tremendously useful and important book. David Corbett delivers in-depth analysis and practical wisdom on every page."

—Sam Barry, author of *Write That Book Already! The Tough Love You Need to Get Published Now*

"Character is the beating heart of fiction, and with *The Art of Character* novelist David Corbett has written a clear, in-depth, and highly entertaining exploration of how to create remarkable characters. This is an essential guide to students of the writer's craft at all levels." —Mark Haskell Smith, author of *Baked*

PENGUIN BOOKS

THE ART OF CHARACTER

David Corbett is the author of four novels: *The Devil's Redhead*, *Done for a Dime* (a *New York Times* Notable Book), *Blood of Paradise* (nominated for numerous awards, including the Edgar), and *Do They Know I'm Running?* His short fiction and poetry have appeared in numerous journals and anthologies, including *Mission and Tenth*, *The Smoking Poet*, *San Francisco Noir*, and *Best American Mystery Stories* (2009 and 2011). He has taught both online and in classroom settings through the UCLA Extension's Writers' Program, Book Passage, LitReactor, 826 Valencia, The Grotto in San Francisco, and at numerous writing conferences across the United States.

THE
ART
OF
CHARACTER

Creating Memorable Characters
for Fiction, Film, and TV

DAVID CORBETT

PENGUIN BOOKS

PENGUIN BOOKS
Published by the Penguin Group
Penguin Group (USA) Inc., 375 Hudson Street,
New York, New York 10014, U.S.A.
Penguin Group (Canada), 90 Eglinton Avenue East, Suite 700,
Toronto, Ontario M4P 2Y3, Canada (a division of Pearson Penguin Canada Inc.)
Penguin Books Ltd, 80 Strand, London WC2R 0RL, England
Penguin Ireland, 25 St Stephen's Green, Dublin 2, Ireland
(a division of Penguin Books Ltd)
Penguin Group (Australia), 707 Collins Street, Melbourne,
Victoria 3008, Australia (a division of Pearson Australia Group Pty Ltd)
Penguin Books India Pvt Ltd, 11 Community Centre,
Panchsheel Park, New Delhi – 110 017, India
Penguin Group (NZ), 67 Apollo Drive, Rosedale, Auckland 0632,
New Zealand (a division of Pearson New Zealand Ltd)
Penguin Books (South Africa), Rosebank Office Park, 181 Jan Smuts Avenue,
Parktown North 2193, South Africa
Penguin China, B7 Jiaming Center, 27 East Third Ring Road North,
Chaoyang District, Beijing 100020, China

Penguin Books Ltd, Registered Offices:
80 Strand, London WC2R 0RL, England

First published in Penguin Books 2013

5 7 9 10 8 6 4

LIBRARY OF CONGRESS CATALOGING IN PUBLICATION DATA
Corbett, David, date.
The art of character : creating memorable characters for fiction,
film, and tv / David Corbett.
p. cm.
Includes bibliographical references.
ISBN 978-0-14-312157-2 (pbk.)
1. Fiction—Technique.   2. Characters and characteristics in literature.
3. Creative writing.   I. Title.
PN3383.C4C67 2013
808.3—dc23
2012031265

Printed in the United States of America
Set in Janson Text
Designed by Spring Hoteling

For Mary Elizabeth Corbett:
In fond and grateful memory

When writing a novel a writer should create living people; people not characters. A *character* is a caricature. If a writer can make people live there may be no great characters in his book, but it is possible that his book will remain as a whole; as an entity; as a novel. . . . People in a novel, not skillfully constructed *characters*, must be projected from the writer's assimilated experience, from his knowledge, from his head, from his heart and from all there is of him. If ever he has luck as well as seriousness and gets them out entire they will have more than one dimension and they will last for a long time.

—Ernest Hemingway, *Death in the Afternoon*

CONTENTS

PART III
Roles | 207

Chapter 17
Meaning and Its Messenger:
The Protagonist and the Premise | 209

Choosing the Protagonist

Summoning the Will

Framing the Conflict—the Protagonist and the Premise

Working Backward—Conceiving the Premise from the Abstract
to the Specific

The Personal Nature of the Premise

Chapter 18
The Challenge of Change:
Three Protagonist Questions | 226

The Mysterious Necessity of Change

What of the So-Called Steadfast Character?

Distinguishing Growth from Transformation

Can I Get What I Want?

Who Am I?

What Do I Have to Change About Myself to Get What I Want?

Chapter 19
Ciphers, Stiffs, and Sleepwalkers:
Protagonist Problems | 250

When the Protagonist's Struggle Is Fundamentally Internal

When the Protagonist Doesn't Know or Is Confused by What
She Wants, or Is Afraid to Want It

When the Protagonist Faces a Problem, an Enigma,
or a Disaster Instead of an Opponent

When the Interconnection Between Outer Goal and Inner Need
Is Insufficiently Realized

When the Protagonist Is Conceived as a Vessel of Virtue
(or the Myth of the Likable Hero)

ACKNOWLEDGMENTS

No writer works in true isolation, and no book appears solely from his effort alone. I owe a debt of profound gratitude to my longtime agent, Laurie Fox, and all the people at Penguin who worked so tirelessly to shape this book into its final form, especially Rebecca Hunt, Taylor Sperry, Katherine Griggs, Cathy Dexter, Ann Marie Damian, Ben Petrone, Stephen Morrison, and Kathryn Court. Leslie Schwerin, filmmaker and friend, read portions of the text in manuscript form and made invaluable suggestions. Mark Tavani has provided considerable support, editorial advice, and simple fellowship over the years, without which my career would have developed quite differently. Fellow writers whose work and teaching have influenced the ideas and techniques presented in this book are too numerous to mention, but those who made specific, direct contributions include most notably Donna Levin, Reed Farrel Coleman, Alexandra Sokoloff, Hallie Ephron, D. P. Lyle, Jim Frey, Elizabeth George, Joyce Maynard, Robert Bausch, Kim

Addonizio, Tom Jenks, and the inimitable Gil Dennis. I'm also indebted to the following people and programs for providing me a venue for my teaching: Linda Venis at the UCLA Extension Writers' Program; Jane Ganahl and Janis Cooke Newman at the San Francisco Writers' Grotto; Karen West, Leslie Berkler, Sheldon Siegel, Jacqueline Winspear, and the three Petrocellis—Elaine, Bill, and Kathryn—at Book Passage; Dennis Widmyer, Mark Vanderpool, and Kara Kilgore at LitReactor; the late Oakley Hall and the extended Hall clan at the Squaw Valley Writers Conference; Ana Manwaring at the Napa Valley Community College; and Maureen Eppstein, Katy Pye, and everyone at the Mendocino Coast Writers Conference. I also need to thank my students and clients, who have taught and helped me at least as much as I've taught and helped them. And last, a word of gratitude is owed Mette Hansen-Karademir, my partner and friend, whose loving support, companionship, and patience sustain me in more ways than I can express.

INTRODUCTION

One can acquire everything in solitude—except
character.

—Stendhal, *De l'amour*

Every story worth telling in some way mirrors our lives,
and to that extent explores four key questions:

Who am I?
Where do I come from?
Where am I going?
*What does it mean?**

Note that I use the word "explores," not "answers."
Storytelling is an art. It can't provide scientific certainty
and it shouldn't try. Though there is considerable craft to
fiction—this book wouldn't exist if that weren't true—it
remains rooted far more in searching than in finding, more

---

* I've inherited this set of questions from the novelist Reed Farrel
Coleman, who shared them during a salon in Berkeley, California, in
July 2010. These questions are hardly unique to fiction, of course. Paul
Gauguin titled his perhaps most famous painting *Where Do We Come
From? What Are We? Where Are We Going?*

wedded to the hypothetical "what if" than any conclusive QED.

As long as we're alive, the question of who we are and how we should live remains open. No one convinces us less than the person who crows, "I have the answer." And ironically, this is precisely why fiction provides a more satisfying depiction of human life than any scientific or otherwise theoretical rendering can offer.

This open-ended quality to life also explains why desire is so central to the exploration of character. As we learned from the very first storybook tales we heard, human want can inspire the indifferent, betray the foolish, and undo the steadfast. And nothing is more ephemeral (or self-deluded) than satisfaction; our wants rise up continuously, propelling us through the hours and days and weeks and years. Though most stories conclude with a gratifying resolution, even a child can intimate an unsettling sense of continuation to the journey in even the most final of endings, the inescapable presence of an implicit "And then . . ." Or the more ominous "And yet . . ."

The importance of character to story lies in this open-endedness at the core of our lives. Stories that emphasize ideas or problems—the conundrums of philosophy, the lessons of history, the truths of science, the consolations of religion—invariably hit rough sailing the further they drift from the shore of character. Ideas too often serve as a digression from the messy stuff of life—ourselves, each other. For some they provide a kind of false salvation. But the core reality of life remains: We die. Ideas, no matter how "eternal," can't save us. And because we can only honestly stand on one side of death, we can never know for certain how our lives will turn out, which is why we experience our existence most profoundly in the interrogative mode, situated in a world premised on, as Constantin Stanislavski put it, the magical "What if?"

The craft of characterization is an attempt to honor and explore the truth of human nature through the art of storytelling. We see in our characters reflections of ourselves, which is why we detect in their stories, no matter how fanciful or dark or grand, an attempt to better understand our lives. And what else is there to discuss, really, than our lives?

Where concept can give us the general outline of a story—the setting and situation, the fundamental problem, the moral dilemma—it's through character that we bring the general down to earth. Characters infuse a story with conviction, nail it to the mysterious details of daily life by revealing the unique and inimitable ways people get things done, the beliefs that guide them and the errors that betray them, their crucial decisions, their hopeless failings, their critical deeds.

Each of us, as the character Murray Burns puts it in the film *A Thousand Clowns*, is trying to reach some understanding of the "subtle, sneaky, important reason why he was born a human being and not a chair." As sagacious as this may sound, it's fundamentally a question of character. The answer lies not in what we believe but what we do. In the stories that affect us most profoundly—whether taken from myth, the Bible, Greek tragedy, Renaissance drama, the novel, postmodern fiction, film, TV—it's the characters that linger most tenaciously in the mind. In some "subtle, sneaky, important" way, they are us.

This book is the result of my own approach to characterization as developed through the writing of numerous stories and several novels, an approach that has evolved to embrace the insight embodied in the quote from Stendhal that began this Introduction: Character is not created in isolation or repose; it's forged through interaction with others and the world. Even in solitary struggles of endurance, such as arduous physical ordeals or battles with illness, there is a contest at the heart of the matter, between the part of us that would surrender and the part that continues on.

The other main distinctive or innovative approaches addressed in this book include:

- Comprehending your characters begins with an honest, unflinching understanding of yourself.

- Scenes, in which characters engage meaningfully and in conflict with each other, are crucial at *all* stages of character development: conception, development, and portrayal. Character biographies created from scenes are intrinsically more useful than those consisting of mere information.

- A clear visual image of a character is a beginning, not an end. If you restrict yourself to a visual image in your "mind's eye," you risk contemplating the character like an idea, rather than forging an intuitive engagement with him.

- An intuitive grasp of your character is formed by exploring scenes of profound emotional import—moments of overwhelming shame, joy, fear, pride, regret, forgiveness.

- Developing a character with genuine depth requires a focus on not just desire but how the character deals with frustration of her desires, as well as her vulnerabilities, her secrets, and especially her contradictions. This development needs to be forged in scenes, the better to employ your intuition rather than your intellect.

- This reliance on intuition provides the best way to respond meaningfully to what I call the Tyranny of Motive: the need to understand what a character wants and why he behaves a certain way. Without an intuitive grasp of the characters, you can all too easily fall into the trap of reducing them to simplistic automatons or "plot puppets," acting in accordance with ideas or story necessities rather than behaving with the complexity of intention that real individuals possess.

- A character can undergo change through either growth or transformation, which can be distinguished by determining to what extent the character exhibits not just strength of will but insight in overcoming a personal limitation.

- Character arcs fall within a spectrum based on which protagonist question they most directly pose:

  - Can I Get What I Want?
  - Who Am I? or

- What Do I Have to Change About Myself
  to Get What I Want?

There is of course a great deal more within these pages, so much so that it may seem daunting. But you can keep from feeling overwhelmed by thinking of this book as a kind of tool kit. Just as no one uses every tool he owns in the course of any project, so should no one consider employing more than what's necessary for the task at hand: bringing a given character to life and rendering him on the page.

This is equally true whether one is working in fiction, film, or TV. The writer outside of academia who can devote herself solely to novels and short stories is a rarity, if not quite an anachronism. It is therefore important to understand both the commonalities in characterization for the various media as well as the distinctions.

In truth, the former are far more numerous than the latter. Novels provide more opportunity for the depiction of inner life, while films and TV demand far more from dialog and action, but beyond that, much of the work in developing vivid, compelling characters is the same—which is the good news and the bad news. There are no shortcuts.

There are, however, dead ends, wrong turns, and long ways around. To avoid them, think of the various areas we're about to cover as opportunities, not necessities. Doing more than that can burden the story, tempting you, after so much work, to shoehorn in the many details you've so meticulously fleshed out, bogging the narrative down with gratuitous scenes, flashbacks, or "insights."

There is perhaps no more crucial discipline in writing than acquiring the intuitive sense of what's necessary and what's not. In characterization, this means developing an ear and eye for when the character has quickened to life on the page and thus engaged the reader, and not belaboring the matter beyond that, no matter how lovely our words. It remains a sad but essential truth that there are, indeed, darlings who must die. Some deserve it more than others, but in all cases it's best to go about the business ruthlessly, and let your grief be short-lived.

More easily said than done, I realize, especially in the realm of character, where our creations do indeed at times seem to possess a life of their own. And that's exactly what we're after. What every writer hopes for—one might even say requires—is a full embodiment of his characters within his imagination, until they seem less like creations than companions.

I realize this makes writing sound like a quasi-functional neurosis, or at least a kind of controlled hallucination—or professional daydreaming. But at some point in your life you've felt that curious, ineffable stirring in your imagination—the shapeless volition that seems to both arise from within and yet come from elsewhere, that pulse of urgency we somewhat crudely refer to as the creative impulse. It's why you're reading these words. You may even believe it's why you're alive. You craft stories. Characters—whether they're demons or angels, apparitions or simply mental stuff—are your inescapable cohorts. This book will help you engage them with greater confidence and deeper insight.

THE ART OF CHARACTER

PART I

Conceiving the Character

Chapter One
Fingering Smoke:
Are Characters Created or Discovered?

Michelangelo believed he was liberating his sculptures from the marble in which they were imprisoned; the true creator, in his mind, was God. The playwright Martin McDonagh experienced something similar. During the six-month outpouring in which he wrote all of his major plays, his characters felt like emanations hovering in the room, jabbering at him so incessantly he had to tell them to shut up long enough so he could jot down their words.

In contrast, Jackson Pollock continued thrashing, dripping, and smearing paint against his canvases until a critical, eerie, ineffable moment when something inside him said: Stop. Translating that to fiction, imagine the writer starting with something very much like Pollock's blank canvas—the empty page—and gradually, through trial and error and persistent refinement, beginning to see something both surprising and yet recognizable that clarifies as the work continues.

The first method seems to point toward discovery, the second toward creation. But both approaches have their issues.

Assume we create our characters the way Pollock created his canvases. How can we be sure we'll ultimately experience that intuitive sense of completion that Pollock felt? How do we know when to stop? There's an apocryphal story about John Coltrane, who late in his career confided to Miles Davis that he was having greater and greater difficulty knowing when to end his solos. Davis supposedly replied, "Put the horn down, John."

That's not the only problem. If we do create our characters—fashion them from a few physical details, some biographical data, a touch of style—how do we explain Martin McDonagh's jabbering hobgoblins? And isn't that what every writer hopes for, the full embodiment of her characters within her imagination, as though they possess willfulness, independence: a life of their own?

But believing we discover our characters is hardly unproblematic. Unless we possess Michelangelo's or Martin McDonagh's gifts, it may not always be clear how to recognize what it is we're searching for. Like scavengers hunting a shipwreck rumored to lie on the ocean floor, we may spend a lifetime looking through the dark stillness only to come up empty.

Myth suggests at least something of an approach; it presupposes a realm where the personified ambitions, fears, hopes, and suspicions of mankind reside. Whether one calls that realm the psyche or the Collective Unconscious or Valhalla, what we think of as characters in our stories, if sufficiently meaningful and profound, seemingly glimmer with the aura of that otherworld.

But how does one work with such things? It's entirely possible that the act of writing serves as an incantation, beckoning the Muse, who in turn lures these evanescent beings we call our characters—which are in fact archetypes—out of the inner darkness over which she reigns. This can be both a consoling and terrifying view of the matter. But inspiration often alternates between consolation and terror.

Even at its most realistic, art remains an approach to the mysterious, and working with the depiction of human life can often seem particularly tricky—like fingering smoke.

But even if I can picture my characters vividly in my mind's eye, hear their voices with perfect pitch, observe them prancing about of their own volition, that doesn't guarantee I've come up with anything unique or even interesting. A great many characters have leapt fully formed from their creator's imagination precisely because they were facile, predictable, clichéd—or thinly disguised borrowings from other books or films. Whatever else can be said of characterization, it is absolutely true that if a portrayal falls flat, it's not the character's fault.

For all but a lucky few, writing requires more than taking dictation from imaginary beings. But you can't just slap a few details together and call it a character, either.

We have to be ready not just to bear witness but to engage the imagination, to ask penetrating, even embarrassing questions of our characters, to mold them, remold them, defy them, even destroy and resurrect them while still maintaining that curious capability to step back, to allow them once again to escape our grasp—dust themselves off, as it were—and reassert their enigmatic independence.

This dialog between deliberate and spontaneous, intentional and unknowable, conscious and unconscious—creation and discovery—is the pulse, the inhalation and exhalation, of the work we call making art.

Speaking personally, I find that a character first takes form as an impression, usually indistinct but sometimes quite clear, as when the impression arises from a real person, or a distinct image such as a photograph.

Even when the initial impression is visually or emotionally distinct, I still know little or nothing about how the character will behave. I learn these things by writing key scenes that evoke conflict, desire and vulnerability, fear and shame, pride and love, gradually crafting something that, while not distinct from my initial impression, is nonetheless more subtle, complex, emotionally engaging, and dramatically interesting.

In short, I alternate between acts of discovery and creation. Through the activity of writing I forge an impression that provides fodder for further development by my unconscious. What returns to me the morning after I "put the horn down" for the day is often richer and more concrete than what I left behind—but only if I supply the necessary raw material.

William James* remarked that we learn how to skate

---

* *Principles of Psychology*, chapter 4, "Habit."

in the summer and how to swim in the winter. By this he meant that only after arduous and often futile conscious effort does our unconscious have what it needs to help us solve a new and difficult problem—a problem we will, ironically, solve once we step away from it. The same is true of characterization. Only by diligent and often frustrating effort, working out the specifics of a character's history, circumstances, and situation, can we supply the unconscious with the raw material it needs, raw material it will fashion into something less clumsy and deliberate, more organic— like the intuition we carry about another person.

In a sense, the work of characterization recalls the story of Geppetto the woodcutter. As writers, we start with a bit of raw material that interests us, and work at it day and night, not just deliberately and attentively but lovingly, until finally, like Pinocchio, through some strange paradox, that bit of material takes on a life of its own.

As for archetypes, I remain a bit of a skeptic. If they work for you, by all means use them. Artists are magpies; we gather up all manner of curious stuff. But mythic heft doesn't come cheap. You can identify a character as Mentor or Trickster, Warrior or Lost Soul, Shadow or Herald, but dramatic urgency isn't created by nomenclature. Too often, such terms just become new rags draped on the same old scarecrow. Even if such catchwords evoke a kind of symbolic or mythic resonance, that doesn't create desire— and desire is what prompts action, and action defines character. Without deep creative imagining and intuitive engagement, a character based on an idea will remain an idea, whether that inspiring thought arose from an ancient heroic saga or something Aunt Milly said. But if you dig beneath the clutter of words and concepts to where the wildness stirs—the depths of your own reckless heart—the myth business will take care of itself.

Exercises

1. Pick two characters from a piece you're working on. Make a point of noting specifically where your impression of them rests at the end of each working day. The next morning, before you begin to write, revisit each character in your mind's eye. Do you hear or see—or better yet, feel—the character differently? Does she suggest an ability to act in a way she didn't when you last visited her? Keep track of your progress over time. How has your intuition of the character evolved? How much of this transformation seems to be the result of your own deliberate work—i.e., creation? How much feels like discovery—i.e., seems to have emerged unconsciously?

Chapter Two
Summoning Ghosts:
Source Materials for Characters

In general, characters arise from five main sources:

- The story
- The unconscious
- Inspiration from art, music, or nature
- Real people
- Composite characters

Each source has its own unique advantages and disadvantages, and limitations in one approach can be mitigated by combining it with others.

More important, a source for a character is just that—a beginning. No first impression, even if wildly inspiring, tells the whole tale. One of the most common errors in characterization is becoming wedded to the emotional, moral, or psychological impact the source for a character first creates. This results in elaboration of the character, not development. Sooner or later, more of the same, no matter how baroquely imagined or beautifully written, stops being interesting. A character who develops is obliged to change, and that requires a capacity to surprise, to contradict that first impression in significant but still credible ways.

Like many of the techniques I describe in this book, these sources for characters should be regarded as opportunities, not obligations. Over time, you may find certain techniques more generally reliable, insightful, or worthwhile—but try to avoid knee-jerk routine. Writing requires a constant pursuit, if not embrace, of the unfamiliar, the foreign, the uncomfortable—and creativity often begins only once we leave our comfort zones.

The Story as the Source for One's Characters

Writers overwhelmingly derive their characters from their story ideas, which can be problematic, since such characters can often be flat or two-dimensional—steely housewives, bitter cops, romantic narcissists, hustlers with a soft spot for kids—the kind of character often derided as a plot puppet.

Such characters more likely fill a role than act as independent agents with needs and fears and affections and concerns "outside the story." Characters are not cogs in the machine of your narrative; it's better to think of them as human beings to whom the story happens.

Consider the following three examples of story ideas:

A Japanese businessman is invited to a birthday party in his honor at the home of the vice president of a small, impoverished Latin American country. The only reason the businessman, an avid opera lover, attends is that his hosts have wisely invited his favorite soprano. During the party, however, guerrillas take over the villa, and the businessman and the soprano become the key hostages in a prolonged standoff.

During the siege of Leningrad in World War II, a starving seventeen-year-old is condemned to death for pilfering chocolate and cognac from a dead German paratrooper. His reprieve comes in the form of a hopeless challenge presented by an NKVD colonel: Teamed up with a charismatic army deserter, the young man has one week to find a dozen eggs for the colonel's daughter's wedding cake.

A detective dedicated to never being fooled again gets tricked into exposing a phony adulterous affair. When he tries to find out who set him up, he uncovers one of the largest land scandals in U.S. history—and rediscovers his own humanity beneath the arrogant, cynical husk in which he's entombed it.

Respectively, these are the core story ideas for the novel *Bel Canto* by Ann Patchett, the novel *City of Thieves* by David Benioff, and the film *Chinatown*.

As it stands, these are mere sketches. To take them to the next level, a deeper understanding is needed of not just the characters who are identified but the other, as yet unknown characters required to make the stories come to life. This is, in fact, how stories get built from a core idea—with a catalog and examination of the people who populate the story's world.

Ann Patchett found inspiration for *Bel Canto* in the 1997 hostage standoff at the Japanese embassy in Lima, Peru, but few books in recent memory more perfectly exemplify the expansion of a relatively simple idea into a fully realized world. The book offers many rewards—an intriguing situation, an exotic setting, elegant writing, deft storytelling— but arguably none of these can compete with the loving examination of the characters who inhabit its pages.

The Japanese industrialist, Katsumi Hosokawa, first comes to life in his remembrance of another birthday, his eleventh, when he sat in the dark beside his father and gained entrance to the passion and sensual extravagance of opera through Verdi's *Rigoletto*. And the impact of that revelation, the lifelong love affair it spawned, along with his helpless devotion to the soprano, Roxanne Coss, inspire in this otherwise unassuming salaryman a capacity for heroic sacrifice, something that feels both shocking and inevitable.

Hosokawa's work requires a translator, and Patchett delivers Gen Watanabe, the selfless facilitator, so quick to help others, so baffled by his own wants; he speaks a broad range of languages with dutiful fluency, though his Swedish is limited to only "the darkest of subjects," for he learned it watching Ingmar Bergman films.

Roxanne Coss, petite and red-haired, takes the stage with all the narcissistic petulance of a matinee diva, flustered by the irritating devotion of her doomed accompanist and convinced the guerrillas will release her—they must, she's the soprano—but as time passes, her voice transforms the very nature of life in the barricaded mansion, not just for her fellow captives but also for the guerrillas, and she takes deeper measure of her gift, as well as of her heart.

I could go on, for the cast is large, with each character delivered with exquisite specificity, a richness of detail that testifies to the author's refusal to be held hostage by her idea.

City of Thieves owes much of its setting and general background to two books that chronicle, in much different ways, the terrible privations inflicted on the residents of Leningrad by the German siege of that city: Harrison Salisbury's *The 900 Days* and Curzio Malaparte's *Kaputt*. And though those sources may have given the author some help with his characters, the precision of detail with which he captures Lev, the luckless, fearful, starving seventeen-year-old, and his flamboyant companion, the sex-crazed and literarily ambitious Kolya, could only come from examination not just of circumstances but of human nature. Lev's desperate desire to lose his virginity, sniffed out instantly by Kolya, whose obsession with the fairer sex is boundless—and who can't help himself from giving unsolicited advice—provides a comically poignant counterpoint to the deathly strangeness of their mission. Kolya's coy obsession with an obscure novel that turns out to be the book he himself is writing—*The Courtyard Hound*—provides him a delicately textured need for Lev's approval that binds the two young men together in a way a strict devotion to the demands of the plot might never suggest. Most important, Kolya's reckless daring, expressed as a kind of detached amusement, as though the horrors of the war aren't really happening, inspires in Lev the courage he's previously felt lacking and will call upon at a crucial moment.

Again, the source materials can provide only so much, no matter how rich or extensive. Imagination and empathy—an engagement with not just the facts of the situation but the wants and fears and strengths of the characters—are what ultimately render the story true to life.

Robert Towne, who wrote the screenplay for *Chinatown*, based his story on the "Rape of the Owens Valley," a scandal in which speculators made millions on the 233-mile aqueduct that brought water to the outer reaches of Los Angeles, while the farmers who lived and worked in the surrounding region were driven off the land and ruined. Towne based the character of Hollis Mulwray on William Mulholland, the engineer responsible not just for the aqueduct but for the St. Francis Dam that failed, resulting in the deaths of nearly 500 people. The notion of using Chinatown as a metaphor for the inscrutable nature of reality was inspired by a detective Towne met who worked in that section of Los Angeles, and who offered a remark the screenwriter borrowed wholesale for the film: When asked what he did in Chinatown, the detective replied, "As little as possible," because nothing was ever as it seemed.

All of that provides a pretty rich vein of material to mine, but putting ourselves in Towne's shoes, knowing we need a cynical detective and perpetrators of a ruthless landgrab doesn't lend us much. We can't get from the story idea to Jake Gittes in one step—it takes imagination to come up with the social-climbing foppery ("Goddamn Florsheim shoe"), the relentless self-promotion (courting the press even at the morgue), the backstory wound (the woman he tried to help in Chinatown, whose death prompted his leaving the police, with a lifelong dread of not knowing what's going on).

We create such details by doing detailed character work, moving beyond the initial story idea to build the fictional world it requires. Fleshing out Jake's workplace, we get his associates, Duffy and Walsh, who reflect, respectively, his more cynical and more compassionate instincts. Exploring Jake's past, we discover not just the police detectives Lou Escobar and Loach—men Jake worked with in Chinatown, one cagey but honorable, the other suspicious and smug—but Evelyn Mulwray as well, the reincarnation of the woman Jake tried to save. Turning our attention to her, we discover the incest angle, which nails the evil at the story's heart: the implicit sense of entitlement and impunity powerful men like her father, Noah Cross, enjoy.

It is sometimes said that genre fiction, crime fiction especially, suffers from poor characterization. And yet virtually all stories belong to some genre or another: tales of revenge, tales of adventure, tales of spiritual awakening or moral reckoning, love stories, war stories, westerns, "test and quest" sagas, family sagas, chivalric romances, picaresque romps, social dramas, historical dramas, horror, sci-fi, satire, biopic, bildungsroman—not to mention hybrids of these various forms.

A genre is just a type of story, with certain conventions established over years, decades, centuries. The writer is charged with both honoring and exceeding the expectations those conventions create. Skill and imagination are required to meaningfully reinvent characters and situations seen repeatedly through history in a certain type of story. How many viewers of *Chinatown*, for example, saw Oedipus there, standing in Jake Gittes's shadow? The problem lies not with genre but with formula, which consists of seeing genre conventions as restrictions rather than mere guidelines, ends in themselves rather than possibilities.

The key, always, is to escape the restrictions of story by giving the characters the freedom to surprise, to step outside the story so they can live it on their own terms while still honoring the core themes and events the story demands. This back-and-forth, between allowing the characters to act at will while also reining them in to the story demands, is done by understanding how and why the characters themselves embody the story's themes and wish the plot's events to take place, without confining them to merely that.

Characters Derived from the Unconscious

The writer and teacher Alexandra Sokoloff encourages all of her students to keep a dream journal: "If not, you're working too hard."

I envy those with vivid dreams, or the capacity to capture them in sufficient detail before they swirl down the drain of oblivion. Far more often than not, my experience with my dream life resembles the following anecdote by the children's writer and illustrator Maurice Sendak.

When Sendak was little, he was often confined to bed with severe illnesses. Once, as his father became particularly concerned that the boy might die, and hoping to distract him from his suffering, he told his son that if he stared out his window and didn't blink, he might see an angel go by. And if he did, he would be a very lucky boy.

Sendak struggled to gaze out his window for increasing lengths of time, always failing to do so long enough to see an angel. Then one day, eyes aching from the strain, he saw it: large as a dirigible, and glowing. He couldn't tell if it was male or female, and it didn't look at him, but years later he distinctly recalled how slowly it moved past his window.

If my dream life provides me with grist for my fiction, then I do indeed feel lucky. More typically, as I discussed in the preceding chapter, I rely on my unconscious not to hand up angels but to provide me with subtly more complicated and nuanced versions of the characters I worked so hard to craft during my waking hours.

But if your dreams deliver the goods, you'd be foolish to reject them. The problem would seem to be the opposite of that discussed in the preceding section—i.e., with a figure that emerges from dreams, where's the story? In a sense, story ideas and dreams create a need to work in opposite directions. In the case of the former, you have to expand on the characters beyond the initial dictates the story and situation require; in the latter case, you move beyond the thematic impact of the dream image to create a sequence of events, driven by cause and effect, that narrates the development of that theme.

Perhaps the most unique use of this sort of material that I've come across appears in a thin volume of brief, odd, mesmerizing character sketches titled *Tropisms*, by the French novelist Nathalie Sarraute. The term "tropism" refers to the reaction of an organism to an external stimulus, such as heat or light. Sarraute based her sketches on what she called "movements"—inchoate dramatic situations—that she believed to be lurking just below the level of consciousness at all times, almost undetected: power struggles, needy requests, dishonest promises, humiliations. For Sarraute, these imagistic tableaus rose before her mind's eye only in moments of quiet reflection, the way plants turn toward light, and they possessed the spectral quality of dreams. She wondered if they weren't a kind of psychological template formed when she was a child, watching the often incomprehensible interactions among adults around her. Regardless, she recognized in them the raw material she would continue to develop for the rest of her writing life.

Characters Derived from Art or Nature

We spot a tree on a windswept hill that has grown crookedly but inexorably over the years and feel a curious kind of sympathy. Its struggle reflects our own. Or we spot a hawk gliding over a meadow and feel a kinship with both the grace of its flight and the focus of its hunt.

When a writer uses this sense of personalization as inspiration for a character, the temptation is to ascribe a fixed personality to the initial impression, because the image formed in the mind is largely a static one. The tree and the hawk remain pretty much as is.

For a more nuanced characterization, the original impression needs to evolve. Let the original image or inspiration be a starting point, not the end point.

So too with artworks—painting, photographs, sculptures. A useful exercise is to open an art book, say of Caravaggio or Vermeer, and imagine the "characters" you see visiting you in your room. How do they affect you? What do they say? What do they want? Better yet, imagine them fighting with you, singing with you, asking for money, raiding your fridge. If you want to use them for inspiration, break the stilted reverence of "art."

Often, when I feel I'm not imagining a character in a sufficiently nuanced or affecting way, I consult a book of photographs, for they possess the kind of powerful immediacy and suggestive depth I'm after. Robert Frank's *The Americans* in particular is a collection I return to often. It's not just the images but their effect on my heart and mind that's critical. Susan Meiselas has also been inspirational in this way, as have Garry Winogrand and Consuelo Kanaga.

I also scan the news (online or otherwise) for compelling photographs—sometimes it's the simple truth that a human face is the most direct and honest inspiration for a character—and I keep a file of these photographs for future use, whenever I feel a need to ground myself and my character work in something concrete. And yet again, the image is merely a start.

Using music for character inspiration can sometimes be more helpful, because most pieces of music manage to engender more than one mood, and they also move in time, thus suggesting the same mobility and capacity for change that people have.

In my novel *Do They Know I'm Running?* I used a lilting, elegiac piano piece by Fauré to help me capture the gentle, wistful side of a Salvadoran truck driver named Faustino. I didn't make it part of the character's biography—Faustino wouldn't know Fauré from the family dog. Rather, it was precisely the use of the music *in contrast to* the rough-edged first impression I had of this man that made consideration of the piece helpful. The music captured for me in an impressionistic way the kinder, more caring, more introspective aspect of his personality—the side he showed almost no one, for it was so different from what people expected of him.

In the end, whether one uses art, nature, music, tarot cards, astrology, Enneagrams, Jungian types, the four elements of antiquity, or any other nonhuman source for inspiring a characterization, the point is to remember that we can personify anything, but we have to leave open-ended our sense of the character's potential, so that his behavior retains the element of freedom and surprise needed to make him compelling.

Characters Based on Real People

The most obvious and immediate source for characters is your own life—where better to find inspiration for realistic, three-dimensional characters than the people around you?

Be careful: We know a great deal about the people in our lives, but not everything—and this is why real people provide excellent but not perfect source material for characters.

We lack access to the inner lives of other people, no matter how much we may believe we understand them.

Our best source for understanding inner life is ourselves—with a special dispensation for novels and memoirs, to the extent we believe what's written there.

And yet reliance on oneself for insight into behavior hardly offers clear sailing. Only the bodhisattvas among us aren't betrayed by self-delusion, and I have my doubts about them.

We commonly think we're more brave, more honest, more attractive, more popular than an objective assessment would bear out. We act on mixed motives more frequently than we care to admit, seldom recognizing in our generosity, for example, the taint of vanity, self-congratulation, or a need to be liked.

Not all this self-aversion is intentional. The overwhelming majority of our behavior—some conjecture as much as 90 percent—is unconscious, a theme we'll touch on often. I may like to think of myself as an expert charioteer manning the reins of a team of horses, but in truth I'm more like a child riding an elephant—or a tiny stowaway on a transatlantic steamship.*

In some ways we may find we know our characters better than anyone in the so-called real world, including ourselves. The appeal of storytelling may in fact lie, at least in part, in the illusory confidence it provides concerning insight into behavior. If only people acted in life as intelligibly as they do in films or books.

But that's a canard. If we know the inner lives of our characters better than we know those of the people around

---

* The charioteer metaphor is Plato's, for reason guiding the passions. The stowaway analogy belongs to the neuroscientist David Eagleman.

us—or even ourselves—it's not because people and characters are irreconcilably different in kind. Rather, we simply devote more time and energy trying to understand our characters than we do our friends, relatives, neighbors, and enemies. Perhaps that's unfortunate. Then again, maybe our characters are just more interesting.

Regardless, don't confuse a wealth of information with complete knowledge. If you know a character completely, you've trapped her like a fly in amber—which is one more lesson to take away from the people we know. No matter how much we may try to confine them in our understanding, they invariably escape, and surprise us. So should our characters.

Review the following list. Reflect upon the person in your life who fits each description given—jot down her name, fix her in your mind, remember a few details about her life: her physical appearance, the effect she had on you, and anything else you think would be important if you were to describe her to someone who didn't already know her.

Pay particular attention first to those traits you consider fundamental, then second to those traits that surprise or intrigue you.

If possible, try to recall a memorable or pivotal event involving you and the person in question:

(a) A family member to whom you feel particularly close *Adilo*

(b) A family member from whom you're estranged or whom you particularly dislike *Jah Cene*

(c) A stranger whose path crossed yours this
    past week   *Shelley*

(d) A person you know personally and admire   *Jake*

(e) A person you know personally and fear   *my father*

(f) The love who got away

(g) The love you wish had gotten away

(h) First love   *Christian Kiki*

(i) Greatest love   *Jake*

(j) Greatest childhood nemesis

(k) Greatest adulthood nemesis   *Olga*

(l) Person from childhood who annoyed you
    the most   *Abdelkrim*

(m) Person in your present-day life who annoys
    you the most   *Kirsten*

(n) Favorite neighbor

(o) Least favorite neighbor   *Mme Abdelchokour*

(p) Favorite coworker   *Pearly*

(q) Least favorite coworker   *Kirsten*

(r) Your mail carrier or someone else you deal
    with on a "business" level daily   *Paule*

(s) An older person who has inspired you   *My mother*

(t) A child who fascinates you   *Jacob*

(u) Someone on whom you have a secret crush

(v) Someone you believe has a crush on you

(w) A person who believed in you *Frank*

(x) A person who thought you'd never amount
     to anything *Grandmother*

(y) A person you envy

(z) A person whose life you would *never* trade
    for your own *Cathy*

The first and most important thing this work should inspire is a deeper and more precise emotional connection to the people inhabiting your memory. Take a moment to register that emotional impact fully and meaningfully. We forget so much in the confusing and relentless demands of everyday life. This exercise is an attempt to dredge up from that oblivion what we have forgotten—but not lost.

It can also be useful to take distinct eras of your life and ask these questions for each time period. A person who believed in you when you were in elementary school is an excellent character; but so is the one who believed in you when you hit your twenties, or middle age.

Once you've done this, try to find some connection between the paired individuals: For example, I realized that my childhood nemesis was an older brother who was a perfectionist, constantly badgering me for being thoughtless and sloppy. My adult nemesis is a neighbor who is—well, guess what—thoughtless and sloppy.

It's important to know these things about oneself, because they inform us about our own emotional inclinations and limitations—and contradictions. They provide a framework for our own choices about our characters, and expose where we might be able to expand our emotional horizons.

Writing out such a list also provides us with a larger cast of characters than we originally might have realized we possessed. We can sometimes unwittingly get into ruts, writing variations on the same characters over and over—the overbearing parent, the needy lover, the insufferable phony. Near the end of his life, John Updike wrote a poem titled "Peggy Lutz, Fred Muth," in which he thanked his childhood friends and classmates—the beauty and bully, the fatso and others—"for providing a sufficiency of human types . . . all a writer needs."

Although the foregoing list tends to emphasize people who have a particularly memorable impact, don't disregard those who may have slipped into the psychological background—childhood neighbors and classmates especially. We spent much of our early life around such people, they had a key emotional and psychological impact on us even when we weren't paying close attention, and thus we remember them more vividly than we might at first believe: the older girl we admired but were too scared to talk to, the elderly neighbor who kept to himself, the wild girl at school, the wild girl's best friend, "the quiet one," the class clown, and so forth. Quickly, one realizes that we carry an entire world inside us, ready to be explored.

Also, though the foregoing emphasizes people with whom you have some genuine familiarity, don't neglect the inspiration that can come from strangers. The actress Sarah Jones patrols the streets of New York looking for intriguing people, eavesdropping on conversations, to fuel her imagination and inspire portrayals and story ideas for her one-woman shows. There is somewhere in your world—a café, a church, a grocery store, a boutique, the welfare office, the yacht club—where the people-watching is particularly rich with intriguing strangers. Go there. Watch. Listen.

Last, don't worry that your life has been too conventional or uneventful to provide you with the kinds of characters who would interest readers. This suggests a lack of imagination or compassion or insight—not a lack of experience. As George Eliot remarked in *Adam Bede*:

> . . . the way in which I have come to the conclusion that human nature is loveable—the way I have learned something of its deep pathos, its sublime mysteries—has been by living a great deal among people more or less commonplace or vulgar . . .

It was a theme Eliot returned to often, that the characters who inhabited her fictive world, which reflected the world of her time, were worthy of not just her respect or even admiration, but her love. The concluding words of *Middlemarch* read:

> . . . the growing good of the world is partly dependent on unhistoric acts; and that things are not so ill with you and me as they might have been, is half owing to the number who lived faithfully a hidden life, and rest in unvisited tombs.

Composite Characters

The sources for character discussed earlier are not mutually exclusive. Combining elements of a character derived from one source (a piece of music or a photograph) with another (a real person), then supplying a few final touches from one's imagination, can generate a composite that exceeds the sum of its parts.

Such characters are particularly useful—and advisable—when relying on real people for source material, for this prevents any one person from feeling singled out and thus exploited, misrepresented, or mocked. (That said, it is one of the mysteries of fiction that people seldom recognize themselves in novels, no matter how blatantly derivative the portrayal.)

The pitfall in composite characters comes when we try to fuse traits we did not realize make an unconvincing whole. One sees the result all too often in action movies, where a woman's name gets slapped on a fundamentally male role, with no thought of the thousands of women in law enforcement or the military who might provide a real-world model for the part. Instead we get the equivalent of a man zipped inside a babe suit.

Another example is what we might refer to as the Reticent Knockout. We can't blithely meld the traits of someone who's physically stunning, and who therefore negotiates the world with ease, with those of a homely person, who feels in many situations the intrinsic insecurity of being overlooked, ignored, even shunned. Ugly ducklings do indeed turn into swans, but without a clear understanding of how and when the transformation took place, and the way the character has dealt with how differently people respond to her, all you've got is a gimmick.

Another example: Suppose you know both a down-to-earth priest and a decorated war veteran, and want to fashion a chaplain from their composite. You will need to ask how much of the veteran's character has been formed by his firsthand knowledge of both the guilt and the satisfaction of killing. If you take that knowledge away from your vet, is he anything like the same person? Do you violate something crucial about him by removing that experience? Similarly, you will need to ask how much your priest's decency results from never having witnessed firsthand the often random butchery of combat. Put him in the thick of a firefight—is he still the same swell guy? Will the soldiers he counsels respect him if he is?

By no means am I suggesting such hybrids should never be attempted—quite the contrary. They can lead to fascinating characters who come alive precisely because of their contradictions—and it is just such characters who seem most lifelike on the page. But one does not create a compelling composite simply by slamming together contrasting traits, hoping sooner or later a well-chosen phrase will make them stick.

A convincing composite character requires particular attention to the formative experiences that molded her. The way to gain insight into that process will be explored in the coming chapters.

Exercises

1.　Take a story idea you're currently working on. Assemble the dramatis personae you'll need to make the story

Use workbook @ home

work. What do you know already about these characters? What's conspicuously lacking—names, ages, physical appearance, family backgrounds, type of work they do, fears, loves, hatreds, desires? What else will you have to learn about them to make the story work? What information is conceivably irrelevant?

2. Give yourself sufficient time without interruption in a quiet place. Let the daily mental business that preoccupies you settle down and fade into the background. Wait until a dreamlike scene or personage forms before your mind's eye. If you simply see a figure, try to guide it into some form of action. If you see a scene, follow it through to some sense of completion. Write down what you observed. Pay particular attention to the setting—do you recognize it? How? Also attend to the power dynamic between the people in the scene, and its emotional tone. Did the scene touch you in some meaningful way? If not, can you think of supplying something consciously that might create a more emotionally affecting scene?

3. Go to a book of paintings or photographs and select a person depicted in one of the plates. Insert that character into a scene you're working on, the less "arty," the better. What happens? How do the other characters react? What of interest changes? What doesn't change? If the insertion feels forced, what could you change or add to make it feel more natural?

4. Select a favorite piece of music and allow it to form a mental impression of a character, or use it as an accent

Jayne loves abstract art!

or contrasting element to a character you're already
developing. Place that new or altered character in a
scene you're currently working on. Again: What happens? How do the other characters react? What of interest changes? What doesn't change?

5. Compare the results of the characters created for the
preceding two exercises. Which of the two character
sources—music or painting—proved easier to work
with, more vivid, more useful? Why?

6. Select at least five of the people suggested in the list on
pages 24–26 and do as the text suggested: Reflect
upon the people in your life who fit the description
given—jot down his or her name, fix him in your mind.
Describe those traits you consider fundamental, then
those traits that surprise you. Recall a memorable or
pivotal scene involving you and the person. Take a moment to register that emotional impact fully and meaningfully.

7. Identify and write a brief biographical sketch for three
persons from your past not identified in the list provided. What makes them so memorable for you?

8. Use one of the characters sketched in exercises 6–7 and
find a way to use him or her in a piece on which you're
currently working. Does the character enrich the piece
or detract from it? In either case, why?

9. Take any two—or if you're feeling ambitious, three—
characters developed in the preceding exercises and

mold them into a composite. Does this new character suggest opportunities for behavior and conflict that none of the sources he's based on possess? Is there anything about the character that doesn't seem to fit, suggesting irreconcilable traits, or a need for deeper, more detailed engagement with the character's backstory or inner life in order to make the fit more organic, more credible?

Chapter Three
The Examined Life: Using Personal Experience as an Intuitive Link to the Character

---

As Anton Chekhov aptly remarked, "Everything I learned about human nature I learned from me." And yet there is perhaps no more stifling and useless advice than to "write what you know," something Eudora Welty wisely acknowledged when she countered, "Write about what you don't know about what you know."

Writers possess only four tools: research, experience, empathy, and imagination. Fortunately, whole worlds can be built from them.

In the preceding chapter, I noted that our best source material for inner life is ourselves. I've also referred several times to intuitive engagement with your characters. In this chapter, I'm going to suggest a way of fusing those two notions, of learning how to plumb emotionally significant events in your own life to hone your intuition, the better to understand and engage with your characters.

Mere information can't provide meaningful insight

into the lives of the people who inhabit our fiction. Information is pretty stale stuff, inert and heady. We need an understanding that's embedded in vivid imagery, a sense of a psychic bond, an imaginative and emotional link between the stuff of memory and the inner life of the character.

We can't hope to accomplish that without a deep and specific understanding of our own wounds, regrets, consolations, joys. This self-knowledge creates the language for communicating with our characters. Words can't get us there. We need to go deeper, into the dark recesses of memory, the messy stuff of emotion, the raw veins of want and fear and pride and shame that pulse beneath the skin of the everyday.

In this chapter we explore how to tap those veins, so we can translate what emerges to our characterizations. In theater, this is called "personalization," and involves trying to bring one's own emotional and sense memory to bear on a portrayal.

The limitations to such an approach suggest themselves pretty quickly. What good are personal memories and experiences when a character's life seems vastly different from my own—for example, when trying to plumb the experience of an orphan with Tourette's syndrome (*Motherless Brooklyn*), a wounded Confederate infantryman struggling to get home (*Cold Mountain*), a street urchin of Mumbai (*Slumdog Millionaire*), or a corrupt Renaissance pope (*The Borgias*)?

As even that short list should suggest, writing by its very nature demands that we explore the unfamiliar. Men must write about women, and vice versa; the educated must be able to portray the ignorant; the shy must convincingly depict the bold, and so on. The point is to build a bridge between what you know and what you don't, though admittedly it's not always entirely clear how to begin.

The great actress and teacher Stella Adler, in the course of a weekend seminar on scene analysis some years ago, bellowed from her seat to a young actress performing with fiery, confrontational insistence a monologue from Schiller's *Mary Stuart*: "Take that chip off your shoulder— you're a queen!"

The actress was "getting in the face" of Elizabeth, her rival for the throne, and thus making the mistake of interpreting Mary Queen of Scots largely from the viewpoint of her own experience, hoping Schiller's language would carry her the rest of the way.

The first step to solving the problem was as simple as realizing a queen assumes her power; she need dare no one to mind her words, because the penalty for defying her is inherent in her crown. So small an insight as that pried open the door to a fuller embodiment of the role.

This is why research proves so critical in building an imaginative bridge between the known and the unknown. For any place, time, or group of people who differ from us, we need to learn the social relationships (with a special eye to who has power and who doesn't), the guiding proverbs (to understand the moral life of that world), and the physical details of daily life (food, work, comfort, hygiene, weather). Only then can we open the doors of empathy and imagination so that we can intuitively share in the sensual and emotional life of the characters who inhabit that world.

We shouldn't—and frankly, can't—leave behind our

own sentiments when we explore the unfamiliar. Rather, we have to let our homework guide us to a point where our experience intersects our fictive world, and build imaginatively from there. The key is to treat with due respect both what we share and what we don't share with our characters. And to do that we must know *ourselves* well, which means understanding the key events in our own lives.

Exacting exploration of our own inner lives also mitigates the tendency to be writerly instead of open and honest. Any composition teacher will tell you that a great deal of what crosses her desk is an exercise in using words to fill the void where a genuine thought, emotion, or observation should be. Not only is meaningful character work impossible without probing your own inner life, you can't develop your own voice. You'll instead have a mannerism unanchored to anything genuine. (Even accomplished writers can succumb. Djuna Barnes at her most obscure strays from the merely evocative to the impenetrable, fearing sentiment so avidly she all too often substitutes a floridly stylized turn of phrase for anything a reader might actually recognize as human feeling.)

The most important emotional incidents to explore in a character's life, and therefore your own, are:

(a) Moment of greatest fear

(b) Moment of greatest courage

(c) Moment of greatest sadness

(d) Moment of greatest joy   wedding day

(e) Moment of deepest shame

(f) Moment of most profound guilt *getting Amos em trouble for ratting him out to father*

(g) Moment of most redemptive forgiveness

(h) Moment of greatest pride

(i) Greatest success (which may not be the same as moment of greatest pride)

(j) Worst failure

(k) Most memorable moment of tenderness

(l) Most shattering incident of violence *father beating mother*

(m) Most life-changing moment of passion

(n) Moment of greatest danger

(o) Worst illness *not knowing*

(p) First experience with death *3 years old thinking I was dying*

(q) Most disturbing experience with death

(r) Most shattering loss other than death

Don't suffer over the superlatives—"greatest," "most," et cetera. Allow the moments that suggest themselves to emerge fully, whether there is one or several—or dozens. Explore them honestly and without judgment. It's easy to be vague or noncommittal—easy and counterproductive. Be specific, down to what you were wearing, what everyone else was wearing, where you were, what time of day. The devil, as they say, is in the details, except in this instance the devil is your friend.

These particular events are revelatory precisely because they expose us. In a sudden shock of raw emotion, the mask of the ego drops, if only for an instant. Stripped of any pretense of control or power, we're obliged to confront a side of ourselves we routinely avoid or actively keep hidden, for better or worse. We turn from creatures of habit to mere creatures. How we handle that helplessness—how profoundly we're undone, how quickly we regain our composure, whether we run or fight or bargain our way back to normal—says more about us than we often care to admit. If it isn't our "true natures" that get revealed, it's at least a more raw, less artful, and deliberate aspect of our natures. Stories are built from such revelations.

The following are some additional "prompts" to key significant emotional moments:

(a) First time as an adult you told someone you loved him (or her)

(b) A time you said "I love you" and wished you hadn't

(c) A time when you were struck or beaten

(d) A time you struck or beat someone else

(e) Most memorable moment with a parent/sibling/child

(f) Most memorable moment with a stranger

(g) "Please stop. I'm scared."

(h) "Don't hurt me."

(i) "Give that to me."

(j) "I'm telling."

(k) "Do as you're told."

(l) "I can't believe I just did that."

(m) "I could kill you."

(n) "I'm not that kind of person." (Or "You can't ask me to do that.")

(o) "I thought you loved me."

(p) "No matter what I do, it will never be good enough."

Again, it's important to be as specific as possible in fleshing out these scenes for yourself. Don't be judgmental, or shrink from scenes that bear unpleasant memories. On the contrary, look for the most conflict-intensive scenes you can, for these are the ones that will best serve your writing. It may seem callous or even glib to say, but artists should never regret their misfortunes. Heartbreak is a gift—it's self-pity that's poison.

As in the preceding chapter with your list of real people, don't restrict yourself to the suggestions I've provided. You'll no doubt begin to imagine other episodes in your life that have proved meaningful, painful, inspiring, profound. Embrace them. Be grateful for them.

Once you've assembled your set of scenes, you may detect a thematic unity connecting some, even many of them: violence at the hands of authority; a need to placate indifferent or even hostile adults; a sense of being second (or third, or last) in line. This thematic unity is the connective thread that can turn these isolated scenes into a possible story.

Similarly, you can connect two scenes of opposing emotional polarity—a horribly shaming incident and a redemptive moment of pride, or an occasion of breathtaking joy and a terrible accident that scarred you with guilt. In this way the scenes you've envisioned become episodes in a journey, points along an arc, not disjointed fragments, and understanding this is helpful not just for your characters, but for yourself.*

Of course, we don't move from shame to pride, fear to courage, misery to joy in a seamless, effortless glide. Our pains, sorrows, miscues, and wrongs misshape us, disfiguring our spirits, our hearts, our consciences. We become brittle, self-protective, mistaken, false. We unknowingly chase the ghosts of our past through the labyrinth of our days.

Our battles with a favored sibling for a parent's love unconsciously inspire a habitual pursuit of married lovers, as we reenact over and over the daily contest for approval and intimacy. This time, we're sure, we'll be the one who is chosen.

A mother's narcissistic flamboyance leaves us desperate for devotion and acceptance, which we ironically seek from lovers as grandly unavailable as she was.

Nursing a loved one through a long and painful death

* I owe my exploration of this territory to the screenwriter Gill Dennis (*Walk the Line*, *Riders of the Purple Sage*, *Return to Oz*), whose Finding the Story workshops at the Squaw Valley Writers Conference inspired my interest not just in honestly plumbing my own emotional memory, but in seeking the connective thematic threads that generate a story. He's a wise man, and I'm grateful for his tutelage.

creates a need for emotional intensity, a daily crisis of profound love, which simple, gentle, accepting affection can no longer fulfill.

Our lives can become a kind of moral and emotional sleepwalk, and it often takes a devastating loss, tragedy, or crisis to shock us out of the habitual behavior that has come to identify us. This crucial moment of insight forms one of the core epiphanies of our lives, and forges the decisions that point toward change.

Anyone who has experienced a therapeutic breakthrough, or been obliged to perform a "fearless moral inventory," as those in twelve-step programs must, know this kind of self-scrutiny. But writers must know it as well.

Such "crises of insight" and moments of decision form the cornerstones of drama. They may take the form of a dark night of the soul, a sudden horrible feeling of *What have I done?*, or a hard-won acceptance of ourselves, warts and all. We can't expect to portray them well in our characters without understanding them in our own lives.

Return to those moments of failure and shame and guilt and loss you've explored, not just to flesh out the scenes that evoke that emotional specificity, but to reflect on how that fear, shame, failure, or loss changed you, made you fearful, untrusting, obsessive, brash.

Then search out those moments in your life where you've wrestled with those shortcomings, faced them squarely, and made the difficult decision to find a new path—toward success, or joy, or acceptance.

Identify the people who inspired you, or obliged you to be honest about who you were and what you were doing.

As long as you put words on the page, those moments, those people, will guide you to the psychological, moral, and emotional territory where your truth lies. Ground yourself there. Write from there.

Remember, don't be dissuaded if your life so far has seemed uneventful. A great many writers have led tame lives, the better to expend their energies exploring their imaginations. It is far more useful to nurture a keen and uncompromising analytical sense of one's own emotional life than to launch off on misadventures for the sake of material.

That said, the number of great writers who have worked as journalists, traveled widely, or engaged in demanding professions that provided a breadth of experience and insight is hardly small. Taking risks in life translates to taking risks in one's writing—and writing requires a high tolerance for risk.

Don't shrink from an adventurous life, but don't think that alone will make you a writer. Writing always takes place in one location—the seat of a chair—and that is equally true of Flannery O'Connor and Paul Theroux.

Exercises

1. Pick five of the suggested events or prompts in the two lists provided in this chapter and sketch the scene that emerges. Can you detect some thematic thread linking the scenes? What is it?

2. Create three events or prompts of your own that spur emotionally significant scenes.

3. Use one of the scenes developed for exercises 1 or 2 and find a way to use it in a piece on which you are currently working. Does it enrich the piece or detract from it? In either case, why?

4. Identify a moment in your life when you've had to face your own misguided, wrongful, or hurtful behavior. Explore the insight that resulted, and how it changed how you acted or even the direction of your life. Provide a similar insight to one of the characters in the scene you've rewritten for exercise 3. How does this insight transform the scene? What decision results from the insight, and how does the character change his behavior? If his behavior doesn't change, why not?

PART II

Developing the Character

Chapter Four
Five Cornerstones of Dramatic Characterization

Imagine a woman in a grocery store at 10 A.M. dressed in evening wear: a cocktail dress, bolero jacket, opera gloves, a string of pearls, patent leather pumps. Her makeup is subtle and tastefully done, her hair neatly combed. She reaches for a can of peaches on a top shelf, straining, unable to get a grip. Glancing around, she sees no one able to offer assistance, stares once more at the unnerving peaches, then suddenly hikes up her skirt, notches the toe of her pump on a lower shelf and starts climbing as though up a rock face. Tongue between her teeth, reaching as far as she can, she wiggles her fingers, finally nudges one of the cans—it totters. Then falls. Several others tumble down with it. She jumps back down, shields her head from the avalanche—she may be hurt, but before anyone can get to her she very slowly drops to her knees, picks up two of the cans, clutches them to her chest, and begins to sob quietly.

There is no description of what this woman looks like

beyond what she's wearing. We presume she's short, but her age, race, weight, height, and so on are all unstated. But it's unlikely anyone who reads the previous paragraph will not form a distinct mental image of her.

What are the most important things that make that visualization and engagement possible—that make the depiction compelling?

- The character *needs or wants something*.

- She is *having difficulty getting what she needs or wants*, and comes up with *a plan for overcoming that difficulty*.

- She exhibits a seeming *contradiction*: She's dressed in evening wear at the grocery store at midmorning.

- Something unexpected happens (she makes a mistake), which renders her *vulnerable*. (She may even be hurt, enhancing this impression.)

- Her sobbing suggests there is more to her predicament than meets the eye—*a secret*.

More than any of the other considerations addressed in this book, these five concerns are key to any compelling character.

That doesn't mean we've uncovered the secret, crazy, magic formula, or that by methodically running down this checklist like the good student you no doubt are you've done all that's required to make a character leap off the page. Characters can't be crafted from a grab bag of traits, no matter how clever or interesting. That's a recipe for an idea, not a character.

For better or worse, art remains a largely trial-and-error endeavor—or, as Hemingway advised: There is no great writing, just great rewriting. Characterization requires a constant back-and-forth between the exterior events of the story and the inner life of the character. This requires training your insight, asking the right questions and not hedging on the answers, and learning to listen to yourself when, from the back of your mind, a voice insists: *No. Not yet. Make it better.*

That said, these five considerations can provide a touchstone as you work. Either while conceiving the character, writing the initial drafts, or polishing a later edit, as you're evaluating the character you may ask yourself if any of these five qualities is missing, or underdeveloped. If so, consider providing such a trait, or bringing one already in existence into greater focus, to see if it resonates with the story, echoes other aspects of the characterization you've already developed, helps clarify or intensify interactions or conflicts with other characters, or in some other way enhances your depiction.

The reasons that these five specific concerns are so central should become clear as we discuss them in greater detail one by one in the ensuing chapters. But in each instance, it's important to bear in mind that a rushed approach to anything will bear only scattered results. To paraphrase one of my favorite math professors: *The difference between great artists, and artists who are not so great, is that great artists think deeply about simple things.*

In the coming chapters, we will try to think deeply about five rather simple things:

- The nature and quality of desire

- How profoundly frustration of one's desires distorts the personality

- What it means to be wounded

- The curse and crutch of secrets

- The inescapability of contradiction

From that foundation we will move on to the physical, psychological, and sociological elaborations that flesh out the character, rendering her and the world she inhabits more real.

But at every stage, it will remain important to be patient; to seek solitude and quiet, the better to think deeply; and to respect the mysterious gravity that resides in the seemingly simple.

Maxine tries to be everyone's mother b/c she virtually had none, and it fills her life enough that she won't need a man —

Chapter Five
Desire as Purpose:
A Driving Need, Want, Ambition, or Goal

The Centrality of Desire

One of Constantin Stanislavski's key innovations was recognizing the central role of desire in our depiction of the human condition. The fundamental truth to characterization, he asserted, is that characters want something, and the deeper the want, the more compelling the drama.

Desire is the crucible that forges character because it intrinsically creates conflict. If we want nothing, then nothing stands in our way. This may lead to a life of monastic enlightenment—or habitual evasion—but it's thin gruel for drama. By giving the character a deep-seated need or want, you automatically put her at odds with something or someone, for the world is not designed to gratify our desires.

And a profound, unquenchable longing almost always forces us to do things we normally would never imagine ourselves doing—even things seemingly contradictory to our natures. When confronted with overwhelming obstacles of a

Jimmy doesn't want her to work so hard at it or he won't get any of it he
she convinces him that getting it is the way to be but he a father —

kind we've never faced before in pursuit of something we cannot live without, we are forced to change, to adapt, to dig deeper into ourselves for some insight, passion, or strength that will give us the power we need to keep going.

In a sense, Stanislavski's desire took the place of Aristotle's *telos*. Where once man lived to fulfill his basic purpose, he now, in Stanislavski's interpretation, lived to fulfill his most basic ambition, craving, or need.

Peter Brooks put it somewhat differently in his book *Reading for Plot*, remarking that, in the absence of desires, stories remain stillborn. This reflects a simple truth: Desire puts a character in motion.

There may be no more important question to ask of a character than: What does she want in this scene, in this chapter, in this story? Thinking more globally, one should ask what she wants from her life—has she achieved it? If not, why not? If so, what now?

The Complexity of Desire—and Thus the Need for Clarity

We often want what we can't have, or would be better off without. Sometimes we don't recognize what it is we're really longing for until someone or something happens along to deliver a swift kick in the teeth, jarring us out of our stupor. Perhaps we actively suppress, deny, or in some other way hide from what we need. Our desires may be layered or nested, with one used to veil another we secretly want more but are too shy, too remiss, too riddled with doubt or scarred by previous failure to pursue. It may even be the case that the real object of desire is intrinsically ineffable: enlightenment, Nirvana, the imminence of God.

All of these situations are dramatically interesting. They're also tricky to pull off on the page. They're complex, and complexity all too often translates into confusion. In storytelling, leaving the object of desire unclear creates uncertainty in the reader or audience. Worse, it grants the author license to meander or verbally navel-gaze—always a temptation to resist.

The answer is often to create an outer objective, a goal or quest, even a mania or an obsession that gives the character something concrete to strive for. Alternatively, you can anchor the character's competing wants in a variety of other characters, who suggest the opportunity to at least partially gratify one desire or the other.

In Junot Díaz's *The Brief Wondrous Life of Oscar Wao*, teenaged Belicia Cabral, growing up in provincial Baní in the Dominican Republic of 1955–1962, cannot name what it is she wants, except that it is "something *else*." She can catalog some of this nebulous longing's more obvious manifestations: desire for a woman's body, "an incredible life," a handsome husband, beautiful children. But what she really wants is *to escape*—not just the circumstances of her poverty but the unchangeable facts of her past, even her "despised black skin." The destination that can provide this escape is less clear, but she shares this unrelenting desire *to get out* with an entire generation under the brutal regime of Rafael Leónidas Trujillo Molina, "the Dicta-tingest Dictator who ever Dictated."

What Díaz does with Belicia is capture the sprawling morass of her longings in a single overt action: *to escape*. We know that simply heading off somewhere will not gratify her wants, but by giving her this single obsessive pursuit, the author clarifies her desire enough that the reader can embrace it. The various strands of want balled up inside her will get teased out along the way, as she interacts with her lovers, her family, her work, her new home.

The same technique appears with Ahab in *Moby-Dick*, Jay Gatsby in *The Great Gatsby*,* and, in a more comic vein, Yossarian in *Catch-22*. Each of these characters has an easily identifiable object of desire: the whale, Daisy, getting out of combat. And yet that's clearly not the whole of the matter, for one senses that killing the whale, having Daisy, and flying no more combat missions would soothe only a superficial itch. Something deeper is at stake, more unknowable, perhaps unidentifiable.

Beginning writers are often intrigued by this vast, inchoate kind of desire, and resist identifying a single ambition or goal for fear of becoming unsubtle. I think the examples I've chosen should squelch that qualm. Subtlety does not come from vagueness in what the character wants; that simply mistakes subtlety for confusion. The obsessive desire need not require a name—affixing a tidy label to a desire does little to ennoble it—but that's easily fixed by identifying the object of desire not verbally but symbolically: the whale, Daisy. Or you can conceive the fulfillment of the want in terms of an intrinsically open-ended goal, like Belicia's *escape*, or a scene that represents—like a fantasy or a sequence from a dream—the state of being the character longs for, such as Yossarian's visions of Sweden, the country to which he hopes to defect.

---

* See Charles Baxter's *The Art of Subtext*, chapter 2, "Digging the Subterranean," concerning his discussion of "congested desires" in *Moby-Dick* and *The Great Gatsby*.

Complication, richness, and texture come from the conflicts encountered in fulfilling a desire. And those conflicts often reveal not just the unexpected difficulty of getting what we want, but how mistaken we can be in judging what it is. This dramatic complexity is created by driving a character toward an identifiable goal, even if it only superficially or partially represents what the character is truly after. Otherwise scenes have nowhere to go, and the drama falters.

The way to flesh out the subterranean, interior wants is through interactions with other characters. An excellent example of this approach can be found in the HBO series *Luck*.

Chester "Ace" Bernstein (Dustin Hoffman), a lifelong gambling kingpin, exits prison after a three-year stint, served for taking the fall to protect others. His exterior objective is to return to his proper station in the world of gambling by buying the Santa Anita Park racetrack and transforming it into a casino. But a variety of more interior needs and wants get explored through a number of other characters.

To help gain entrance to the horse-racing world, Ace decides to buy an Irish thoroughbred named Pint of Plain. Because of his felon status he needs a "beard" for the purchase, and his longtime friend Gus Demitriou (Dennis Farina) fills the role, serving also as driver, bodyguard, and confidant.

The issue of trust gets complicated by the various former gambling associates and business executives Ace needs to fulfill his scheme—men who "lie as easily as they breathe," and who suspect Ace has more than a little anger built up over his fall, and may be out for some kind of revenge. It's clear they're right, and Ace has the patience to serve up his vengeance cold.

Into this den of thieves walk two creatures who reflect a wholly different side of Ace: Claire LeChea (Joan Allen), a woman who runs a foundation that hopes to rehabilitate prison inmates by allowing them to care for aging race-horses, and the Irish thoroughbred himself, Pint of Plain.

Claire—dowdy, shy, almost a nun to her cause—presents an opportunity for Ace not just to act on his altruism but to reacquaint himself with female companionship, something he feels has passed him by, so much so her presence renders him boyishly skittish.

Pint of Plain wins a race despite being badly wounded in the leg when struck by another horse's loosened shoe. Ace, clearly moved by the horse's spirit, insists on keeping vigil outside the stall. At one point during the night Pint of Plain nuzzles Ace awake. Ace stares into the thorough-bred's night-black eye, and the gangster and the animal share something unique, transcendent, a moment of purity.

The outer goal of buying the racetrack permits us to see Ace negotiate the viper's nest of gambling and the legitimate businesses it feeds; we see his steely calm in the face of opposition, his patience at carrying out an elaborate scheme, his rage at having his loyalty questioned. In contrast, through his interactions with Gus, Claire, and Pint of Plain, we see the humbler man beneath the hardened mask, the need for companionship, affection, and something much deeper—for lack of a better word, his soul. Desire lies at the heart of all of these encounters, with the outer ambition, buying the racetrack, providing the opportunity for the pursuit of the others.

Variety in the Depiction of Desire

There is a variety of ways to portray the pursuit of a need, desire, or ambition so that the character's through-line is more interesting than a headlong pursuit, and that honors the complexity and layering we've just discussed. Here are a few examples.

When Conflict Clarifies or Transforms the Object of Desire

Michael Corleone begins *The Godfather* by explicitly distinguishing himself from his father and brothers, telling his fiancée: "That's my family, Kay. It's not me."

But then his father is almost murdered, and Michael's blood loyalty quickens. Revenge is required. Michael, a "civilian," is the perfect candidate to do the killing, after which he's obliged to go into hiding, where he marries—only to have his Italian bride murdered in his stead. This trail of blood proves there is no safety except deep within the bonds of loyalty and love only family affords. And so he returns, and exacts his revenge on all those who harmed or betrayed or continue to threaten his family, men who routinely justify their actions with "It's only business." For Michael, it's never business. Throughout the story his motivation always revolves around family, but the trials he endures transform his understanding of which family deserves his devotion—from the one he could choose freely to the one he cannot escape.

In *Thelma and Louise*, two women seek a weekend on the wild side. It turns step-by-step into a tragic refusal to endure prison, a condition which metaphorically defines their prior lives. Like Michael Corleone, they have one overarching desire—in this case, freedom, rather than family—but the progression of conflicts transforms this desire from the recreational to the absolute.

When the Character Suffers Two Irreconcilable Desires

Sometimes a character faces an inescapable choice between two options that conflict so utterly he's stuck. This usually takes the form of a decision between a moral compromise he finds unacceptable or death. Classical and Renaissance tragedy abounds with examples:

- Orestes must avenge his father's death or face the wrath of Apollo, but this means killing his mother, and thus enduring the rage of the Furies.

- Antigone must decide between honoring her familial obligations by burying her brother, the rebel leader Polynices, or obeying the state. She bravely chooses the former, and is executed.

- Coriolanus, to rise to the position of consul of Rome, must bow to the whims of the people, but this grates against his warrior's pride. He stands by the latter, which leads to banishment, rebellion, and ultimately his betrayal and murder.

The drama in these stories is provided by the hero's struggle between the competing options, a state of moral paralysis that gets broken once the unavoidable choice is made. Without the struggle and the choice, there's no drama, which is the problem at the heart of a more recent example of the genre, Joyce Carol Oates's *Little Bird of Heaven*. The story has a potentially dramatic concept: A teenage girl named Zoe Kruller, living in a small town in upstate New York, is faced with a standoff between her mother and brother, who represent home, and her much-loved rake of a father, who is accused of murdering a singer with whom he was having a secret affair. Note the phrasing: *is faced with*. It's static, and so is the novel. The story goes nowhere because Zoe simply reacts to the situation, and lacks any desire to escape, change, or even affect it. There's nothing she wants. She doesn't struggle, she just laments her fate.

You convey emotional or moral paralysis and the angst of going nowhere by showing the character trying to achieve a goal, make a choice, go somewhere, and failing. Otherwise, she's just waiting.

Don't worry about diminishing your character through failure. It's the desire that counts. In George Eliot's *Middlemarch*, Edward Casaubon could easily be every bit as static as Zoe Kruller. His "soul was sensitive without being enthusiastic; it was too languid to thrill out of self-consciousness into passionate delight; it went on fluttering in the swampy ground where it was hatched, thinking of its wings and never flying." But Eliot spares Casaubon from narrative lethargy by giving him a quixotic quest—a "Key to all Mythologies" that he never completes. Dorothea defends him from ridicule by noting, "Failure after long perseverance is much grander than never to have a striving good enough to be called a failure."

Another variety of this story is when a character's conscious want contradicts a deeper, unconscious, denied, or suppressed want. Such stories are marked by two layers of conflict: one, the dramatic action as the protagonist pursues the misbegotten object of desire he's convinced he wants; and, two, the dramatic tension created as the increasingly unsatisfactory results of his quest slam him again and again into the key truth he's trying to avoid—he wants something else.

Joe Buck in *Midnight Cowboy* fails repeatedly in his misbegotten bid to become a New York hustler, only to finally realize what it was he was truly craving all along: intimacy.

The conflict begins with Joe's realization that the people he has loved and desired have all deserted or betrayed him: His mother dropped him off at his grandmother's house one day and never came back. Sally Buck, his grandmother, showered him with saccharine lies. The other teenagers with whom he's had sex, boys and girls both, enjoyed his body but never seemed to care very much that "Joe Buck was inside it." Some have been savagely cruel.

The only person who ever seemed to take a real interest was a cowboy lover of Sally's, and so Joe decides to adopt the persona of the Midnight Cowboy—the way Indian braves assume a warrior identity during their rites of initiation. This will be his mask, his shield against the pain of rejection and betrayal. He heads to New York and becomes a hustler—a warrior of love, a lady-killer, slaying the matrons of Manhattan with his down-home manhood.

Unsurprisingly to everyone but himself, Joe repeatedly fails in his quest, befriended only by Enrico "Ratso" Rizzo, a tubercular polio victim with a hustling streak of his own. Rizzo is streetwise and sees Joe as naïve to the point of stupid; Joe is handsome and considers Rizzo physically repulsive. Each exemplifies what the other most fears in himself, but out of intersecting needs—Joe for someone who knows the ropes, Rizzo for a cash cow—they form a testy mutual aid society that bit by bit inches toward friendship.

But Rizzo grows increasingly ill. When Joe returns from his first successful trick, with promise of more wealthy women clients to come, he finds Rizzo near death, demanding to be taken to Florida for the sake of his tuberculosis. Joe must choose between his mask and his heart. He does so—and rediscovers the sad but inescapable truth about love: Our loved ones are wildly imperfect, and they leave us. They die.

Midnight Cowboy exemplifies a psychoanalytic view of man's condition: We are wounded psychically, often early in childhood, and live with continuous anxiety over abandonment, rejection, or abuse. To protect ourselves from further wounding, we develop a shell, a false persona, a defense or adaptation—we drink, do drugs, becomes perfectionists, work ourselves to death, pursue only meaningless affairs, get stuck in unfulfilling marriages, shy away from the risks necessary for true success, adhere to Pollyannaish optimism, hide away in cynical isolation. Often this false strategy in some way symbolically reenacts the traumatic incident. But underneath there continuously abides an implacable impulse toward health—and truth.

These equal and opposing cross-purposes—to survive and avoid pain, to heal and move beyond it—define our existence. The crucial event is usually an encounter with someone who provides the confidence or faith that it's safe at last to let down our guard.

This obviously doesn't mean everything will turn out swimmingly—as *Midnight Cowboy* makes clear. Dropping our defenses opens us once again to the core reality of love: It obliges vulnerability. Which means we'll most likely get hurt. Perhaps worse than before.

When the Object of Desire
Is Ultimately Found to Be Worthless

This story line, the theme of which often translates to "Be careful what you wish for," typically pitches worldly ambitions against more traditional values such as dignity, family, honor, and love.

Erich von Stroheim's *Greed* (1924), adapted from Frank Norris's novel *McTeague*, dramatizes the pitiless side of good fortune when a winning lottery ticket destroys the lives of three people involved, a theme echoed in the 1948 film *The Treasure of the Sierra Madre*, adapted by director John Huston from the novel by B. Traven.

In a more recent variant, *Frozen River*, the female protagonist, Ray Eddy, struggles throughout the film to obtain the money needed to buy the double-wide trailer she's promised her sons. Frustrated in her attempt to do so legitimately, she turns to crime (immigrant smuggling). In the end she faces a choice that obliges her to realize what's become of her soul; in obsessing about getting the trailer, she's actually betrayed the reason she wanted it in the first place: to protect her family. Here it's not so much that the object of desire is tarnished or found to be worthless; rather, the hero realizes that what the prize symbolizes— home—is far more important than the object itself.

When the Character Wants One Thing but
Gets Something Else Altogether

This variety of story typically results in a kind of cosmic irony where the protagonist must resign himself to what he's received, or else it prompts a deeper understanding of what it is he truly wants.

Will Freeman in Nick Hornby's *About a Boy* goes to a single-parents group hoping to pick up women, and even invents a fictitious son to perfect the ruse. But instead of a lover, he ends up with a twelve-year-old friend named Marcus. The friendship leads him to a deeper awareness of himself as a man, providing him the maturity to finally love.

Another variant, with a similar plot device, is the film *Roger Dodger*. Here again, an emotionally constrained adult male, Roger Swanson, has the benefit of an adolescent sidekick, his nephew Nick. But instead of this prompting reflection on his own misguided desires, Roger uses Nick as a shill to get women interested in him for sex. The plan backfires when Nick makes it all the easier for women to see right through Roger's bitterness and cynicism.

The foregoing examples demonstrate the range and variety of stories available simply by looking at the issue of desire in creative ways—and this is hardly an exhaustive examination.

If you find yourself puzzling over what it is your character wants or why, explore these various alternatives again and see if something clicks—your character wants one thing but gets something else altogether, your character has pursued a goal he comes to realize is worthless or destructive, your character's desire is defined by a helpless reenactment of a definitive trauma. It may help crystallize your story for you, or guide you to a variation you'd previously not considered.

Identifying the Core Desire

Clearly, pursuing a desire is not as simple as it might seem, at least not in dramatic writing. The exterior goal echoes interior ones, or disguises them, betrays them, contradicts them. We choose the exterior goal to provide dramatic urgency, to create movement, and to offer clarity, even though that outer goal often only incompletely represents what the character truly wants.

Regardless of whether it's the exterior or interior goal that's more central, it's the deeper, more resilient want we most need to understand. It's the thing that, if taken away, would cause the character to dissolve before our eyes. It's the force that, perhaps openly, perhaps secretly—but always relentlessly—drives him forward.

In trying to identify your character's key want, begin with *what he believes it to be*: romantic love, family, vengeance, wealth, fame, power, respect. He may want all these things, something deeper that they all represent, or something else altogether, but for the sake of dramatic clarity choose one and write from there, at least until you have a clearer sense of where your story is headed.

One way to determine which object of desire is fundamental, or represents the best stand-in for the others, is to strip it away, make it unattainable, but fulfill the character's other wants. Is the character content? If not, why?

Don't just supply a pat answer: Picture scenes in which

the character is pursuing this desire, imagine how it shapes her life, changes her interactions with others. For example, imagine her dealing with someone who has access to what she wants—the man she believes is the love of her life, the boss who stands between her and success, the mentor whose approval means everything—but refuses to give it to her, or demands something for it she cannot possibly pay. What does she do?

This work should not be limited to one's characters. If we are honest with ourselves, we almost always recognize that despite our many ambitions and wants, one stands out among the others as preeminent. It may be home or family, it may be romantic love, it may be social justice or respect from one's peers. Knowing this about yourself hardly cheapens or trivializes you. On the contrary, it provides an essential perspective, a focus that permits you to value your other endeavors meaningfully. It also better enables you to step outside your own wants and imagine what it might be like to live differently, in pursuit of a different desire or ambition.

Many of my students have had trouble identifying their characters' core needs and wants because they're as yet uncertain of their own, or are afraid to admit them. As a fundamental step in doing this work, every writer needs to look within honestly and ask: What do I truly want? How have I gone about getting it? Why and how did I get it, or not? Another way to pose the question is to ask: When was I happiest? When was I most miserable? Why?

Do not be put off by the fact that the catalog of human desires often seems embarrassingly narrow. The particular form in which this person or that wants fame, or wealth, or love, or revenge, and the specific manner in which a particular desire can be sought or thwarted, is seemingly infinite and richly nuanced—and thus gratifyingly unpredictable.

Besides, who said desires need to be subtle, unusual, or complex to be compelling? In Don Carpenter's *Hard Rain Falling*, Jack Levitt, a teenage orphan runaway who joins a pack of rough boys on the streets of Portland, Oregon, states his simple wants with clarity and force: some money, a piece of ass, a big dinner, and a bottle of whiskey. The myopia of those unoriginal longings foreshadows the disaster lying in wait just beyond their gratification.

Examples of characters with compelling core desires with ripple effects throughout the story include:

• Macbeth, though initially skeptical of the witches' prophecy, becomes emboldened when the first half comes true—he is made the thane of Cawdor—and, urged on by his ambitious wife, obsessively pursues fulfillment of the second half: becoming the king of Scotland. The desire first to gain the throne, then to retain it, consumes him, to the point of murdering not just his enemies but their innocent families.

• In *Death of a Salesman* Willy Loman, despite his advanced years and the loss of his job, clings to his need for greatness, which he equates with charisma and "being well-liked." He also wants his sons to believe as he does in the great possibility of the American Dream, and constantly invokes the lesson of his brother Ben, who went to Africa and Alaska and "got rich." That unquenchable desire for wealth, greatness, and being liked consumes and ultimately destroys him.

- In *House of Sand and Fog*, Kathy Nicol[o] [wants to]
  keep the house she has inherited fr[om...]
  just for the roof over her head it provi[des...]
  its loss will strip her naked, revealing to her t[he]
  truth she has been concealing: Her husband has [left]
  her, she has descended into debilitating depression,
  and she has lost her capacity to function in the real world.

- Kathy's situation is similar to that of Blanche DuBois
  in *A Streetcar Named Desire*, who has lost the family
  home and now has nowhere to stay. She is desperate,
  and has come to New Orleans to find her sister, Stella,
  and ask to be taken in.

- The prostitute Beth, a secondary character in Jess Walter's *Citizen Vince*, is pursuing a real estate license, which
  is almost certainly beyond her grasp, and yet she has
  come to want it so badly, "It hurts my head to think about.
  It's stupid how much I want this." But of course what she
  really wants is normalcy, a respectable life: Vince.

- Walter White, the protagonist in the TV series *Breaking
  Bad*, learns he has terminal cancer, and wants to provide
  financial security for his family, something he realizes is
  impossible on his high school chemistry teacher's salary.
  But this awakens in him something deeper, a need in the
  truest sense of the words "to live."

Exercises

1. Select three books or films you've recently enjoyed.
   Identify the core desire, need, or ambition in at least
   three main characters.

2. Do the same for three characters in a piece you're currently working on, as well as three to five characters you developed in doing the exercises for chapters 2 and 3.

3. Take the same characters chosen in exercise 2 and ask what would happen to them, what would happen to their stories, if their desires, needs, or ambitions exhibited any of the following:

- The overall desire was an obsessive totem for multiple underlying desires.

- The object of desire changed or became clearer due to conflicts endured.

- The character suffered two irreconcilable desires.

- The conscious desire conflicted with an unconscious one.

- The object of desire was ultimately found to be worthless.

- The character wanted one thing but got something else altogether.

Don't answer this question simplistically. Chart out how the story would change if it exhibited any of the foregoing characteristics. What have you learned about your characters by asking these questions?

Chapter Six
Desire Denied: Adaptations, Defense Mechanisms, and Pathological Maneuvers

How We React to Conflict
Defines Our Capacity for Success

Since desire creates conflict, we're obliged to ask: How does the character react when her desires are thwarted? What sort of response does conflict engender? This turns out to be a crucial question not just in drama but in life.

For seventy-two years, researchers at Harvard tracked the lives of 268 subjects—healthy young men from the college's 1942–1944 graduating classes. The study's principal analyst for forty-two years, George Vaillant, wrote two books on the insights he gained from the study: *Adaptation to Life* (1977) and *Aging Well* (2002). What he discovered was that the greatest single factor in determining whether a subject led a happy, successful life was rooted in how he responded to the stress of failure and life's inevitable setbacks.

Vaillant drew on the research of Anna Freud concerning what she called "adaptations" or "defense mechanisms"—

organic, unconscious thoughts and behaviors each of us uses in response to pain, stress, loss, conflict, disappointment, uncertainty, even betrayal.

These adaptations normally change as we mature, becoming more socially functional as we proceed from infancy to adolescence to adulthood. Some of us, however, never outgrow certain adaptations, clinging to them unhealthily, and these inhibit how we interact with others and the way we manage the turbulence of life.

Sometimes the conflicts we face are internal. For example, I may suffer unwanted thoughts or emotions—racist obsessions or homosexual longings—and then deny them or project them onto others. Other times the adaptation arises when I'm facing an overwhelming crisis or ordeal—I drink to "steady my nerves," I stubbornly "stick to my guns" rather than admit I need to adapt to new circumstances. Either way, the defense mechanism defines my response to conflict, and fundamentally shapes how I view myself and my situation.

Vaillant, again relying on Anna Freud, developed a four-tier hierarchy for these adaptations, from least to most adaptive:

Psychotic adaptations: paranoia, hallucination, megalomania

Immature adaptations: passive aggression, hypochondria, projection, fantasy

Neurotic adaptations:

> *Intellectualization* (turning feelings and sensations into thoughts)

Dissociation (brief but intense removal from one's feelings)

Repression (inexplicable naïveté, memory lapse, denial, ignoring physical stimuli)

<u>Mature adaptations:</u> altruism, humor, anticipation, and:

Suppression (postponing attention to the problem in order to address it at another time)

Sublimation (finding "acceptable" outlets for feelings/passions—e.g., sports or career for aggression, courtship for lust)

As useful as I find this approach to be in my work, I'm also aware that psychoanalysis creates a more intellectual than emotional approach to fleshing out a character. The result often more resembles an idea than a person. But as I stress often in this book, the antidote to overintellectualization is to envision dramatic situations—scenes—in which the issue plays out: in this instance, how a character responds to conflict and stress.

The Normality at the Heart of the Pathological Maneuver

Unfortunately, writers often grant their protagonists only mature adaptations, giving them an intrinsically sanguine psyche that automatically responds to stress and conflict with wit, patience, greater resolve, or determination. This may underscore the broad appeal of the old college try, but it's a lost opportunity.

The author Elizabeth George hints at the neglected advantages of the seemingly bizarre when she refers to adaptations somewhat colorfully as "pathological maneuvers."* As much as I enjoy this turn of phrase, and find it perfect from a writerly perspective, not even the more primitive defense mechanisms are inherently dysfunctional. Toddlers commonly employ psychotic adaptations, for example, just as adolescents routinely exhibit immature ones. Despite the unfortunate label "neurotic," the adaptations in this category define how most "normal" people respond to stress.

But though not all adaptations are pathological, a great many of the more interesting or vivid ones are: obsession, addiction, denial, hallucination, irrational hatred or rage, harming oneself, harming others, mania, hypochondria.

Don't get caught up in the garish terminology. These responses are best understood in specific and human terms, meaning it's best if possible to explore how a given adaptation has been exhibited in yourself or someone in your life.

When I think of dissociation, for example, I recall a Salvadoran woman I know whose husband was murdered by a death squad during that country's civil war. The couple was taking their nightly walk outside their home when a motorcycle appeared. The man riding pillion produced a gun, fired, and hit the husband in the heart—clearly the work of a trained assassin. As the motorcycle sped off, the wife knelt beside her dying husband and tried to stop the bleeding. But after a moment she went psychologi-

---

* Elizabeth George, *Write Away*, chapter 5.

cally blank, stood up, and walked half a block with no knowledge she was even moving, covered with her husband's blood.

One way to find such examples in your own life is to return to the emotionally charged events we explored in chapter 3, specifically moments of profound fear, shame, or guilt. How did you respond? How have you responded to similar episodes since?

Do you drink a bit too much when fearing judgment, ridicule, or rejection? Do you jabber away when you meet someone you're attracted to? Does loneliness prompt eating, drinking, or spending binges?

Putting your character in similar pressure situations can also vividly open him up to you. Envision your character getting his face slapped in a crowded room; being confronted by a gunman who demands his wallet and car keys; having to save a high-chaired infant from a sudden, out-of-control kitchen fire; dealing with doctors treating a dying spouse, child, or parent.

Sometimes we're perfectly capable of handling stress in one environment and helpless in another. Patrick Fitzpatrick in Thomas McGuane's *Nobody's Angel* is a former tank commander who felt perfectly at home in the military, but who, out of uniform and back in Montana, falls increasingly victim to drink as the misadventures of romance and the demands of his eccentric family task his capacity to deal. Combat maneuvers are a snap compared to a gifted, much-loved but psychotic sister.

The key point is that when confronted with stress, we feel anxiety—the echoes of abandonment, ridicule, rejection, violence—based on the details of our lives. And given that unique personal history, each of us has developed an organic response, often unconscious, and often less than optimal. The most common defense is denial—we simply stifle whatever we're feeling and go on as though nothing has happened. But whatever the specific defense used, it routinely contains elements of both deceit and cowardice: deceit, in that we refuse to face the situation before us in all its emotional intensity or sensory impact; cowardice, in that we can't muster the will to return to the moment and deal with it honestly, no matter how painful, fearful, or shameful. As a result, overcoming the so-called pathological maneuver often requires both insight and courage—which is precisely why it provides excellent grist for drama.

Dramatizing Growth from One Level of Adaptation to Another—The Ghost and the Revenant

Your story may demonstrate how the character grows from less-adaptive adjustments to healthier, more mature ones. Tales of recovery, personal growth, and redemption are premised on just such an arc, even though the progress to sobriety, maturity, or self-reclamation seldom follows the graceful trajectory the word "arc" suggests.

In the film *Crazy Heart*, based on the novel by Thomas Cobb, Bad Blake (Jeff Bridges) is an aging country singer–songwriter who has boozed and womanized his way to the end of the line—where, through drunk luck, he meets and falls for a single mom named Jean Craddock (Maggie Gyllenhaal). Having avoided commitment his entire life, Bad falls prey to the great lie every inebriate knows like his own name: This time will be different. The stress of responsibility and openness, which Bad experiences as boredom, obliges him to seek out a drink when he's supposed to be watching Jean's young son. The boy goes missing, prompting the inevitable crisis that Bad has sought out time and again, a crisis that reveals his gift for failure, and which provides an excuse for even more drinking and the oblivion that ensues. Though the film portrays his whiskey-addled fall well enough, his recovery feels like a magic act— in one scene he enters rehab, in the next he exits sober. Regrettably, this robs the audience of the real conflict at the heart of the story: How does this man learn to stop running from his fear of being seen honestly by people he loves?

One finds a more compelling and realistic dramatization of recovery in the TV series *Breaking Bad*. Due to poly-drug abuse centered on a methamphetamine addiction, Jesse Pinkman (Aaron Paul) has internalized the negative view most adults have of him: He's the inveterate screwup, "the bad guy." This self-image gets perfected when his girlfriend Jane (Krysten Ritter) slips back into heroin addiction because of his influence, then dies of an overdose. In group therapy afterward, he smugly believes his pain and guilt are greater than anyone else's, only to learn that the group's leader ran over his own daughter when backing out of his driveway to buy vodka. The leader advises, "You're not here to become a better person. You're here to learn to accept who you are." That realization leads Jesse back to temporary sobriety, but the mounting stresses of his subsequent return to the meth trade create the perfect triggers for relapse, and this seesaw captures all too well the day-to-day life of someone dealing with this particular pathological maneuver.

In the film *Secretary*, based loosely on a short story by Mary Gaitskill from her collection *Bad Behavior*, Lee Holloway, a dowdy, shy, almost pathologically self-conscious young woman, exits a psychiatric facility to find her alcohol-afflicted family unchanged. She reverts to cutting herself, which she has done since she was twelve; it's her way of coping with the psychodrama of anger and denial that characterizes her home life. Answering an ad for a legal secretary, she meets attorney E. Edward Grey, who has a bit of a quirk, a fantasy life he has lived out with other secretaries: He finds fault with their performance, then spanks them voluptuously into self-improvement. Lee is not put off by this—on the contrary, she feels found. Not only does she relish the attention, it provides her a way to externalize and share the ritual with pain she's conducted since puberty. Her sense of herself and her sexuality blossom, the dowdiness falls away like a shirked cocoon. But then Mr. Grey recoils. Afflicted with self-loathing and guilt, he breaks things off cruelly and fires her. But Lee's come too far to return to who she was. With her newfound self-awareness, she proves to him that not only is she not disgusted by his wants, she embraces them and wants to share them.

In the personal redemption arena, consider the film *Michael Clayton*. The eponymous hero (George Clooney) is a legal chameleon who works as his law firm's fixer. He's good at it, the best—the bigger the problem or seamier the fallout, the headier the rush—but every solution leaves a taint, if only on his soul. People regard him as "the garbageman," even the lawyers who rely on him—worse, even members of his own family. And as he's spent years now solving other people's problems and neglecting his own, he's internalized the garbageman persona. At the same time he loves the action, the flirtation with disaster it suggests—it comes so much more naturally than the boring steadiness of responsibility—and this need for an adrenaline high has led to a gambling addiction. Luck, after all, is the one problem you can't fix. He's flirting with ruin when a lawyer associate and close friend (Arthur, played by Tom Wilkinson) goes off his meds and has a manic episode he interprets as moral clarity: He can no longer defend a corporate client who has manufactured a toxic weed killer, causing the deaths of hundreds of small farmers. The corporate clients, ensnarled in a multibillion-dollar lawsuit, kill Arthur to contain the damage when Michael proves unable to do so. This failure prompts Michael to decide he can no longer be who he's been, moving from gamble to gamble, crisis to crisis, fix to fix, feeding off ego and adrenaline rather than owning up to who he is, who he cares about, and what he needs to do. The crucial turn occurs when Michael must explain to his son why the boy's not going to be like his coke addict uncle—and, by implication, his gambling addict father. Michael decides to stop helping everyone, including himself, avoid responsibility for the messes they create. Instead of being "the guy you buy," he becomes "the guy you kill."

In each of these examples, the character's adaptation—drink, drugs, cutting, gambling—is anchored at least symbolically in two other characters, one who represents *past* failures to respond well to frustration of some fundamental want or ambition, and another in the *present* who forces the character to deal with the problem once again. Different teachers and texts refer to these characters by different names. I prefer "ghost" and "revenant"—ghost because of the haunting effect of the past, revenant because of that problem's return within the present.

Although it is useful to conceive of the ghost and the revenant as characters, the ghost can also be a generalized problem from the past, or a succession of encounters that all create within the main character a single sense of loss, vulnerability, or failure. Joe Buck's ghost in *Midnight Cowboy*, for example, could be considered his history of aborted love: being abandoned by his mother, glad-handed by Sally Buck, used by his teenage trysts. But it's still at times dramatically useful and more powerful to epitomize that legacy of pain in a single character. For Joe Buck, this is Crazy Annie, the town slut he was too naïve to realize wasn't the girl you fell in love with, and whose memory resonates even more painfully than the others.

The revenant, on the other hand, is almost always best conceived not as a problem or a situation but as a person within the drama. Otherwise the main character will be obliged to work out his emotional conflicts internally, which creates the risk of interminable rumination.

If the ghost is a single character, the adaptation or pathological maneuver is in many ways an attempt to drown out the sound of that character's voice, to turn away from that character's gaze, for she embodies the habitual failure to overcome the odds and be genuine, be strong, achieve the core desire. And the revenant embodies the inescapable realization that no one can hide from himself forever. Life doesn't work like that, whether because of fate, karma, Freud's concept of the repetition compulsion, or our unconscious drive toward psychic health.

Jean provides Bad Blake his latest chance to get it right, and thus serves as his revenant. But we hear his failure echoing deep into the past, a legacy of drunken womanizing and irresponsibility. No one epitomizes that legacy more painfully than the son he's long neglected. As Bad edges toward recovery, he tries to reconnect, but that bridge turned to cinders long ago—and created the ghost that haunts Bad into the present, a reminder that growth never comes easy or cheap.

In *Breaking Bad*, Jane serves both as revenant and ghost, switching from one to the other with her overdose and death. For much of the season in which she appears, Jane is very much a revenant, creating circumstances that Jesse could use to look at his own history of poor choices and lost chances, his weakness and addiction. But he fails that test. After Jane's death she comes to epitomize every failure that preceded her. Jesse feels stained forever by what happened, even as, in the present, his counselor tries to shake him out of the egotism of self-pity.

In *Secretary*, Lee's alcoholic father represents the emotional powerlessness she's felt in the past, while Mr. Grey provides an opportunity to turn that around—ironically, in the role of sexual submissive, which provides her a way to ritualize and understand her inner woundedness. She grows from secretly cutting herself to deal with her pain to openly sharing her understanding of that pain and her need for intimacy with the man she has come to love.

Michael Clayton's lawyer associates and clients all

personify the desire to escape the damage one creates, and thus they represent Michael's own history of shirking responsibility, but the real anchor character for that insight is his son, Henry, whom he can sense he's failing. Meanwhile, in the present, the madness-tinged crisis of conscience created by Arthur, the bipolar attorney, forces matters to a head. Michael accepts that he must either change and live up to what his son deserves, or fall back into a kind of twilight of the soul, the living death of being "the man you buy."

If the protagonist grows beyond the maladaptive defenses we see him employing at the story's onset, he will achieve some new relationship or state of awareness with both characters:

- Bad accepts he can never pretend to reconcile with his son, prompting an honest reflection on the damage his drinking has done, which helps him accept the pain of losing Jean as well.

- Jesse also must accept he can never bring Jane back, and whatever peace he achieves depends on his ability to face himself and what he did—literally a monstrous task, as the course of Jesse's behavior through the rest of the series demonstrates.

- Lee's growth helps her demand a more involved, caring, and accepting relationship not just with Mr. Grey but with her father.

- Michael Clayton, though unable to save
  Arthur, will embrace the call to conscience
  he embodied, and will turn against his former clients and associates, achieving a dignity that will permit him to look into his
  son's eyes and not feel ashamed.

Core Versus Secondary Desires and Adaptations

There are two levels to consider: how the character handles the frustration of his *core desire*, which goes to the very
essence of his life, and how he handles inevitable minor
frustrations on any given day. The two may well be related,
but don't take this for granted.

Consider a character whose core desire is romantic love,
but as yet it's remained out of reach. How has he responded:
In bitterness? Resignation? Sexual adventurism? Drink?
Devotion to his parents or siblings? Platonic friendships?
His students? Such a man might tell himself that romantic
love isn't really that important—which could be a sign of
denial (a neurotic adaptation) or sublimation (a mature
one), depending on how productively he applies the energy
he'd otherwise direct toward a lover.

The only way to answer the question of how this character reacts to romantic setback is to put him in a scene of
heartbreak and watch as he responds, then follow his trajectory afterward: Does he deny the pain, react in anger,
descend into black despair or self-loathing, chuckle to
himself about the absurdity of life, then move on to someone else? Take your time. Sit with the character as he reacts; visualize the scenes in all their emotional texture.

You may well find the scenes you envision are crucial to the story you intend to tell, so it's hardly wasted effort.

But how the character responds to heartbreak may not tell you how he responds to more minor or situational frustrations unrelated to his core desire.

He may be perfectly capable, for example, at fix-it projects, so that the wear and tear on his home or car is just a chance to exhibit his expertise. Here, he responds maturely, accepting setbacks as challenges, not intrinsic defeats.

On the other hand, his love life may color everything, and frustrations there may poison every other aspect of his life, so that a hole in the roof becomes just one more sign of how inadequate, unlucky—unlovable—he is.

It is essential you know how the character responds to frustration of his core desire. There's a bit more latitude when it comes to ancillary desires, but notice how much texture is gained by contrasting mature adaptations in one aspect of life with neurotic or immature reactions in others. This provides an opportunity for contradiction, which we'll cover in greater depth in chapter 9.

Tracking the examples we discussed in the last chapter, and will continue analyzing in the next three chapters to come, we find:

• Though Lady Macbeth's adaptation is the more extreme—paranoid hallucination—Macbeth's guilt prevents him from interpreting clearly the witches' final prophecy, and he becomes mired in false confidence (fantasy) and indecision (repression) in the face of mounting opposition to his reign.

- Willy Loman in *Death of a Salesman* deals with his job loss and other mounting failures with a redoubled, almost shrill belief in chasing the American Dream—a form of fantasy and denial—while at the same time secretly plotting his suicide.

- Kathy Nicolo in *House of Sand and Fog* blames the county, her lawyer, and Colonel Behrani for her own negligence (projection), retreats into depression, uses her sexual charms to manipulate an attractive man into rescuing her, and falls back into alcohol and drug abuse as she increasingly fails to deal with the mounting stress of losing her home.

- Blanche DuBois, another would-be siren confronted with the disgrace of losing her home, drinks, scapegoats, guilt-trips her sister Stella, and escapes into dreamlike fantasy all as a way to deny the core recognition that the culprit for her ruin is herself.

- When Beth, the prostitute who wants to be a real estate agent in Jess Walter's *Citizen Vince*, realizes Vince won't be attending her (most likely one and only) open house, she pushes her disappointment aside in favor of fantasy, saying "in a voice rich with delusions, 'Well, you'll just have to come to the next one.'"

- Walter White in *Breaking Bad*, when faced with the threat of violence or arrest that constantly attends his newfound métier as meth cook, invariably overcomes his paralyzing panic by reverting to his most reliable strength: intelligence. Once he's able to think the situation through, his fear becomes manageable, and he's able to deal with the problem at hand.

Exercises

1. Return to the characters identified in your responses for the first two exercises in the preceding chapter. Envision each character in a highly stressful situation: a robbery, a violent fight, an accident with a loved one, the need to end medical treatment for a terminally ill spouse or child or parent. How do they respond? Take your time; let the scene develop organically.

2. For each of the same characters used for exercise 1, answer these questions:

   • What is the character's core desire? How have previous attempts to gratify that desire been thwarted? Is there a single character who epitomizes the frustration of that unfulfilled desire? How does the ghost of the past revisit the character in the time of your story? What forms do his adaptations or defenses take? At what level is he stuck?

   • Is there a galvanic character in the present who serves as a revenant, someone who forces the main character to deal with his continuing inability to act honestly, bravely, responsibly?

Chapter Seven
The Power of Wounds: Vulnerability

When people appear wounded or in need of our help, we are instantly drawn to them—it's a basic human reaction. And if people are open with us, revealing themselves in an honest way, "warts and all," we feel more willing to trust them.

As in life, so in fiction. Vulnerability creates a kind of undertow, pulling us toward a character who is wounded or imperfect, and that attractive force is far more important than whether the character is "likable." People will accept a certain degree of unpleasantness, even outright evil, in a character as long as she remains compelling, which relies far less on her being pleasant than on her being engaged in a meaningful struggle.

There are a variety of ways a character can be vulnerable, each with its own particular power.

Some are existential—she is wounded badly or terribly ill or facing some sudden danger. There is a strange, inexpressible power to physical wounds and crippling illness, and when they occur within a story the stakes are instantly raised and our interest almost always intensifies—unless the wounding or illness feels contrived. Create a wound or an illness for mere effect and you'll more likely alienate your audience than engage it. As for sudden danger, it's true that Raymond Chandler suggested sending a man through the door with a gun whenever the action flagged, but I don't recommend it. Sooner or later, the reader knows you're bluffing.

Some vulnerabilities are situational: The character is out of work, in the midst of a streak of bad luck, stranded by the side of the road, in a strange place during a power outage, wandering unknown rooms in the dark.

Some are moral: Something the character has done places her in jeopardy—she will be judged, rightly or wrongly.

Implicit in all vulnerability is the notion of threat, whether it's to our physical, emotional, spiritual, or psychological selves. That's what makes vulnerability, or the wounds that represent it, a key means of revealing what is at stake in any given scene or story. Just as people are drawn to you when you are wounded, so readers or audience members are drawn to a scene in which genuine vulnerability is shown.

Vulnerability reacquaints us with what Camus described as the "benign indifference of the universe," and our relative insignificance in the scheme of things. But it also reacquaints us with our need for others, and their help. And regardless of the kind of vulnerability, the fact we face some form of real jeopardy implicitly draws others toward us—or pushes them away out of guilt or dread. In either case, the potential for drama is obvious.

If the vulnerability in the present of the story echoes back to a past wound or wounds, that history, or one character who epitomizes it, may serve as the main character's ghost. And whoever comes to the main character's aid in the present, and forces her to deal with that history of pain and overcome its debilitating effect, will serve as revenant.

There is a special connection between vulnerability and shame, one of the most intriguing (and useful) emotions both in real life and fiction.

Shame is the excruciating fear of disconnection that arises when we feel we have done something, or something about us has been revealed, that will prompt others to recoil from us—out of disgust, contempt, disillusion, anger, loathing. The shame creates in us a sense of unworthiness, as though we don't deserve the honest affection of others.

Connection—whether it takes the form of a filial bond, romantic love, solidarity, or some other kind of belonging—is routinely ranked highest in people's assessment of what's valuable in their lives. Anything that threatens connection therefore strikes at the heart of our existence, which means nothing could be more crucial for characterization.

A great many stories are premised on the protagonist's struggle to achieve a sense of self-worth that is stronger than his shame, which means the character will have to grow to the point where being vulnerable in front of others doesn't create a crippling sense of unworthiness.

Consider the film *Precious*. The protagonist begins the

film numb to the history of abuse she's endured. She's literally walled up inside a fortress of flesh, hiding from her life. It's only as outsiders take her seriously, feed her sense of dignity and self-worth, see her for the person she *can be* rather than the depressed underachiever her mother has created and crippled, that Precious realizes what she wants—to raise a family free of abuse and indignity, in which everyone is allowed to love, and is loved in return. Precious learns that worthiness can come only with an honest self-compassion. Absent a realistic awareness of her faults and virtues, assessed not just with truthfulness but kindness, she is incapable of being meaningfully open and caring.

The key word is "realistic." Precious does not become foolishly all-forgiving. Once she understands what real love is, she no longer feels compelled to make excuses for her mother, or deny the horrific abuse her mother condoned.

Vulnerability is not the opposite of strength. It takes courage to be truly vulnerable, for openness is all too often its own reward. No one is comfortable exposing himself; some are just better at managing the discomfort due to their sense of worth. But having a strong sense of connection and worthiness does not assure us we will be loved, because love is a gift, not a right. It's given, not earned.

Key questions to ask of your characters therefore include: Do they believe they are worthy of love? If so, some person or persons demonstrated that worthiness to them; picture the person, the moment, envision the scene. Despite

THE POWER OF WOUNDS: VULNERABILITY { 89

that sense of worthiness, what elements of shame and vulnerability persist—and what moments and people created such tenacious insecurities?

If your character believes she isn't worthy, what event or events created that conviction? Does she possess a terrible secret that inhibits her ability or willingness to be vulnerable? When was the last time she was truly open with someone? How did it turn out? There is perhaps no more devastating scene than one in which the character risks vulnerability only to earn exactly what she feared: rejection, disgust, betrayal, contempt.

There often is no more crucial question to ask in the course of a scene than what within it renders your character vulnerable, since that so often ties in to what she wants. What are the stakes, what is at risk, what is the harm that might be done?

Returning to our ongoing examples:

- For all the evil in Macbeth's murderous climb to power, there is also the threat of retribution. Even though it's eminently deserved, and we hope to see him suffer for his crimes, that peril increases our interest in his fate. His guilt and fear, his gnawing conscience, his full awareness of his crimes—his insight—also render him vulnerable.

- Willy Loman, beneath his bombastic sloganeering, is a desperately frightened and lonely man, fearful he has not lived up to his own expectations, and is thus unlovable.

- In *House of Sand and Fog*, Kathy is helpless before the power of the county to take away her home, and that opens the door to other forms of helplessness: her addictions, her need for a strong man, her fear of her mother's scorn, her desire to die.

- Blanche DuBois is homeless, in desperate need of a safe place. And the tawdry nature of her secrets threaten to shame her beyond redemption if revealed, which is why she inevitably relies on "the kindness of strangers."

- Beth in *Citizen Vince* is so broke she lives with her mother, where she shares the sofa with her young son. She is also vulnerable because of her love for Vince, who is fond of her but "not that way."

- Walt in *Breaking Bad* has terminal lung cancer, and is expected to live only two years. He also knows he lacks the money to both pay for his treatment and provide for his family after his death. His powerlessness, combined with his love, inspire our empathy.

Exercises

1. As before, select three characters from a piece you're currently writing. Do any of them exhibit: A physical vulnerability—a wound, an illness, a disfiguring scar? A situational one—what threat(s) do they face in your story? A moral one—what sort of guilt are they risking due to the actions they commit? If none of these applies, supply one kind of vulnerability and see what happens.

2. Once the three characters addressed in exercise 1 possess a vulnerability, identify what other characters in the story are drawn in because of that. Does the wounded character come to rely on the help of one of these other characters? How does that need for help play out? (For example, is there a successful outcome?) Or is the character betrayed or abandoned by his helper? Does the character, out of shame, blame himself for that betrayal or abandonment?

3. Taking these same three characters: Do they believe they are worthy of love? If so, what person or persons in their past convinced them of this, and how and when did that happen? What elements of unworthiness persist, and what incidents and people are responsible? Picture the moments specifically; play them out as scenes.

4. Again, the same three characters: When was the last time they were truly open with someone? How did it turn out?

Chapter Eight
The Gravity of the Hidden: Secrets

———

What we refer to as subtext—the "thing beneath the thing," as filmmaker Leslie Schwerin calls it—is premised on the tension between what is revealed and what is not.

This speaks to the power of secrets. If we believe someone is hiding something, we can't help but pay more attention to him. Few drives are as strong as the one to find out—ask Pandora, or Psyche, or Bluebeard's wife.

Christopher Vogler* calls this the Law of the Secret Door: Put a barrier between something and the hero and his curiosity will inevitably require him to tear that barrier away. The power of secrets speaks to this insatiable need to know.

Secrets need not necessarily be shameful, though many are, sometimes unreasonably. But they always speak to an aspect of what has happened to us that we can neither forget nor share.

———

* Christopher Vogler, *The Writer's Journey: Mythic Structure for Storytellers & Screenwriters* (Michael Wiese Productions).

In Kate Atkinson's *When Will There Be Good News?* Joanna Hunter, whose mother, sister, and baby brother were murdered by a lunatic when she was six years old, explains to a police officer why she tells no one about this: "People look at you differently when they know you've been through something terrible. It's the thing about you that they find most interesting."

What we choose to keep hidden, and why we do so, says a great deal about what we believe others expect from us, and about the limits of who we can be and still be loved and accepted.

Secrets represent what we fear, if exposed, will destroy forever our standing among our friends and families, community and peers. That fear may be unreasonable, out of all proportion, but that's far less important than that it exists—especially for writers.

The mask we call our ego or persona is crafted on the premise of concealing our fears, our weaknesses, our vulnerabilities—our secrets. The threat of being exposed or found out and therefore ostracized or abandoned is one of the key dreads of existence. In a sense, secrets are a premonition of the isolation we associate with death, and our keeping them hidden is part of the magical thinking we perpetuate as part of the ritual of life.

A great deal of modern drama is premised upon the peeling away of the mask that conceals our secret selves, and the struggle to summon the courage and honesty to deal with the consequences of being known more truly and completely. In such stories, the secret serves as ghost, and the character who obliges the main character to expose the secret and deal with it serves as revenant.

• • •

Although there is a diagnostic distinction between secrets, which are consciously concealed, and repressed traits or behaviors, from a dramatic perspective they reflect more a difference in degree than kind. Repression, from a writer's point of view, is simply what happens when the concealment of a secret has been rendered habitual by years of deceit. It's fear of exposure that makes what's hidden dramatically interesting, and for both secrets and repressed desires or traits, that fear is fundamentally the same. What's at stake is our public identity, the person others believe us to be, and all we have built by assuming that role.

Both repressed traits and secrets can be unearthed straightforwardly by exploring the character's backstory—whether they've been buried for a moment or a lifetime. What is the character afraid of or ashamed of, what does she feel guilty about? And remember that these past incidents almost always involve *other people*, and thus can be conceived in scenic terms.

It may be that there is no such thing as living without a mask, and that the stripping away of one simply predicates the donning of another, or relying on one already in place. It may be that what I think of as my honest self is really just a different one: slightly less dishonest, defensive, deluded—or not. But it remains true that each mask is there not just for concealment, but for protection.

Patricia Highsmith in *The Talented Mr. Ripley* provides a chilling example. Tom Ripley, with his perpetual deceits, is a character whose every action conceals a secret—it's what makes him fascinating to us. And yet the frisson at the heart of the story is provided by the fact that Ripley's inner conception of himself reveals just another layer of fraud.

There is something deeper but untouchable, unknowable about Ripley, because it's not just his worldly persona that's self-fabricated. Though articulate and seemingly self-aware, he's in fact utterly and terrifyingly self-deluded. And Highsmith's art lies in never spelling out for us what's "really" at the bottom of things, but capturing that eerie sense of disequilibrium created by that lack of a center of gravity.

The book's power lies in its depiction of that impenetrable void at Ripley's core, which accounts for his chameleon-like (or parasitic) behavior. He only truly comes to life when assuming the persona of Dickie Greenleaf, without ever fully realizing why this is true about himself.

It's a far more chilling portrayal of evil than, say, Scarpia in the opera *Tosca*, who states openly that he takes greater pleasure in seizing by force what objects of desire are refused to him than accepting those that are freely given. As terrifying as that is, his self-awareness renders him knowable, even predictable. In contrast, Ripley's self-delusion renders him utterly *un*predictable, and thus far more horrifying.

Though not a role player like Ripley, Freddie Clegg in John Fowles's *The Collector* provides a similar portrait of delusion at the heart of evil. Freddie is largely blind to his own wickedness. Again, the interior world of the character is no more true than the deceitful exterior. At his core, there is a kind of emptiness instead of a human soul.

But ironically this lack of a center doesn't render either Freddie Clegg or Tom Ripley less vulnerable to exposure, which again testifies to the power of secrets. Both men retain an *idea* of who they are and protect it fiercely, even though—or perhaps because—it's a fraud.

It is not just protagonists and other main characters who benefit from harboring—or revealing—a secret. In the film *Tumbleweeds*, the libertine mother, Mary Jo, and her wise-beyond-her-years daughter, Ava, provide the core of the drama. But at their most recent stop on their parade of misbegotten landings, they encounter a man named Dan, who possesses a kindliness tinged with sorrow. We gradually learn he is a widower, but that still seems to get us only so far. We see him tutor Ava, who is preparing for a Shakespearean role for her high school drama class, and he shows her that the rhythm of iambic pentameter mimics the pulsations of the human heart. He also offers Mary Jo and Ava use of a camper he keeps parked outside his house. He and his late wife had bought the camper in preparation for a cross-country trek they'd planned for some time. Their friends threw a lavish going-away party the night before the couple was going to head off. "It was a great party," Dan says with slightly more wistfulness than usual. Then: "I shouldn't have been driving."

The fact that Dan was responsible for his wife's death comes as a thunderbolt. We now see in his kindness not just sadness, but a guilt for which he can never atone.

This demonstrates not just that even secondary characters can benefit from secrets, but that timing is crucial in their revelation. Since secrets automatically provide suspense, don't disclose them until necessary—usually not until well into the story, and as close to the end as possible if they lie at the heart of the conflict.

Following through with our recurring examples:

- Macbeth's murder of King Duncan and his plying the two chamberlains with drink so they can be set up for the crime is one of many secrets Macbeth is obliged to conceal through the course of his rise and fall. His lust for power is itself a secret until he seizes the crown.

- Willy Loman conceals not just the loss of his job but his plans for suicide.

- In *House of Sand and Fog*, Kathy lies to her mother about her husband's leaving, her return to smoking, and the loss of the house to back taxes.

- Blanche DuBois's secret in *A Streetcar Named Desire* is that she lost the family home not because of understandable money troubles—she was living on a teacher's salary—but because through drink and illicit sexual liaisons she became so emotionally and physically dissipated she lost hold of the rude realities of her life.

- Beth in *Citizen Vince* is obliged to conceal her romantic interest in Vince, for if she makes the first move she risks being laughed at. How can a hooker presume to be "something that you wanted like that," i.e., a girlfriend?

- In *Breaking Bad*, Walt, desperate for money, turns his chemistry expertise to cooking methamphetamine, which he conceals from everyone, especially his DEA agent brother-in-law.

Secrets are not essential for a portrayal, but they do provide an economical way to depict vulnerability. If you're going to use a secret, don't think small, unless you're trying for comic or ironic effect. Imagine something deep and fiercely protected—the thing that, if known by others, would change forever your character's life as he knows it. Even people he loves and who love him would recoil in disgust or fear or condemnation if they knew.

Exercises

1. Take three characters from a piece you're currently writing and identify whether they possess any secrets. If so, how do those secrets affect their behavior vis-à-vis the other characters? Are any of the characters actively trying to unearth another's secret? Why or why not? What would happen if one character were to disclose her secret to one of the other characters? (If nothing, choose a more damning, shameful, or devastating secret.)

2. Analyze the secrets you developed in your response to exercise 1. How long has the character been hiding this secret? How habitual is the concealment? Has that concealment become second nature? If so, what might force it back into consciousness?

3. For any of the characters you explored in the previous two exercises, does a secret form the ghost of the story? If so, who serves as revenant, to expose the ghost and force the main character to deal with bringing it into the open?

Chapter Nine
The Paradox of This but That: Contradictions

> The spirit of creation is the spirit of contradiction—
> the breakthrough of appearances toward an unknown
> reality.
>
> —Jean Cocteau

The Nature and Dramatic Purpose of Contradiction

Simply stated, a contradiction is something about a person
that piques our interest because it betrays what we expect,
given what else we know or observe about him. Like secrets, contradictions instinctively arouse our curiosity—we
can't help ourselves—and they therefore, in characterization, provide a useful tool above and beyond considerations
of verisimilitude or inventiveness.

In truth, once one trains an eye to seek out contradictions, they can be seen virtually everywhere. They express
a seeming paradox of human nature: that people do one

thing and exactly the opposite; they're this but they're also that.

Some are physical, like the bully's squeaky voice, the ballerina's chubby knees—or the mother's "hideous smile of malice" in Paula Fox's *The Widow's Children*, or the old woman's "intimate menacing voice" in Eudora Welty's "A Visit of Charity."

Some seemingly go no deeper than nicknames—the killer in Richard Price's *Clockers* named Buddha Hat—or an otherwise unassuming housewife's suggestive tattoo, as in John Hawkes's *Travesty*. And yet even these seemingly inconsequential incongruities raise a suspicion of unexpected complexity, enigma, or depth.

Some contradictions are dispositional: A man is both garrulous but shy, outgoing but suspicious, brutal but childlike. Omar Little from the TV show *The Wire* isn't just a shotgun-toting vigilante who lives by robbing drug dealers—asked how he earns his money, he replies, "I rip and run"—he's also an open homosexual who treats his lovers with startling affection and tenderness. The ultimate effect: We never know exactly which half of the personality will assert itself in any given situation.

Some contradictions are behavioral: We feel divided—optimistic and yet wary, accepting and yet guarded. We're both generous with family and friends but fearful of strangers, apologetic to our superiors, and resentful of our inferiors (or vice versa). Such contradictions routinely speak of a tension between whom we trust and whom we don't—and why. Whatever their cause, they remind an observer that what she sees in any given situation is not the whole story.

Beyond purposes of verisimilitude, contradictions serve two key dramatic purposes:

- They defy expectation and thus pique our interest.
- They provide a straightforward method for depicting complexity and depth. Specifically, they provide a means by which to portray:
    * Subtext (the tension between the expressed and the unexpressed, the visible and the concealed)
    * The situational subtleties of social life
    * The conflict between conscious and unconscious behavior
    * Suspense: We want to know what the contradiction means, why it's there.

Contradictions can be used as foreshadowing. In the opening pages of Raymond Chandler's *The Long Goodbye* Marlowe sees Terry Lennox for the first time as he's all but falling down drunk from a Rolls Royce—a case of ironic juxtaposition. This is followed by even more contradictions: Despite Lennox being blotto, his enunciation would suggest he hadn't had anything stronger to drink than orange juice. In fact, he's the most well-mannered drunk Marlowe can remember ever encountering. That alone piques our curiosity, but there's more: "He had a young-looking face but his hair was bone white." On closer inspection, Marlowe discovers the right side of Lennox's face is "frozen and whitish and seamed with fine white scars . . . A plastic job and a pretty drastic one." Why Lennox would go to the trouble of such an extreme alteration of his features but not dye his hair is, well, a mystery. But then that's Marlowe's line of work.

There are limits to what is credible. If we say someone's behavior is "out of character," we normally mean it doesn't mesh with what else we know about him—a perfect case of contradiction. But in a script or a piece of fiction, if something feels "out of character," we usually mean it's not believable. Contradictions that seem too extreme or implausible may enhance a comedic portrayal—the Mob boss with the Yorkie, the cop who's terrified of cats, the chain-smoking nun—but they can undermine a dramatic one.

It's often useful to ask whether the contradiction draws you, the writer, toward the character, or permits you an emotional distance. If the latter, you are "looking at" the character rather than emotionally engaging with her. The contradiction you're considering therefore more likely resembles an idea, not a viable characteristic. If you can justify it, root it in backstory—unearth scenes from your imagination that reveal how this character developed these seemingly contradictory inclinations—it will become less conceptual, more intuitive and organic.

Some people, especially those with pious standards of appropriate behavior, will always rankle at contradiction no matter where they find it. But rectitude is the enemy of creativity. For the writer, things are thankfully a bit more fluid. Even so, you can't just stitch two opposites together and consider it a job well done.

With the understanding that, in writing, nothing is trivial, let's discuss these various kinds of contradiction in descending order, from the seemingly most superficial to the more substantial and meaningful.

Contradictions Based on Physical, Ironic, or Comic Juxtaposition

Anyone acquainted with gang culture, specifically street handles, has come across a kind of contradiction based on ironic juxtaposition: big guys named Tiny, brooders named Smiley, killers named Sweet.

But there is also:

- The beautiful young woman with the dwarfed limb—or a wig to conceal her chemotherapy-ravaged hair

- The middle-aged mother who dresses like her teenage daughter

- The scrawny bespectacled titmouse with the shameless comb-over who, with one drink down the hatch, can't help but play the Romeo—or pick a fight with the cretin sitting one stool down

- The aging gigolo shaving with a Lady Remington—as Richard Bone does in the opening scene of Newton Thornburg's *Cutter and Bone*

Contradictions Based on Our
Need to Serve Multiple Social Roles

In his novel *Rameau's Nephew*, Denis Diderot proposed that each of us is obliged to assume a seemingly endless number of masks to fulfill the various roles or multiple obligations demanded of us. If one of those masks feels more solid or firmly rooted, that's only because habit, created by the daily assumption of that particular role—dutiful daughter, querulous neighbor, taskmaster boss—has made it more routine, familiar, and natural. But all it takes is a sudden or drastic change in social setting and we find ourselves asking: What's expected of me here? Who am I supposed to be? What do I need to do to blend in?

We conduct ourselves appropriately in a variety of different social situations: the dinner table, the office, the stadium, the chapel, the bedroom. We feel differing degrees of freedom to "be ourselves" in each of these environments, depending on who else is present, our relationship with them, our status. The persona that excels at the office presumably will not serve in the bedroom, and vice versa—unless one's workplace is decidedly forward-thinking. But most people effortlessly navigate such diverse circumstances daily.

Consider, for example, the single working mother. At the office and at home she is a whirlwind: decisive, blunt, practical. Then a man with whom she's very much smitten arrives to take her out on a rare date. Her children barely recognize her: She's not just dressed to the nines, she's charming, soft-spoken, giggly, deferential. They might well ask themselves: Who is this stranger, and what did she do with Mom?

And in a completely different circumstance—say at the hospital with her dying father—the very same woman may reveal but another side: impatient, petulant, needy, scared.

Contradictions Based on Competing Morals or Goals

We consider ourselves upright and conscientious—until we encounter an envelope filled with cash (David Mamet's *House of Games*). You have been faithful to your spouse for years—until one night alone in a strange place (Tobias Wolff's "An Episode in the Life of Professor Brooke"). In Peter Carey's novel *Theft*, Michael Boone is torn between his helpless love for the mysterious Marlene, who appears out of a driving rainstorm one night, and his duty to his severely disturbed brother, Hugh.

Some of the greatest drama in history has been premised on such conflicts: Antigone must choose between loyalty to the state or love of her brother; Orestes must choose between incurring the wrath of Apollo or being set upon by the Furies; given the foreknowledge that he will die during the sack of Troy, Achilles must decide whether to continue and earn a warrior's glory (*kleos*) or accept the chance offered to him by his goddess mother, Thetis, and return to Attica and live out his days in peace.

These are core conflicts at the heart of the drama, but similar, smaller conflicts premised on contrasting morals or goals can also be employed to enhance characterization, portraying the many contradictory forces tugging on the character: the pitiless nun (*Doubt*), the criminal psychologist with a gambling problem (*Cracker*), the prostitute mother (*Bellman & True*).

Contradictions That Result from a Secret or Deceit

The fact that someone is hiding something provides an obvious opportunity for contradiction, since sooner or later the thing concealed will inadvertently slip out, supplying the kind of inexplicable behavioral turn that by its very nature intrigues.

In Daphne du Maurier's *Rebecca*, the impact on Maxim de Winter of the death of his wife, a woman he both cherished and despised, festers just under the surface of his civility only to erupt in inexplicable bursts of caustic temper that over time take on such a menacing aspect that his character seems increasingly likely to crack apart—suggesting that Rebecca's death might not have been a tragic accident after all.

In Baroness Emmuska Orczy's *The Scarlet Pimpernel*, Marguerite St. Just wonders what happened to the man she married. Once a charming baronet of soldierly confidence, filled with romantic ardor, Sir Percy Blakeney's become a parody of himself, playing the part of the slow-witted dandy when out in society and refusing to so much as touch her when the two are alone. Ultimately Marguerite will learn the foppery is a disguise, intended to conceal Sir Percy's role as the leader of a band of English noblemen dedicated to saving the lives of French aristocrats facing death under the Reign of Terror. His affection will return once he learns that rumors he's heard, that Marguerite was responsible for the Revolutionary Tribunal's execution of the Marquis de St. Cyr, failed to state that she'd denounced the Marquis because of his savage treatment of her brother, and had never intended that he be killed. In both cases, Sir Percy's concealment of the truth—his identity as the

Scarlet Pimpernel, his belief his own wife was a French conspirator—creates the behavior his wife finds so bafflingly contradictory.

Contradictions Based on Conscious Versus Unconscious Traits

This kind of contradiction shares common ground with both those based on serving a number of social roles and those based on deceit. The entire construct of the ego, the persona we project to others, relies on a certain level of repression, concealment, and camouflage. This says a lot about who we want to be, who we pretend to be, who we're afraid of becoming—and where we stand among others. To this extent, we all live a lie, or at least conduct a certain amount of psychological legerdemain, every moment of every day with everyone we meet.

And yet one of the key attributes of suppressed traits is that the suppression secretly increases their power. By bottling up an impulse to be openly flirtatious or reckless or mean, we secretly create the pressure cooker that guarantees someday, somehow, it's going to slip out.

The tension created by these two antagonistic impulses—to control our behavior so we "get along" and to let go and "be ourselves"—forms one of the core conflicts of our lives. And conflict is inherently dramatic.

Understanding this intrinsic war within can be helpful when allowing the character to act unpredictably. For every trait we publicly exhibit, its opposite lurks somewhere in our psyches. These shadow traits may be feeble and ill-formed from lack of conscious use, but they exist— meaning that if a character acts unbelievably, we can make what he does seem more organic if we find a way to root it in the battle between the character's conscious and suppressed behavior.

Contradictions can show both what the character intends and what she's unaware of in her own nature—and they do so in one quick stroke, no belabored psychoanalysis necessary. Attempts by authors to portray the working of the unconscious often devolve into laborious explanatory exercises, or else the author stands in for the unconscious, reducing the character to a psychological specimen—or a puppet.

In the TV series *Mad Men*, Don Draper (Jon Hamm) fully embraces the übermale ethos of 1960s Madison Avenue. He's not just the rainmaking prince of Sterling Cooper, he's the alpha in virtually every group of men he encounters. Part of this is charade—he's assumed a false identity to escape his shamefully poor upbringing and to hide other problematic aspects of his past, and diligently protects the mask he's assumed—but it also speaks to his need to fit in, to succeed. His role in the rise of Peggy Olson (Elizabeth Moss) seemingly contradicts the narrow-mindedness of this ethos, even though his support is by no means unqualified or even consistent. But he's the one senior member of the firm to see her talent and promote her rise in the creative department, a tribute to a sense of fairness he tries otherwise to conceal. More important, he sees in her a decency and a lack of artifice that he secretly admires—and envies.

Dispositional Contradictions

Each of the main characters in Charles Portis's *True Grit* is intriguingly contradictory: Despite Mattie's youth, she is indomitable, and savvy in business. LaBoeuf is courageous despite a foppish concern for appearance. Cogburn, the one-eyed drunken fat man, is relentless, cunning, and, in the end, valiant.

Jimmy McNulty of the TV series *The Wire* is a devoted father and a dogged cop, plus a hopeless drunk and an inveterate womanizer.

In her short story "The Other Place," Mary Gaitskill deftly conjures a thirteen-year-old boy using nothing but his name (Douglas), his age, and three contradictions: The first is that he is keenly intelligent but hates to read; the second is that he has inherited an "essential tremor" that causes involuntary hand movements, and yet he loves to draw, and does so exquisitely; the third is that he draws both beautiful sketches of crows—they fascinate him because they are one of the few animals that are more intelligent than they need to be to survive—and detailed, vivid drawings of men with guns, or hanging from nooses, or cutting up other men with chain saws.

This type of paradox is hard to attribute to a cause—which doesn't necessarily indicate a shortcoming. Readers and audiences do not need or want everything explained. But in devising a character like Cogburn or LaBoeuf or Mattie or McNulty, it's necessary to intuit the psychic whole that embraces the contradictions and not simply slap them together and hope they gel. It's likely, for example, that Mattie's precociousness is partially due to her need to step into the role of responsible adult because of her mother's lack of business sense and her father's absence. But the fact that she possesses the ability and the determination is constitutional. She's not her mother's daughter; she's her father's.

Following through with our examples:

- Macbeth is both audaciously violent and cringingly fearful, exceedingly ambitious and haunted by his conscience. He is both daring and terrified.

- Willy Loman pontificates about the importance of being liked by others, while he is undeniably the most isolated figure in the drama.

- In *House of Sand and Fog*, Kathy is an attractive and intelligent young woman—who, since her teen years, has been haunted by a palpable desire to die.

- Blanche DuBois is desperate and weak, hopelessly vain, with an alcoholic's capacity for denial and delusion—but she is also fiercely proud and resourceful with a surprising steeliness.

- Beth in *Citizen Vince* has a broken arm and is obliged to turn tricks with a cast (an example of "comic juxtaposition" mentioned earlier).

- Walt in *Breaking Bad* is both an underachieving chemistry teacher and a brilliant cook of methamphetamine. And his turn to criminality unleashes a previously suppressed confidence and assertiveness, which demonstrates itself in both defending his son, who has cerebral palsy, from a group of bullying classmates, and a sudden surge of lust for his pregnant wife. Others see these traits as "coming from nowhere." Walt says that, for the first time in years, he is "awake."

Above and beyond all the other considerations discussed so far, contradictions are useful because they are inherently interesting. Our perceptions are instinctively geared toward seeking out what doesn't fit. This is evolutionarily adaptive: It alerts us to threats. That unexpected sound we hear could simply be the wind in the grass—or a predator approaching. Your normally placid neighbor's bout of cursing could be nothing—or something you ignore at your peril. The underlying message of every contradiction is: Pay attention.

Exercises

1. Select three characters from a work of fiction or film you've recently enjoyed and ask if they exhibit any of the following contradictions:

   - Physical, ironic, or comic juxtaposition

   - Need to serve multiple social roles

   - Competing morals or goals

   - A secret or deceit

   - Conscious versus unconscious traits

   - Dispositional or constitutional contradictions

2. Do the same for three characters taken from a piece you're currently working on.

3. If a character chosen for exercises 1 and 2 does not possess a contradiction, supply one. What happens? Does it feel contrived or organic? In either case, why?

Chapter Ten
Serving and Defying the Tyranny of Motive

> More often than not, people don't know why they do
> things.
>
> —William Trevor, "The Room"

The Mystery at the Heart of Character

Sophocles described his heroes with the term *deinos*, which translates loosely as "wondrous and strange." A character who lives up to that description possesses a kind of incandescence, reminding us of the unpredictable capacity for loving sacrifice, heroism, fierce persistence—or craven selfishness, cowardice, vacillation—that each of us carries within his heart.

But creating stories and characters is a practical matter too, requiring craft. The chasm between the ineffable thing we're after and the simple tools we have at hand can feel discouragingly vast. It's simple to say: The writer's task is to balance expectation against surprise, word for word, action by action, scene by scene. Like many things that can be simply put, it's incredibly hard to pull off. In characterization this balancing act requires creating an initial impression of the character that feels coherent or whole, then shoving her through a doorway toward the unknown, into a gauntlet of trials and reversals, revelations and confusions, that will shred her familiar, coherent sense of self and transform her utterly.

That's the trick, as it were, and it's true across the spectrum of narrative. And though many of the most satisfying stories reveal to us the capacity for growth or even transformation, the ability to rise above what we thought were our fixed natures, there remain limits to what a writer can get away with, not just in serious drama but in comedy. Wile E. Coyote cannot stop wanting to catch the Roadrunner, no matter how many anvils fall from the sky.

And so we find ourselves once again in the unyielding grasp of desire. No matter how many other elements of characterization we explore, we keep returning to that one core understanding, the thrumming engine of life that seemingly makes everything else go. The inescapable urgency of what a character wants, the vibrant way her craving and need defines her, creates what I call the Tyranny of Motive. Like all tyrannies, it demands obedience—and inspires rebellion.

How Much Do We Need to Know About a Character?

We can't possibly know everything about anything, and this is no less true of our characters than the cosmos. The fact that we exhibit unconscious traits reveals we don't even know everything about ourselves. How could a character without this quality be compelling? Besides, a character about whom you know everything is a limited, static, necessarily predictable entity. Why bother?

Even the author can benefit from a sense of mystery before his own creation. The vibrancy of characters, rooted in their capacity to act seemingly of their own volition, also generates perhaps their most important attribute: their ability to instill a craving to know more about them. This is not created simply by playing an elaborate game of hide-and-seek, withholding information until you're ready to eke it out—Reveal to Conceal, as it's called.

The quality most necessary for defying expectation lies within that curious human quality known as freedom. Exploring this in a character requires contemplating, given what is already known, what she would most likely do at a given point in the story, then asking: *What if she did something else instead—specifically, what if she did the exact opposite?*

We touched on this in the preceding chapter on contradictions, but what I'm after here is a bit more fundamental. Gauging the limits of what choices are credible in any given situation relies on an understanding of the character that goes deeper than our work so far allows. We need more, and will address that in the chapters that follow.

What we are trying to do as writers is to learn just enough about a character so we form a coherent intuition that we can observe "behaving" in our imaginations with clarity and specificity. Some writers start with detailed outlines and character sketches; others improvise and revise as they go. Either way, the writer over time develops an intuitive sense of what needs to be understood for his scenes to hold up.

We need to feel comfortable enough with a character to begin writing—enough to be able to imagine how she negotiates the world of the narrative, how she interacts with other characters, and at least a little of why she behaves the way she does. To use a sports metaphor, we are seeking the "sweet spot" where we have a sufficient grasp of a character to allow ourselves to let go of her and let her surprise us.

This is not a science. It's barely a craft. Although we can learn techniques and tricks, characterization remains somewhat elusive, like trying to shape a figure from mercury. There are times I wonder if it isn't a symptom of a basically benign mental disorder. In my most productive moments, I consider it the adult version of having an imaginary friend.

Whatever this curious faculty is, it requires an ability to envision our characters clearly and feel as though we're in dialog with them, observing them as we observe a dream—*not* controlling them like marionettes. And this returns us to a notion I've mentioned earlier, and will explore more carefully now: the need to engage not just your mind but your intuition in developing a character. This is how, to the extent it's possible, we defy the Tyranny of Motive.

The Limits of Intellect

Go back to that first day on the playground, try to remember how strange your new classmates seemed, and how your impressions of them formed and evolved. It's doubtful you told yourself, "Jennifer needs constant attention and therefore will react resentfully if I befriend Jack." Rather, you gathered in what you saw, what you heard, what you felt, and without a conscious thought you fashioned these perceptions into a mental impression that helped guide your interactions with prickly, jealous Jennifer.

Not much has changed in adulthood—except perhaps that you allow logic, specifically cause and effect, to influence your judgments. But it's unlikely your inner impressions of others are constructed of syllogisms. And yet, this is typically what happens in bad writing.

Too often, writers feel obligated to be able to explain why their characters do what they do at every stage of the story. They believe, not without some merit, that to leave things incomplete, ambiguous, or untidy is just sloppiness. Unfortunately, though there's much to admire in this sort of rigor, in the realm of characterization it's sadly misplaced.

Where rigor is necessary is in how vividly and creatively we conceive our characters, but this can't be accomplished through intellect alone. The actor Dustin Hoffman, invoking Miles Davis's legendary quote "Don't play what's there, play what's not there," remarked, "We think the conscious is the determining factor, and actually it's the least reliable instrument."*

We don't get to know someone new through a recitation of biological data; we get to know them through interacting with them—especially during emotional, unpredictable, or demanding times. So too we get to know our characters

---

* Giles Foden, "The Tao of Hoffman," *New York Times Style Magazine*, March 2, 2012.

by engaging with them in meaningful scenes that reveal the most significant aspects of their lives.

The problem is that we don't have external stimuli—a real human being—for cross-checking how accurate we are. All we have is our intuitive sense of the character, the image we see of her, the emotional impression she makes, and some idea of what she would or wouldn't do—which ironically we're constantly challenging, even undermining, through conflict and contradiction, not to mention revision.

So where is that fine line between being puzzled by behavior and finding it unbelievable—worse, contrived? The answer lies in letting the seemingly enigmatic behavior emerge *from the character*, not the writer. This may seem like a step into madness, but, as noted at the very start, a great deal in characterization has an element of the irrational to it.

We need to create enough of a vivid and concrete intuition of a character that the possibility for real, unpredictable, unpremeditated action *on the character's part* seems not just possible but credible. The only way to do this is to continue working on a character until she has, at the very least, the same shape and substance as the inner representation of a real person—and, as we shall see in the coming chapters, this requires envisioning the character in emotionally demanding scenes, filled with conflict, pathos, and risk.

Readers and audiences shouldn't be vexed by a character's behavior, but they should never feel entirely comfortable either, or they'll be several steps ahead of the story at every turn. This may mean that at some level the character's motivation isn't yet clear—but will be clarified as the story proceeds—or it may mean that the motivation is more complex than simple reductive explanations can justify.

In Linda Seger's *Making a Good Script Great*, she identifies seven "motivators" that drive the character through the story: Survival; Safety and Security; Love and Belonging; Esteem and Self-Respect; the Need to Know and Understand; the Aesthetic (a need for order, balance, or purpose); and Self-Actualization. As reassuring as this list may feel at first, that effect fades pretty quickly once you truly dig in with a character. Perhaps the first thing you realize is that these motivators aren't mutually exclusive—absent self-respect, a sense of purpose and self-actualization, how does one truly love?—but seem to be artificially abstracted from something more organic and complex.

This may seem counterintuitive to those who've been browbeaten in English or composition classes to identify the root cause of a character's actions, but this is a fool's errand. One sees the same sort of error in the usual understanding of "tragic flaw." If actors portrayed Medea solely by focusing on her jealousy, Coriolanus his pride, Hamlet his indecision, Macbeth his ambition, the results would be ridiculously wooden. Such an approach fundamentally misconceives the very nature of these characters.

The reason that Abel's death at the hands of Cain never feels as compelling as Oedipus's murder of Laius—or Adam and Eve's disobedience, or Prometheus's theft of fire—is because Cain's violence is so tidily explained by envy. In the other three examples, we're never quite sure exactly why they committed their crimes. Oedipus's hot temper, Eve's unbridled curiosity, Prometheus's compassion for man—they never seem to tell the whole story. Which is why those tales continue to intrigue us centuries later.

Robert McKee makes this point in his writing guide, *Story*:

> Generally, the more the writer nails motivation to specific causes, the more he diminishes the character in the audience's mind.

This is a sneaky, subtle, maddening truth. A character most predictably fascinates at precisely the moment you set her free, and permit her to defy your own and your audience's expectation of what she might do.

Explaining your character kills her. Whatever she does, the reader or audience needs to feel her actions arise not from this or that identifiable source, but from the whole of her personality, her wants and contradictions and secrets and wounds, her attachment to friends and family and her fear of her enemies, her schooling and sense of home, her loves and hatreds, her shame and pride and guilt and sense of joy. As important as a character's core desire is, it doesn't exist in a vacuum, nor can it be teased out and separated from everything else about her.

Simply tying actions to motives is too simplistic to feel satisfying. It smacks of an overly rigid and unsophisticated view of behavior. And the more the reader sees the writer's hand in a character's behavior—the more the behavior can be reduced to readily explainable causes—the more that reader will feel shackled to the Tyranny of Motive, rather than introduced to something more elusive and intriguing, something wondrous and strange.

Exercises

1. Go back to a novel or film you've enjoyed recently. Take three characters from it and analyze a particularly key action each of them makes within the story. Ask yourself if there is a single identifiable motive for any of these actions, or whether there is instead a complex of factors prompting the action. Don't be vague—tease out those multiple factors.

2. Repeat the above exercise with two characters from a piece you're currently writing.

3. Envision what would happen if the two characters from exercise 2 did exactly the opposite of what you've already written in the scenes you've chosen. Does that reversal violate or enhance your sense of what the character is capable of? If it feels wrong or forced, examine what causes this—is it possible, for example, that your sense of the character is needlessly limited?

Chapter Eleven

Dynamic Versus Static: Creating a Biography from Scenes

What is character but the determination of incident?
What is incident but the elucidation of character?
—Henry James

Lajos Egri in his seminal *The Art of Dramatic Writing*, a book that profoundly influenced a generation of novelists, playwrights, and screenwriters, urged writers to construct detailed character biographies focusing on three principal areas:

- Physical (appearance, sex, race, age, health)

- Psychological (love, hate, fear, pride, shame, guilt, success, failure)

- Sociological (class, education, work, family, friends, religion, politics)

I agree with this approach, with an important caveat: I do not compile a list of facts about my character such as her height, eye color, marital status, religion, occupation, and so on. Instead I envision these things scenically, focusing on the question: *How does my character's physical, psychological, and sociological makeup affect her interactions with others?* The specific way I recommend going about this is the subject of the next three chapters.

A static laundry list of information about your character may aid a description of him, but it often proves less than helpful in dramatizing how he behaves. The screenwriter Frank Pierson (*Cool Hand Luke, Dog Day Afternoon, Presumed Innocent*) recommended writing scenes outside the script to see how the characters act in moments of embarrassment and conflict not tied to the story. The approach I propose here and in the following three chapters is an expansion on this, though to the greatest extent possible I try to focus on envisioning scenes that reflect meaningfully on the story I intend to tell. Although I cover a lot of ground in these chapters, I seldom if ever explore everything I discuss there with any single character. I go as far as I need to at any point of the writing to give me a deep, vivid, living impression of the character. That said, imagining emotionally textured and revealing scenes that I ultimately discard is not a waste of time; it's part of the inevitable process of exploration that writing requires.

I don't craft these scenes into final form. A mere sketch will do, enough to give me a vivid visual and emotional impression of the character engaged in some meaningful act that explores how he interacts with his family, how he goes about his work, how he treats someone he's attracted to, to what extent he relies on his education, the care he takes in his appearance—Why? For whom?—the way he responds to shame, to fear, to danger.

In many ways, this work resembles what I recommend in chapter 3 as a means of self-exploration, but the focus now turns toward the character. I delve into key moments of real emotional impact, but still with an eye to fleshing out the physical, psychological, and sociological touchstones that define his life.

Imagining my characters through scenes opens them up in a way that descriptive biographies can't, which exposes a simple, fundamental truth about writing: *Characters reveal themselves more vividly in what they do and say than in what they think and feel.*

This is not just a principle of dramatic portrayal. Twentieth-century philosophy, from Heidegger and the existentialists through Jürgen Habermas and the deconstructionists, has emphasized that the self is created not through reason (thought and feeling) but by engagement with the world and others. Thought and feeling can be revoked, superseded, or countered by other thoughts and feelings; action requires commitment. It has consequences.

Put differently, as my favorite aunt used to say: *You don't know yourself by yourself.* Reflection and introspection are necessary aspects of any life, but our actions define us, specifically the way we behave toward others. Much of what we carry around in our minds and hearts isn't the result of contemplation but the aftereffect of how we've been treated by someone else, especially someone we cared about, or wanted to care about us. How can we come to know a character without exploring that?

How we act, especially in conflict, reveals what we want, what choices we make to pursue it, how desperately we want it, how far we will go to obtain it, and what we think of ourselves and others.

None of which is to say a character's feelings or thoughts are irrelevant. But telling the reader what a character thinks or feels is often far less effective than showing how it influences her behavior, or by showing her wrestling with those ideas and emotions instead of simply having them.

Scenes test character. And we reveal ourselves most unequivocally when we're tested. It often matters little how we feel or what we think. The key issue is: Can we make those thoughts and feelings count for something? Can we strip away their airiness and reveal the wants and needs and convictions pulsing underneath, bring them to bear in our life among others, let them guide or inspire us as we struggle to live meaningfully, lovingly, courageously? Do we have the will, the clarity, the determination—the force of *character*—to do that?

Chapter Twelve
Flesh and Blood and Shoes:
The Character's Physical Nature

Is Physical Description Necessary?

Before the widespread accessibility of film and TV, elaborate physical descriptions in books were prized, even though they seldom if ever dealt solely with the exterior. Joseph Conrad's ability to sketch a character's soul by describing his gait, his posture, his clothing, his face—"of pasty complexion and melancholy ugliness" (from *The Secret Agent*)—continues to awe me every time I read a passage from one of his books. Katherine Anne Porter described the interplay of inner life and outer appearance as deftly, subtly, and astutely as anyone ever has.

In contrast, Elmore Leonard relies almost exclusively on action and dialog for characterization, feeling his descriptive skills are lacking; but readers embrace his books primarily to delight in his characters, whom they "see" despite the relative lack of detail.

Some writers deliberately omit or limit physical descriptions altogether, especially of protagonists, for they believe the lack of detail permits a better opportunity for engagement from the reader. And writers for TV and film can rely on actors, actresses, and costume designers to do at least some of the heavier lifting.

Physical considerations are hardly moot, but beyond giving the reader enough information to picture the character sufficiently—whether that's accomplished directly through description or indirectly through action and dialog—the crucial questions are:

- How does her outward appearance reflect her inner life?

- How does her appearance affect her behavior?

- How does her appearance affect others' reactions to her?

Such considerations are far more important than hair color, waist measurement, and exact height.

The Senses

How a character interprets the world through her senses provides one of the most cunning ways of using physicality for the sake of characterization. The simultaneous use of both outer sensation and mental evaluation anchors the character's inner life to external events, serving two functions at once.

In Don Carpenter's *Hard Rain Falling*, Jack Levitt waits with his friend Denny for two girls to arrive, and when they do he's a little disappointed—despite the excitement that new things, especially girls, always bring. They have "wolfish faces and children's mouths grown hard"; they wear black dresses with bright blue pumps; their voices are "toneless and brittle with self-imposed coolness." Jack can see that beneath the façade both girls are plain, but their attempt to emulate "four-bit New York whores" arouses him despite his disillusion. The point is, how they look and sound provides insight into *both* the girls *and* Jack.

In *The Brief Wondrous Life of Oscar Wao*, Oscar's innocent lustful astonishment could not be more aptly portrayed than in his letter to the narrator in which he confesses that he finally lost his virginity: "She tastes like Heineken."

The film version of *The Maltese Falcon* tried to capture the scent of Joel Cairo (Peter Lorre) by having Spade (Humphrey Bogart) sniff the odd little man's handkerchief and chuckle. In the book, Hammett first describes Cairo visually—down to his fawn spats and his short mincing steps as he approaches—then concludes with: "The fragrance of *chypre* came with him." The effect is multilayered. It lets us know that Spade knows what *chypre* is— a scent created by François Coty and named for Cyprus—and it enhances the impression of Cairo's femininity. More important, it creates the feeling of intrusion only a thick scent can.

Sex Versus Gender
Your character's gender can sometimes feel like an automatic decision, but it shouldn't be. With the simple issue of

sex comes the far subtler, more complex, and thus more interesting question of gender role.

Men and women act differently—and get treated differently—in every culture on earth. By simply asking yourself—Does this character *need* to be a woman or a man?—you're probing key questions regarding what you believe this character will need to do and say, how he or she will need to respond, what goals and desires will be permitted, what interior and social obstacles will rise up in the character's path, and what actions will be available to overcome those obstacles.

The difference between men and women in this regard is not as stark as it once was. House husbands have become a staple of romantic comedy, just as women characters like FBI Special Agent Clarice Starling in *The Silence of the Lambs* and the combat helicopter pilot Karen Walden (played by Meg Ryan) in *Courage Under Fire* now populate the crime and action genres. But each of these characters is still obliged to swim upstream against what others believe her proper role should be.

When you make the decision what sex your characters will be, don't cheat yourself by conforming them too comfortably to cultural stereotype. So-called real men and real women are largely figments of our imaginations. Our gender role almost always violates some aspect of our personality—gentleness and pity for men, for example, aggressiveness for women. Why deny yourself this rich source of conflict?

Sexual Attractiveness

One of the most tender scenes in Jake Arnott's *The Long Firm*, set in 1960s London, is when the gangster Harry Starks beds a rent boy he collects at a coffee bar. After sex, transacted upright against a full-length mirror, Harry tells the young man he's a nice-looking kid, then says, "I ain't very pretty am I?" His face is battered, making him look older than he is, and his eyebrows have a tuft of hair in the middle. He tells the young man this makes him look like "a bloody werewolf," and that his grandmother used to tell him it meant he was "born to hang."

Pete Dexter's *God's Pocket* is filled with scenes that use sex and sexual attraction to devastating effect, especially in portraying vulnerability.

Peets, a construction foreman, watches his wife, who's a nurse, get ready for her shift. "Watching her dress always worked on him the way watching her undress was supposed to." He reaches to smooth the back of her skirt and she subtly backs into his hand.

Things are not so easy for Mickey Scarpato, "who doesn't understand women the way most people don't understand the economy." He likes to have his wife, Jeanie, name his body parts as they make love, which she does with good-natured indifference. She listens to the whistling of his breath through his nose as he gets close to climax, settling her chin on his shoulder "to wait it out," and taking note of "the hedge of black hair on his shoulders." Where she once tried to arouse the local wives' jealousy by describing Mickey as "a jackhammer," she now thinks of his penis as "something real hungry with a little bitty mouth. Like a guppy." Mickey knows he's lucky to have Jeanie, and spends almost the entire book doing everything he can think of to please her, because he can sense she's got one foot out the door.

If we're handsome or beautiful or sexy we enjoy perks that the plain, the homely, and the repulsive do not. People smile at us more often, pay more attention to us, take our requests more seriously (or at least try to fulfill them more enthusiastically), and generally do us more favors.

But people also want things from us they don't want from others—they want us to like them, laugh at their bad jokes, indulge their pets. They may project their sexual longings onto us or their dreams of success. Beauty, like fame, can be a decidedly mixed bag.

It's not important to know how tall, how pretty, how under- or overweight a character is. The numbers are irrelevant. The questions to ask are: How does my character's appearance make her feel? How does it make others feel about her? How do these feelings translate into behavior?

The aspects of sexuality that pertain to the character's inner life will be covered in the next chapter, but the main question to ask here is: How does my character's *appearance* affect her sex life?

- Does she consider herself not just attractive but sexy? Do others?

- When was the last time the character had sex? With whom? If it's been a while, why?

Is it missed? How much? If not, why not? (Conventional wisdom suggests that men crave and miss sex more than women, but conventional wisdom greases the wheels of mediocrity in many endeavors, characterization no less than others. Resist the obvious.)

- Is your character comfortable with sex? Is it easy? Complicated? Embarrassing? Frightening?

- Who have her most memorable lovers been? What did they think of her face, her body, her kiss, her lovemaking?

- Has anyone been disgusted by the way he looks? How deep and long-lasting is that wound?

- Combining this with age: How has her sense of sexual attractiveness changed over the years?

Remember: Each of the above questions should be answered by *envisioning a scene*. Outside of porn, sex on the page or on the screen is about vulnerability, not wish fulfillment. An episode of life-changing sexual revulsion, the wedding reception where your character's spouse flirts with a good-looking stranger, or that moment when your middle-aged character enters a room and realizes heads no longer turn, opens her up in a far more interesting way than the kind of breezy going-at-it one finds all too often in fiction and film.

Not that your work should be populated only by the erotically challenged and perpetually frustrated. But in writing, great sex is a lot like true love: Where's the conflict?

Race

Ask yourself what advantages or indignities are enjoyed or suffered by your character because of her skin color. As our society grows more integrated, exchanges across race occur more frequently and in more places. And yet, for some, this still creates confusion and anxiety.

There is no shortcut to obtaining a better understanding of people who are different from you, whether the difference results from sex, race, age, or whatever. Pete Dexter writes with particular brilliance across the racial divide. He was a newspaperman in the South and in Philadelphia, as racially charged a city as exists in America, and being a journalist requires you to meet people from every walk of life, and to listen. Richard Price has a similar gift, and his devotion to street research, riding along with cops, talking to people, is legend.

Guesswork won't do. There is always a self-serving lie in a convenient assumption. As a writer, demand more from yourself than tolerance. We're supposed to be curious, compassionate, and concerned with getting it right. Without that, our portrayals across race lines all too easily fall into caricature or stereotype, demeaning not just our characters but us.

Age

As you consider what age your character will be, think of how it affects her ability or willingness to engage with others. Is she in the prime of her life and thus relatively fearless? Is she too young to know how harsh life can be, and thus too trusting? Is she young but wise, having suffered some wrenching loss? Is she old and wise? Old and frightened? Old and sheltered? How deeply does she feel her regrets?

The young provide an excellent vehicle for portraying bafflement with the ways of the world. Scout's curious, obsessive need to know what's going on in *To Kill a Mockingbird* allowed Harper Lee to envision Maycomb County, even in its everyday familiarity, with a lingering sense of puzzlement.

Daniel Woodrell routinely uses teenagers as his protagonists to ensure that violence and betrayal are felt as intimately and savagely as they should be. Even the Missouri irregulars of *Woe to Live On*, despite the bitter, world-weary, amoral wisdom they embody—the result of unapologetically savage warfare—are barely into their twenties.

In Mike Leigh's film *Another Year*, Mary (Leslie Manville) has entered middle age with nothing but 500 pounds from her divorce and a failed love affair with a married man she calls her "great love." She is only too aware that every passing moment skims her chances a little thinner—clinging to the people in her life, especially the men, with cloying desperation—while numbing the loneliness with drink, which only sabotages matters all the more. She's mirrored by the character Ken (Peter Wight), similarly and just as bitterly divorced, overweight, smoking too hard, drinking too much, resentful of the young, weepy at the memory of a friend's funeral. He of course is smitten with Mary, who sees in him everything she despises about growing old gracelessly and refuses to accept in herself.

Health

Just because your character appears in your mind's eye as in the pink doesn't mean she hasn't at one time or another been on the brink of death. Use your imagination. Considering this question alone—when in her life was she most ill?—can often open up a character in a revealing way. And if your character has had the good fortune of rosy health, ask who close to her has not been so lucky. How did this affect interactions between them?

In *Midnight Cowboy*, Ratso's polio and tuberculosis turn him into a needy user—which makes it all the more *affecting when he expresses real gratitude for Joe Buck's kindness.

Angels in America recounts how AIDS ravaged not just individuals but couples. Louis reveals a narcissistic dread of death and the messy details of illness, fleeing his lover, Prior, who has the disease. Prior is obliged to see himself through alone, and comes out in the end with a fuller, deeper understanding that permits him to forgive Louis. In contrast, Roy Cohn denies the true nature of his illness just as he denies his own homosexuality, equating it with weakness and thus, now, death. He instead claims he's suffering from liver cancer, and we watch him drown in his own bile.

Sometimes it's not illness but injury that provides the telling insight. In David Benioff's *The 25th Hour*, Frank

Slattery's tenuous position as a Wall Street bond trader resonates with his body, which still bears the scars of his years wrestling in high school and college. He's had his nose broken four times, his ears cauliflowered, his front teeth chipped "from an accidental head butt sophomore year of college." All of this embodies the restless aggression he brings to every task, every encounter.

Deportment and Fashion Sense

Balzac equated sloppy attire with moral suicide, while another Frenchman, fashion designer Jean Paul Gaultier, remarked that badly dressed people are always the most interesting. Despite the disagreement, both are avowing the importance of what we wear.

Even those who claim to pay no mind to how they dress are making a *social* statement, however halfhearted it might be. We dress for other people—or not, ignoring what others think, which amounts to pretty much the same thing.

Beyond the issue of shabby versus neat, comfy versus haute couture, questions worth considering include:

- Does your character have a sense of style? In what way—Goth? Bohemian? Label conscious? Does she disdain style as a narcissistic bother?

- Does she suit her dress to the occasion, or wear whatever she wants whenever she wants, occasion be damned?

- How crowded are her closets? Does this make her feel proud or uneasy?

- How old is the oldest thing she owns? How new is the newest? What does this tell you about her?

- Is there a favorite item of clothing? When was the last time he wore it? (Even a man as obtuse about women as Mickey Scarpato has a favorite shirt; it's yellow, a color he believes suits him.)

Remember, these questions should not prompt answers but *scenes*. Put another person in the picture if one isn't there already. Attire reflects how comfortable we feel both in public and "in our own skin," and dictates how others respond to us.

In Mark Costello's *Big If*, the secret service agent Tashmo favors yoked suits with slashed pockets and wears his graying hair in a pompadour with long sideburns. His supervisor—a woman—won't let him wear bolo ties, but a yoked suit without a bolo looks, to his way of thinking, ridiculous. "Never mind, fuck her—he loved his dudeish suits. They made him look, with the 'burns and the pomp and the zippered boots, like the carny-barking car impresarios he had worshipped as a kid."

In Ellen Sussman's *French Lessons*, Josie Felton is a high school French teacher grieving the end of an affair she could tell no one about; worse, she's pregnant. Fleeing to Paris, she enlists a tutor to get her language skills up to local level, a young man named Nico, who is startlingly handsome. On their first walk together he drags her into a shop at the carrefour de la Croix Rouge and has her try on a pair of turquoise patent leather pumps. They hug her feet like "a new skin," and she thinks that's exactly what she needs.

It's not just how one dresses that's important, though:

- How much time does your character spend getting dressed? Imagine it. Watch him. Allow the scene to unfold.

- How does she put on her makeup?

- How does he shave? Meticulously? In a rush? (How often does he cut himself?)

- What is the first thing to come off when she gets home—the jacket? The shoes?

Picture these small and simple events with care. By some curious magic they can enliven your character in your own mind's eye, helping you bring her to life on the page.

Physical Description in Screenwriting

Casting doesn't solve everything. Screenwriters also use physical description to provide a sense of how a character's exterior reflects the way he faces the world and other people. But the economy required by a script forces the screenwriter to get as much as he can from as little as possible.

In Tony Gilroy's script for the film *Michael Clayton*, senior partner Marty Bach is described with this: "Big power. Sweet eyes. A thousand neckties. A velvet switchblade."

In Vince Gilligan's pilot episode for the TV series

Breaking Bad, he describes Walter White, whom we see stumbling out into a pasture from a Winnebago dressed only in underpants and a gas mask, as being a pasty forty-year-old we'd barely notice if he passed us on the street: "But right now, at this moment, in this pasture? We'd step the fuck out of his way."

Not all writers for film embrace this technique—Steve Zaillian doesn't, for example, in his excellent script for *American Gangster*—but novelists who've written for the screen often carry it with them when they return to their fiction. Desmond Lowden employed a scriptlike economy, blending the inner and outer, in his novel *Bellman & True*. A character named only The Boy has a face that's pale and "sharply pointed with the effort of being eleven years old." Anna, a former high-priced call girl, wears no makeup, "like a fashion model walking from one job to another, her face and hair in her handbag, and no expression for the journey in between."

What all of these examples show is how to convey with remarkable economy not just the character's appearance but her essence.

Exercises

1. Take a piece on which you are currently working and reflect on what would happen if you changed the sex, race, or age of one or more of its major characters. Has anything become possible or impossible with the change? If so, why?

2. Using the same piece as chosen for exercise 1, imagine one or more main characters fumbling through an act

of terribly unsatisfying sex (don't make it solely the other character's fault). Do you learn anything about your character? Why or why not?

3. Taking these same characters, ask how their ages influence the way they view the world and interact with others.

4. How do the characters chosen for the preceding exercises feel about their sexual allure? Do they feel comfortable in their own skin? Is their self-image consistent with an objective appraisal of their sex appeal? If not, why?

5. Using the same characters, explore the issue of health: Have they ever been mortally ill? When? Have the effects of this illness lingered in some way? What if one or another of them were to suddenly become ill? Who would care for them? How would the character respond to that helplessness?

6. For the same characters, explore their fashion sense and deportment. Put them in uncomfortable or out-of-the-ordinary clothes. How does their behavior change?

Chapter Thirteen
The Tempest Within:
The Character's Psychological Nature

This is perhaps the single most important area to explore, which explains this chapter's length. Take it in bits as you wish. There's a lot to consider.

By psychological I mean what makes up the inner world of your character: her emotions, her feelings (not quite the same thing),* her passions, her fears, her abiding loves, her poisonous hatreds, her hopes, her shame, her reservoirs of swagger, her echoing doubts.

Again, it is important to picture these things specifically and to give them life in a scenic context—to imagine what event caused the shame or pride or fear or confidence,

---

* The difference between emotion and feeling is more one of degree than kind. Feeling is emotion that has been habituated and refined; it is understood and can be used deliberately. I know how I feel about this person and treat her accordingly. Emotion is more raw, unconsidered. It comes to me unbidden, regardless of how familiar it might be. Rage is an emotion. Contempt is a feeling. Both, obviously, are valuable in characterization.

and to follow through by envisioning how it affects the character's interactions with others.

Desire

In chapter 5 we covered this topic at some length, so we needn't go over the same ground again. But it's important to reemphasize the need to visualize in a scenic context your character pursuing, possessing, or losing the thing or person she most wants or needs in life, or at least at that stage of life when your story takes place.

The overwhelming majority of stories are premised on the pursuit of an identifiable desire, with the drama arising from the conflicts endured to fulfill that want. There is nothing "less literary" or "less artistic" about such stories, unless you consider *The Odyssey*, *Antigone*, *The Aeneid*, *Richard III*, *The Tempest*, *Pride and Prejudice*, *Moby-Dick*, *Madame Bovary*, *For Whom the Bell Tolls*, *The Great Gatsby*, *All the Pretty Horses*, and literally thousands of other masterworks "less than artistic."

Yes, there are characters who do not know what they want, or who want more or something other than what they seem to be pursuing. But don't confuse the character's lack of clarity with your own. You must at some point be able to visualize a climactic scene where the character achieves or renounces some sense of fulfillment, justice, insight. And as you revise, you will trim and rework each scene leading up to that climax with this emotional impact clearly in mind, and with an understanding of how and why any particular scene places the character nearer to or further from the climactic resolution. You'll also need to discern why the character can't identify or refuses to admit her desire, and what might force her out of that denial—or cause her to cling to it. Otherwise the story will meander, sag, lose focus. Its impact will falter.

Fear

A vast range of feelings and emotions lies within the fear spectrum, everything from panic attacks and existential dread to the creeps and the heebie-jeebies. But in all cases, fear arises largely outside of conscious control, which is what makes it so crucial to characterization. It's the invisible companion in every meaningful scene. When a character faces conflict, she confronts not just her adversary but her fear—of defeat, humiliation, loss, death. She can't overcome one without conquering the other.

Fear is primal, and often lurks behind other emotions. Anger in particular serves as a mask for fear, a way to project power when battling a sense of helplessness. Resentment conceals a fear of being overshadowed, overlooked, left behind.

Mickey Scarpato in *God's Pocket* has a gambling habit. He wants to think he controls it, but instead it controls him, and this makes him feel weak. That weakness conjures a constant sense of dread, and he enters every scene with a premonition of downfall.

Brian Remy in *The Zero*, afflicted with gaps in his memory, lives in constant dread that down one of those mine shafts of oblivion lies the thing he needs to remember most of all, whatever that might be.

Be imaginative in probing your character's fear. Place him in a scene that arouses that fear, amplify it, dim it:

What nudges him toward panic, what eases him back to mere caution? Search his past, asking how old fears haunt the present, inhibiting love, confidence, intimacy, success. And don't neglect the positive things he actively avoids for fear of having them taken away: love (like Joe Buck and Precious), success (like Dick Diver in *Tender Is the Night*).

Courage

Given the essential role of fear, your story may well turn on how your protagonist learns to master or control a debilitating terror or dread—or how it ultimately undoes her. Know her moment of greatest courage up to the point your story begins: Does she draw upon it or exceed it in the course of your story? Does she fall short? Why?

One of the most compelling forms of courage is the willingness to love. Annie Proulx covers this terrain expertly, especially in both the novel *The Shipping News* and her story "Brokeback Mountain." Joe Buck ultimately discovers this courage in *Midnight Cowboy*.

Bravery of one sort or another is the crucible required in redemption stories. Ham in *David Copperfield* loses his betrothed, Little Em'ly, to another man—Steerforth—but then transcends his status as a cuckold through an act of selfless valor, dying while trying to rescue a man cast overboard in a terrible storm off the shore of Yarmouth. (In inimitable Dickensian fashion, the drowned castaway turns out to be the man who stole Little Em'ly in the first place, Steerforth.)

Don't neglect quieter forms of courage, like the capacity to endure one's disenchantment, to be patient, or to bite one's tongue if that's what a scene requires. Not every door needs to be axed open, or every blowhard put in his place. The measure of every act of courage is the fear it over-comes. In trying to determine the best way for your char-acter to show her spine, return to the underlying fear and write from there.

Love

What your character loves is deeply connected, if not iden-tical, to what she wants. Ask yourself: Is that thing or per-son currently in her life? Why or why not?

If she has what she loves, has it proved to be enough? Has it engendered hardship—a loving mother with a ter-minally ill child (*Lorenzo's Oil*)—or consolation?

If your character doesn't have what she loves, was it lost or has it yet to be found? Again, picture a specific scene or scenes, place her and the loved one together, have them touch, watch them eat, let them fight.

In the film *21 Grams*, Cristina Peck (Naomi Watts) loses what she cherishes most, her two children and husband, in a hit-and-run accident. The family moments portrayed before the deaths are everyday, small—meals, schoolwork, a neighborhood walk—the easily forgettable stuff of life, things one does not foresee getting cut short. That ordi-nariness actually serves to enhance, not undermine, Cris-tina's devastation, justifying her subsequent obsession with revenge.

Ironically, the issue of love is perhaps more important for your opponent or villain than your protagonist. First, it provides an excellent opportunity to show contradiction. And many villains appear cartoonish precisely because the writer has failed to see them as three-dimensional persons, with loves—even a capacity for tenderness—as well as hatreds.

Tony Soprano is not the only gangster (or autocrat) who is also a devoted family man. Men of his kind are notorious for valuing family above all else, despite cheating on their wives, spending lavishly on mistresses, covering up their paramours' suicides (or murders), and supporting children born to other women.

Don't fall victim to the kitschy promise that "all you need is love." This illusion deflates a great many romantic comedies. Prisons are full of men who've been loved—perhaps not enough, perhaps not wisely, but all too often Mom or the wife or the most recent girlfriend (if not all three) stood by her man at the sentencing hearing. Sentiment cheapens everything, love especially. In Willa Cather's *My Mortal Enemy*, Myra forsakes her inheritance to elope with Oswald Henshawe. She marries strictly for love. As the title implies, it's not a happy story.

In the film *Love and Other Drugs*, what keeps the two lovers apart is Jamie's terror of commitment and Maggie's fear that her early-onset Parkinson's disease makes her unlovable. Her verbal dagger—"You are not a good person because you pity-fuck the sick girl"—lays bare both their limitations: Jamie's saccharine belief that his lack of commitment is blameless if it has a whiff of charity, and Maggie's dread of lacking enough of a future to make her worth loving. The drama results from their gradual, trial-

and-error battle to tear down the barriers their fears have so stubbornly erected.

Hate

Just as villains gain greater solidity through the things they love, even good people can turn nasty. Righteousness is often just sentimentalized loathing. It's a rare do-gooder who isn't sharpening a knife in his mind, a theme Flannery O'Connor lustily embraced.

Pain often forges hatred, as is the case of Ruth Fowler in the story "Killings" by Andre Dubus (the basis for the film *In the Bedroom*). Ruth suffers the senseless murder of her son and cannot find much solace in the prospect of forgiveness. Her heart is understandably, bitterly, insatiably set on vengeance. A mere trial is not good enough; the killer will live, perhaps be out on the streets someday soon, and she can't abide that. She becomes obsessed with killing the killer, which feels about right until, of course, it doesn't.

Hatred can be a sustaining force, as it is with the columnist J. J. Hunsecker (based acidly on Walter Winchell) in the classic film *The Sweet Smell of Success*. His contempt for the groveling, unscrupulous press agent Sidney Falco is epitomized by the line "I'd hate to take a bite out of you. You're a cookie filled with arsenic." It's probably the nicest thing he says about anybody except his sister in the entire film.

Hatred can be irrational and even unconscious—it often again speaks to some deep-seated fear, or reflects a part of the character's own personality he or she is ashamed of, feels guilty about, or fears will be exposed. This helps explain closeted homosexuals like Roy Cohn (*Angels in America*), or rabid counterrevolutionaries like Chauvelin (*The Scarlet Pimpernel*), who hide behind a sanctimonious and virulent persecution of those who possess the courage or idealism they themselves lack.

Shame

Better the trouble that follows death, an old Irish saying goes, than the trouble that follows shame. This racking emotion rises up when you've done something that undercuts your standing in a valued group, even a group of one: a close friend, mentor, spouse. The act needn't be something immoral—though it often is, since doing something wrong exposes you not just to punishment but also to scorn. Rather, a shameful act causes withdrawal of love, approval, or status, whether or not it is also wrong.

Shame can result from having your fly down at a cocktail party—or being marched through the streets with a shaved head to hoots of mockery and hate, as were women collaborators in France after the German Occupation in World War II.

The screenwriter Frank Pierson argued it was far more productive to envision a scene where your character vomits in a public place than to know where he went to high school. Shame makes you feel as though you've no place to hide—others treat you with disgust, disdain, pity, or ridicule. And the greater the humiliation, the more strength of character will be required to overcome it.

Sports stories routinely traffic in shame. In the film

The Hustler, Eddie Felson feels the humiliation of his loss to Minnesota Fats bitterly, like most born competitors—so much so that even after he turns a corner, finds a girl, changes his life, the lure of a rematch haunts him to the point that it destroys everything but his skill.

Stories about small-town life often have a strong subtext dealing with shame. In *The Last Picture Show*, Sonny mollifies his loneliness by bedding the town widow—secretly, he thinks—and is humiliated when he finds out the affair is common knowledge.

Other than love, fear, and desire, the most fruitful area to explore with your character might be shame, precisely because it requires *other people*, and is thus particularly amenable to visualization in scenes: When has your character felt most ashamed? Who else was there? How does that embarrassment echo into the present, not just for your character but for others?

Shame may play a vital role in your character's secret, some mortifying incident in her past she prays to God never comes to light. What if it gets exposed? What happens? Who uncovers it? Why?

Guilt

In contrast to shame, guilt concerns doing something you know to be wrong. It involves a violation of your own moral code, however that's defined.

Although shame's also often part of the freight when you do something wrong, especially if others know about it, guilt is between you and your conscience. Acts of cruelty, cowardice, theft, murder, deceit, betrayal—even if known by only the perpetrator—inspire guilt. Or not, depending on how finely tuned your character's conscience is, and how easily she silences it when pursuing something she wants.

Redemption stories obviously require a previous act of guilt or shame—they remain vastly popular with audiences and readers, for what better fantasy than to foul up everything only to find oneself back eating pancakes with the family by story's end? And yet the best redemption tales recognize something inherent in guilt—its stain is often indelible, and the struggle to stay straight is never over. The pancakes have to wait.

Conrad wrote of such characters often and devastatingly. In *Lord Jim*, the pirate Gentleman Brown, recognizing in Jim the festering influence of his earlier cowardice, senses that the good captain's fragile sense of honor will keep him from doing what he should: kill Brown outright. Jim's indecision leads to the death of an ally's innocent son, and once again hoping to atone, Jim approaches the dead man's father, who shoots him dead.

Sports stories don't always traffic in mere shame; guilt can claim a place on the bench as well. Often this takes the form of a sense that one has violated an inner code, something all competitors feel—games have rules, after all—even if they don't always honor that code.

In *The Color of Money* (screenplay by Richard Price), Paul Newman returns as an older but wiser version of Eddie Felson, whom he played in *The Hustler*. He starts off training a young hotshot on the poolroom hustle, but then ultimately feels disgusted at what's become of his life, his soul. He's betrayed something honorable and lost his way. Rediscovering his pride and his love of the game, he hones his skill until he's ready to compete at the tournament level, ultimately facing off against his former protégé and beating him—only to learn the kid threw the game to win a major stake he's made against himself. Eddie remains haunted, if not quite condemned, by his past.

Sometimes, however, redemption remains out of the question. In Kate Atkinson's *Case Histories* and its sequels, Jackson Brodie suffers a guilt that's messy, irrational, and out of all proportion. He's in no way to blame for the murder of his sister and the suicide of his brother, but that makes no difference. He feels more than just grief or despair. It's guilt that haunts him. And ironically, it's a guilt he can't shed precisely because he did nothing to earn it. It's like original sin but with no grace to alleviate it, which is why he's always trying to rescue women in trouble, or falling in love with women who embody it.

Again, thinking scenically: When and where did your character commit the sin or crime or moral mistake that filled him with an overwhelming sense of guilt? Was he punished? Was he forgiven? Who else knew about it? Was it a secret? Has it remained a secret? Who else now knows? What would happen if someone found out?

Forgiveness

True forgiveness is rare—very rare, given the human heart's lust for grievance. To know when your character has been forgiven, or when she has forgiven someone else, is to know a lot about her heart, her conscience, her soul—and her luck.

Obviously, this question twins with guilt: Was your character forgiven when she committed the worst sin of her life? By whom? Who didn't forgive her? How has that forgiveness affected her? Has she forgiven herself? If your character is the one doing the forgiving, is that impulse inspired by a time she herself was or was not forgiven?

The film *Ordinary People* revolves around a young man's struggle with survivor's guilt in the aftermath of his older brother's death in a boating accident. The principal force preventing any breakthrough is the mother, whose favorite was the son who died; she simply can't find it in herself to let go. Ultimately the father recognizes his wife's cold, controlling intransigence, sides with his surviving son, and helps the young man reclaim his life.

Often, however, the issue is not so simple, and the magic doesn't click. In Frederick Busch's *Girls*, Fanny and Jack lose their infant daughter in an accident that resulted from Fanny's negligence. She has no recollection of that, however, and Jack, out of love and understanding of her frailty—she could never withstand the guilt—tells her it was his fault. This lie creates a heartbreaking irony: Though Fanny still loves Jack, she cannot forgive him, as he has secretly forgiven her. Jack bears his fictitious guilt willingly, but also wishes somehow he could reclaim what he once recognized as himself, his marriage, his life.

Although in creating background for your characters, you needn't worry about crafting perfect scenes, it's worth noting that forgiveness is difficult to pull off convincingly, in both life and drama, precisely because it needs to be earned—and yet, it's a gift. Where is the turning point when someone relents and provides what's been his to offer freely all along?

This is true of love as well, of course, but the back-

and-forth interactions that build a credible fondness are not so elusive as those that portray a believable turn toward mercy. It's sad but true that contrition doesn't automatically get you off the hook.

Though people forgive—or pretend to—they have trouble forgetting. This can result from the gravity of the transgression or the pain it created; it can result from fear; it can result from the sanctimonious vindictiveness that often masquerades as virtue. Whatever the reason, simply being sorry seldom turns the trick.

There's no way to get inside the head of someone else to see if his remorse is motivated by self-reproach or self-advantage. Con men, narcissists, and sociopaths prey on this lack of insight, mocking up elaborate smoke screens of contrition that fool not just the gullible. And penance, no matter how punitive or arduous or sincerely carried out, can never return the world to the way things were before the crime—and the graver the stakes, the more this is true. Even in cases of theft, restitution feels like small recompense. Memories are never so long as when clutching a grudge.

To render mercy plausibly, one often needs to portray something less than full absolution, as in Guy de Maupassant's story "Forgiveness," in which a wife, deceived viciously concerning an adulterous affair, is ultimately willing, a year after the other woman's death, to make her husband an offer of friendship.

Another approach is to have the offering and the withholding of forgiveness battled out between two secondary characters, as with the father and mother in *Ordinary People*.

However you choose to go about it, to dramatize forgiveness, you have to show the guilty party working hard to demonstrate real contrition while, at the same time, revealing the wounded party working equally hard to let go of her pain, her fear, her resentment, her claim to the moral high ground, and then just giving in. Try as you might, that magic moment will always feel a little gratuitous, as when Stella, who's been slugged by a drunken Stanley, ultimately caves in to his begging and moaning and descends like an aggrieved queen from the upstairs apartment in *A Streetcar Named Desire*. With every step down she tells him: *You owe me.*

Failure

No one achieves everything he sets out to do, and how your character responds to failure will be one of the cornerstones of who he is.* The job he lost, the marriage that fell apart, the love that got away, the friendship he couldn't salvage: Has he bounced back? Become wiser? Or has he let that failure haunt him, define him, limit him, embitter him, provoke an ongoing fear that he doesn't deserve what he wants, and will not be able to have it? Has he set his goals lower? Higher? Has he changed them at all?

In *Slumdog Millionaire*, Jamal's first loss of Latika to his brother Salim only intensifies his obsession with finding her again, claiming her for himself.

In Joe Connelly's *Bringing Out the Dead*, Frank Pierce is a Manhattan paramedic who failed to save the life of a young girl named Rose. Her death haunts him into the present with workaholic insomnia and an obsession with

---

* See chapter 6, "Desire Denied: Adaptations, Defense Mechanisms, and Pathological Maneuvers."

saving everyone, even those who might gratefully thank him for letting them die.

Salesmen and others who live by chasing down the next hot prospect often serve as totems of failure. Willy Loman's haunting sense of having missed the big chance that was right there for him to grab is accentuated by his bloated veneration of success, and creates a crippling falsity. Disgrace hangs like a shroud over both the real estate hustlers in *Glengarry Glen Ross* and the aluminum siding salesmen in *Tin Men*. And Sidney Falco, the cookie of arsenic in *The Sweet Smell of Success*, runs like a relentless machine gassed by the terror of failure.

In picturing the scene of your character's failure, don't forget to ask: Did he let someone else down when he failed? Who? Is that person still in his life? How? Why didn't he overcome whatever stood in his way? Has he learned to overcome it since?

Success/Pride

Just as with the other opposites we've explored here, so with failure and success. You need to know when your character set out to do something and achieved it, and felt that swell of pride in her own heart. Has that success given her the confidence she'll need to withstand the travails that lie in wait during the course of your story? Was she allowed to bask in the glory or did she need to suppress it, for fear of looking vain or presumptuous, or because circumstances simply didn't permit it (as in combat)? Looking back on her life, what would she consider her greatest triumph or "golden moment"?

It is also wise to reflect on how pride may have affected your character's relationship to her shame. The golden moment can mask more humiliating episodes in one's past: I can forget about my disgrace now that I've earned a couple attaboys. Has the tension between pride and shame led your character to regard her reputation anxiously, for fear someone may see through the mask? Has her pride ossified into vanity or a sense of privilege, giving her a false impression of her own worth? (This was a concern of UCLA's legendary basketball coach John Wooden, who counseled his players to be more concerned with their character than their reputation.)

Sometimes success comes not with pride but instead with indifference or even shame (if the success is dubiously merited), a theme common to stories about the folly of envy, or which advise: Be careful what you wish for. Helmholtz Watson in *Brave New World* feels nothing resembling self-esteem for his various gifts, which puzzles his less generously endowed comrade Bernard Marx to the point of apoplexy.

Don't neglect to consider the possibility that your character has been ruined by success. Dick Diver in *Tender Is the Night* and Macbeth are both examples of men who get exactly what they're after, and pay.

Religion/Spirituality

Religion remains a vital if not crucial aspect of most Americans' lives. And yet a great many writers disregard faith. This is a missed opportunity, and belief or nonbelief has little to do with it. For all the vehemence of his atheism, few writers depict the daily devotions of their characters as astutely as did James Joyce.

One of the most touching portrayals in *God's Pocket* is of Minnie Devine Edwards, an avid churchgoer. On the morning that her husband, Lucien, for the first time in thirty years (except for his wedding and his mother's funeral), refuses to go to work, she pores through her everyday Bible for half an hour—her church Bible sits safe in a drawer, waiting for Sunday—hoping to find something that might supply guidance. She goes over "the familiar comforts" but can find nothing that goes to the heart of the matter, and so she touches the picture of Christ she keeps near the sink and prays: "Dear Jesus, don't let this be nothin', please."

The work of Canadian writer Brian Moore, a devout Catholic, addresses faith as the persistent want for reliable love, but not without insight into its capacity for stubborn, bigoted blindness. This is portrayed with particular power in *Black Robe*, about the Jesuit effort to convert the Hurons (adapted into film by the author with director Bruce Beresford).

If examining the religious or spiritual life of your character serves the story you intend to tell—or if it allows you to look deeper into how she views her life, morality, community, death—ask yourself the following:

- Was your character raised in a certain religious tradition? Does he still practice it? If not, why? If so, how devoutly? If he no longer believes, picture the moment when he lost his faith. What happened? Why? What friends or family members did he leave behind?

- Has your character embraced religion as an adult? If so, when and why? Augustine, Ignatius Loyola, Francis Xavier, and T. S. Eliot all notoriously embraced faith as adults. Often the conversion is forged in a crucible of gutting emptiness or corruption of spirit. I know someone who, though raised Catholic, fell away, only to embrace evangelical Protestantism in his battle to stop drinking. Memoirist Mary Karr famously converted to Catholicism for the same reason. Joe Loya, in *The Man Who Outgrew His Prison Cell*, talks about renouncing his criminal self and turning to Buddhism. Again, picture the exact moment when your character found his faith—the place, the time of day, who if anyone was with him, what *specifically* prompted his turn toward God.

- How does faith shape his conscience? What is forbidden and encouraged in his tradition? What virtues does he honor? What sins does he regularly commit? What sin has he never committed, but might if the circumstances were right? What sin would he never commit?

- How has his faith shaped his sense of purpose? Does he believe life has meaning because of God's plan for him? Does he believe in an afterlife? Does this prompt solace, dread, both? Does he believe God guides his actions or takes an active role in his life?

- Does he believe in secondary spiritual beings: Satan, the angels, the saints, demons, fairies, gremlins, ghosts?

- Does he see the world as inert stuff, the devil's playground, or a sign of God's beneficence? Is there something beyond, or within, the visible that testifies to the spiritual nature of all things? How does this guide or inform his actions?

- If your character is an agnostic or an atheist, what forces shaped his conscience: Family? Schooling? Was he raised religious only to discard his faith, but not his morals, in adulthood? What gives his actions purpose? Does he see some life force or other abstract entity inhabiting or animating the world? Is he a scientific rationalist, a materialist, a cynic, a nihilist?

Even if you disagree with faith's response to the issues of virtue and death, meaning and community, the universe and love, no writer who wants to be taken seriously can disregard the questions themselves.

Food

It may seem curious to include food as an aspect of a character's mental makeup, but it's often a stand-in for gratifications the character can't find elsewhere, and thus speaks to many things: desire, love, companionship, home.

John Harvey's Nottingham police inspector Charlie Resnick is something of a wistful bachelor gourmand. He prizes Czech Budweiser and the espresso served only at a stand near the station where he works. Come midnight, he forages through his fridge for scraps of bacon and Stilton cheese, a slice of onion or tomato, which he assembles into a sandwich on a heel of oven-toasted rye, slathered with stone-ground mustard. The patience and devotion he demonstrates in preparing these meals reveal both his capacity for pleasure and his loneliness.

In *God's Pocket*, Minnie Devine tries to exorcise her worry by hand-making sausage, trimming the fat from a pork roast, cutting the meat into squares, then doing the same with the fat, putting them both through the grinder, spicing the meat with salt and pepper and garlic and coriander, measuring by eye. She puts the skins in a pan of water, adding vinegar to soften them. Finally she crushes a red pepper and adds it to the meat, begins working it all with her hands, praying as she does, continuing until the ache in her arms lets her know that Jesus is listening.

In James Joyce's short story "Two Gallants," Corley plans to hit up a prostitute he knows for money. His mate, Lenehan, is obliged to wait until the transaction is complete. He walks for hours and hours until he comes to a "poor-looking shop" with the words REFRESHMENT BAR over the window, beyond which lies a cut ham on a blue dish and a serving of plum pudding. He's not eaten since breakfast, except for some biscuits he begged off "two grudging curates." He enters and sits and asks the "slatternly" waitress the price of a plate of grocer's peas. Learning they're three and halfpence, he orders a plate and a ginger beer, and when the peas arrive they're hot and seasoned with pepper and vinegar. "He ate his food greedily and found it so good he made a note of the shop mentally."

No American novelist writes of eating and cooking with more unadulterated sensual gusto than Jim Harrison, even when he's merely frying up a ground-beef patty in an iron skillet with salt and pepper.

The rewards of food transcend nourishment. Favorite

dishes often echo far back into childhood, and an adult tends to embrace or renounce the kinds of meals she grew up with. Food is solace and ritual. Its preparation is work and yet almost as enjoyable as the eating. It conjures two of the senses hardest to get right on the page: smell and taste. It speaks of desire and pleasure and camaraderie, or their lack, all at once. Food mitigates hardship and rewards patience. It's generosity. It's love.

Few things can enliven a character as vividly as the specific details of what she cooks, what she eats, for whom, with whom. It may well define home, as for Resnick and Minnie Devine, or the want of a home, as for Lenehan. Or it may be a momentary resting place, a savory respite on the irreversible and ultimately solitary march toward death, as with virtually every Jim Harrison character you can name.

If you're having difficulty picturing your character, sit her down at a table, serve her what she's hungry for, or show her dishing it up for someone else.

Death

I can imagine you thinking: Couldn't we have left things at food? Sadly, no.

Christopher Vogler observes that every hero must suffer a fundamental confrontation with mortality for his story to be meaningful. The death may be metaphorical: the dissolution of the ego, the destruction of one's vanity or reputation. Or it may be secondhand: the demise of a cherished love, a devoted friend, a trusted comrade. But the experience must be life-changing.

The guiding principle that character is developed through engagement with others finds its most significant qualification in our experience of death or some other shattering loss. This is because the engagement that existed is gone; the connection with the other person has been severed forever. We're obliged now to reconstruct our idea of who we are and what our lives mean in the face of this gutting disconnection.

The novelist Cheryl Strayed recounts in her memoir *Wild* that it was only through the solitude of her 1100-mile trek along the Pacific Coast Trail that she could turn away from her need to placate or appease others—or to find acceptance or escape through them—and confront the suffering that continued to consume her in the wake of her mother's death, the disintegration of her family, and a heartbreaking divorce. The isolation of grief obliged her to embrace *acceptance*, not just of death and loss and suffering, but of the small, scared, vulnerable woman who had to endure it: herself. She forged a new sense of her own worth and her place in the world by sloughing off the denials, the sexual adventurism, and the substance abuse and associated psychological legerdemain by which she'd negotiated her pain up to that point.

Death transforms us by forcing us to reshape our wants, our identities, our lives in the face of inescapable disconnection. The baroque elaborations of personality drop away when we're obliged to confront the simplest truth of life: It ends. To paraphrase the Buddhist nun Pema Chödrön: Life becomes much simpler when we realize there is no escape.

Obviously, our own experience of death so far is vicarious, but we know what it means to feel its presence in our lives. Before exploring this with your characters, look into your own past for the most poignant, devastating, revealing moments when you and death have come eye to eye.* Remember the confusion. Recall the curious sense of normalcy, or the shapeless void, or the terrifying immediacy of it. Our mortality forms the unfathomable hole around which all the rest of life is anxiously, tenderly, obsessively arranged. Death is the thing that never truly makes sense, no matter how much we comprehend the why of it. This is because of the sneaky implicit sense that things continue, an assumption that unwittingly animates all our thoughts and sentiments. As Adolfo Bioy Casares notes in his story "Miracles Cannot Be Recovered," the most disturbing thing about the dead is that they simply *vanish*.

Death teaches us that time is inescapable, that some doors never open, and that everything sooner or later is lost for good.

The reason so many mysteries and crime stories fail to truly satisfy often lies not just in the pornography of violence they rely upon, but in their trivialization of death. But this is also true of the vast majority of commercial storytelling, given its obsession with happy endings. Syd Field speaks prudently but not wisely in his seminal *Screenwriting* about avoiding "downer endings," given the financial realities of Hollywood. This trivializes the culture, it dimin-

---

* This is part of the work recommended in chapter 3, "The Examined Life: Using Personal Experience as an Intuitive Link to the Character."

ishes the audience, and in the end it undermines the film industry it claims to speak for. Sooner or later, people do get weary of being lied to, or treated like children.

Examples of death portrayed in fiction and film are far too numerous to address here, which is perhaps good. Better that you find your own best examples, analyze why they affect you as powerfully as they do, and bring that to your own work. And though characters don't die in the same sense you and I will, they don't know that. If they aren't as terrified, mystified, or motivated by death as you are, you're not paying enough attention.

Exercises

1. Take two characters from a piece on which you are currently working and explore as discussed in this chapter each of the following psychological components of their makeup:

   - Desire
   - Fear
   - Courage
   - Love
   - Hate
   - Shame
   - Guilt
   - Forgiveness

- Failure

- Success/Pride

- Religion/Spirituality

- Food

- Death

Has this work inspired any additional scenes, or suggested changes in scenes you've already written? If so, how? If not, why?

Chapter Fourteen
The Teeming World:
The Character's Sociological Nature

———

Where one's psychology defines one's inner life, sociology defines how your character navigates the world of other people, and this covers at least as much ground as we explored in the preceding chapter. Again, take it in pieces. There's no need to swallow it whole.

For every significant bond between two people, you can often ask many of the same questions you ask of a specific character: What was the moment of greatest joy? Greatest fear? Greatest shame and guilt? Success and failure? Forgiveness? Keep this in mind throughout the following discussion. It's central to all of the suggestions that ensue.

Family

> It's like you were saying about children. The
> parent is so often either the problem or a lie.
>   —Aimee Liu, *Flash House*

Your role within the family is a key factor in determining who you consider yourself to be vis-à-vis others, how confident you feel in the world, and how valuable you consider your contributions to be. It is also the crucible in which much of your psychological life is forged: What episodes from your character's family life inspired her, shamed her, baffled her, created boldness, fostered uncertainty, deepened fondness and appreciation, curdled into envy or hate?

That said, heroes are often orphans, precisely because this allows them to travel light, without the psychological baggage of family. Dickens in particular had a lifelong love affair with orphans and foundlings. Unless the story's core conflict deals with how the hero defines himself with respect to his relatives—how he grows beyond a parent's wishes or fears or demands, for example, or a sibling's envy—family members, freighted with backstory, can create incredible drag on the action. In *Slumdog Millionaire*, for example, Jamal loses his mother early on, the better to facilitate and intensify his search for love solely from Latika.

And yet, since the search for identity and one's place in society is often a struggle against parental or family influences, it's hard to imagine how any meaningful story could exclude them altogether, if only as atmospherics.

If parents per se are missing in the story, their presence is often assumed by some other character or factor—a mentor, a jailer, the nemesis or villain, the rescuer who never quite arrives—or an internalized guilt, strength, or reassurance.

That said, potentially key considerations in examining your character's family background—if that background is relevant to the story you intend to tell—include the following relationships.

Father

Was he present or absent? If absent, picture the scene when he left. If present, was he there all along or did he disappear at times? If he came and went, why, and for how long at a stretch?

If he's a dominant force in your character's life, then picture them together, a moment of fondness or scorn or indifference or sacrifice. Think in scenes: a drunken rage; a request for guidance—or money; a sanctimonious lecture on sobriety; a brutal "leathering"; the purchase of a car for your character's sixteenth birthday; its repossession because of nonpayments; a turbulent union meeting in the basement; a call from the road when he's been gone for weeks on a sales junket; a trip to the principal—or the local jail—when for once he takes his troubled child's side.

In Pete Dexter's *God's Pocket*, Mickey recalls a childhood conversation he had with his father, Daniel, a longhaul driver. Daniel seldom required Mickey to attend school, and actually preferred having his son along on these drives, because there was no one to look after the boy at home. During one routine trip between Miami and Atlanta, Mickey remarked on how pretty the sunset was beyond the pines, to which his father retorted, "If it is, you can't make it no better, sayin' it." This moment crystallizes not just Mickey's relationship with his father, but his own adult inability to express anything resembling his feelings—"He kept [them] in order, and to himself."

Mother

One should ask the same questions of the mother as for the father, but with the added understanding that the mother is the emotional and sensual core of a child's existence, a connection that routinely extends far into adulthood, if not to the end of one's life. Beyond the questions you might ask of the father, add:

Was the mother nurturing or undermining? Warm or cool?

Was she the father's ally or his adversary in raising the family?

Did she encourage the child's pursuit of skills and opportunities that would expand his horizons, or was she resentful, secretly or openly, of the child's ability to one day escape?

Did she represent a kind of helpful older sister or an obvious adult?

Did she have an active sex life with the father (or a lover)? Were the kids aware of it? How did they feel about it?

Remember, picture your answers scenically: a fight with the mother that defined everything thereafter, a trip to the hospital with her to visit a dying sister, a Sunday breakfast she prepares when hung over, a flirtatious visit with a strange man one afternoon. Try to form an imagistic impression of the woman, a full intuition not reducible to a checklist of traits.

The capacity of the mother to bind the child in unseen ways forms the premise of the family curse, or *fukú*, at the heart of Junot Díaz's *The Brief Wondrous Life of Oscar Wao*. Both mother and son suffer at the hands of hopeless love, and are blinded by romantic desire to the sadistic brutality lying in wait. The mother's story is told first, so that when we see Oscar following a similar path, as touched as we are by his sweetness, we recoil at his gullibility, even as our hearts break for him—and then, when his mother learns what has happened, for her as well. Her hold on her daughter, Lola, is equally fierce, but in different ways. Lola resorts to an almost spiteful cruelty to break free of her mother's crushing, suffocating influence, even as both women understand that the hatred crackling between them is the necessary price for a daughter's separate identity.

Mothers sometimes disappear just like fathers, and how such separations get managed largely define for the rest of our lives our relationship with anxiety, affection, belonging, trust. The core revelation of Janet Fitch's *White Oleander* involves the daughter's repressed memory of a woman named Annie, whom she ultimately learns was a babysitter in whose care her mother left her for a year, which resulted in an almost crippling terror of abandonment.

Sometimes the mother's grip on a child slips away, or seems to, despite her strength. In David Benioff's *City of Thieves*, a teenage son intends to stay in Leningrad to defend the city while his mother and sister flee to the safe interior countryside. The mother, who uses "idiot" as an endearment, tells her son point-blank that she and his young sister need him. But he refuses, saying that if Leningrad falls, Russia will, and if Russia falls, fascism will conquer the world—a conviction so deeply felt he still believed it a half century later. It provides him the strength to stand up to his mother for the first time—no small feat, for even though she was barely five feet tall, he had been "afraid of her from birth." And yet he doesn't shake her ruthless influence completely: He falls in love with Vika, a redhead who teaches him how to slit a man's throat.

Remember that even lovely mothers have their spells, preoccupied mothers have their bouts of clarity, judgmental mothers aren't entirely devoid of tenderness. And even the most tormented mothers are forever remembered not just for their failings but for those one or two moments when the dark cloud lifted, and a gentler spirit materialized.

Grandparents

Did they live far away, nearby, with the family? Were they actively involved in the character's life, as confidantes perhaps? Or were they a cantankerous burden?

In the film *Queen of Hearts* (1989), Sibilla lives with her daughter, Rosa, and her family. Sibilla has never accepted Danilo, Rosa's husband, detests his "beatnik" father (who of course arrives midstory), and is a pious Catholic who acts as moral scold for everyone in the family—which provides numerous opportunities for ironic comeuppance.

Returning to David Benioff's *City of Thieves*, the grandfather is "the smiling watchman of my earliest memories," who takes the narrator's hand and walks him several blocks to the park where the boy harasses pigeons while the older man reads his Russian-language paper. Through him, the narrator learns what it was like to survive in Leningrad during the winter of 1941–1942; he learns of miserable cold and starvation, the eating of every living thing except each other, even pets. He learns what it means to be truly alive.

Siblings

Some believe that a child's peers, and especially her siblings, have as much influence on her behavior as parents—perhaps more. The bonds of sibling love are especially crucial in large families and poor families, as portrayed so well in Christy Brown's *My Left Foot*. And sibling rivalry has informed literature since Cain and Abel—a contest revisited repeatedly, from Shakespeare's *Richard III* to Arthur Miller's *The Price* to John Steinbeck's *East of Eden* to the film *Amores Perros*, where the assassin hired by one brother to kill the other instead ties them both up and leaves a pistol between them, saying as he leaves, "Settle it yourselves."

Nor is it merely brothers who indulge in such contests: Ask King Lear.

One of the first questions to ask of your character is who among the other children is an ally, who is an enemy or a competitor—for a parent's love, for respect at school or in the neighborhood. As always, between any two people but especially brothers and sisters, envision the quality of the love between them—picture scenes of shared or neglected chores, help with homework, a fight, a sincere compliment, a visit to the doctor, a tedious party, Christmas Day.

How many siblings are there—several, one, none? What are their sexes? What is the age range? Where does your character fall in the hierarchy? How does this affect her worldview?

In the film *The Fighter*, the primary tension lies between the brothers Mickey and Dickey, but Dickey has allies, not just their manipulative, guilt-afflicting mother but the gaggle of weirdly nicknamed sisters—Pork, Tar, Red Dog, Beaver—who serve as her Furies. Mickey's fight for the championship pales before his battle to get free of his family's cancerous loyalty.

Perhaps no one explored with greater psychological acumen the intricacies of sibling affection and rivalry than Jane Austen. In the modern era, Kate Atkinson tracks the same filial terrain to marvelous effect in her novels, especially *Case Histories* and *When Will There Be Good News?* Julia and Amanda Land conduct an almost perpetual competition for attention, even late in adulthood—and yet when the long-unloved Amanda contracts cancer, no one is more heartbroken than Julia. And Jackson Brodie can never escape the nagging despair that has haunted him since the murder of his sister Niamh when she was sixteen, a despair amplified by the subsequent suicide of his brother Francis, who held himself responsible for the girl's brutal death (he refused to pick her up at the bus stop the night she was killed).

The gangster genre returns often and famously to the issue of family, and therefore siblings. Absent the love between Sonny and Michael, the disdain between Michael and Fredo, and the suspicion between Michael and the "outsider" stepbrother Tom Hagen, the Corleone family would have a much different Godfather. And Tony Soprano's unending battles with his narcissistic, freeloading, manipulative sister Janice was one of the most engaging family conflicts in a television series defined by them.

Spouse

> Marriage is so unlike everything else. There is
> something even awful in the nearness it brings.
> —George Eliot, *Middlemarch*

> Sooner or later, at best, your wife turns into your
> sister. At worst she becomes your enemy.
> —Louis de Bernières, *A Partisan's Daughter*

No other relationship is so potentially fraught with
conflict—and therefore rich in potential for fictional depiction—as that of the married couple. The fact that the
bond begins in romantic heat and transitions into family
creates a tension that sabotages not a few pairings. It combines the best and worst aspects of friendship, family, and
sexual passion. It pits commitment against desire, stability
against adventure, loyalty against freedom. And as every
engagement between two people is unique, so every marriage has its inimitable compromises, rewards, gratifications, and resentments.

Marriage is almost as central to storytelling as death, and
literary examples run the gamut, from the savage (George
and Martha in *Who's Afraid of Virginia Woolf?*) to the
merely heated (Stella and Stanley in *A Streetcar Named Desire*), from the resigned (Newland and May in *The Age of
Innocence*) to the conniving (Maggie and Brick in *Cat on a
Hot Tin Roof*), from the artificial (Michael and Kay in *The
Godfather*) to the star-crossed (Gal and Deedee in *Sexy
Beast*), from the hard-won (Katherina and Petruchio in

Taming of the Shrew) to the sweetly amiable (Tom and Gerri in *Another Year*), from the embattled (Tony and Carmela in *The Sopranos*) to the unlikely (Jean and Charles in *The Lady Eve*) to the doomed (Mickey and Jeanie in *God's Pocket*).

As rich as the literature is in examples, however, don't neglect to draw inspiration from the real-life marriages you know. Tolstoy claimed that all happy families are happy in the same way, but this is certainly not true of marriages. The ways in which couples build a life together are as infinite in variety as human personality itself, the unforeseeable result of two people lashed together by love and need, habit and trust, hope and luck.

At the core of each marriage, however, is a fundamental question: How willing was each to give up something he or she wanted for the sake of staying together? What was it, and has what's been gained compensated for what's been given up? Was there a breaking point, and what was it? What role did children play or not play?

All of which points to the quality of love between the two people concerned—a question that gets answered by pursuing the work outlined in other chapters: What does each character desire, love, fear, regret? What are the pressures of family, work, community, faith? Once you have two characters formed this way, and put them together, do you see sparks or the drawing of knives? Do they dance? Go silent? Lie? Did their love save them, fail them, strand them? Again, ask of the marriage what you would of a character: What was the moment of greatest desire? Love? Fear? Resentment? Shame? Forgiveness?

In William Trevor's short story "The Room," Katherine has remained with her husband Phair for nine years despite his having been charged but acquitted for the murder of a "classy tart" he was seeing on the side. Katherine has finally taken a lover herself, a man separated from his own wife and who remarks with awe at how remarkable Katherine is to have loved so deeply, to which she responds, "And yet I'm here." Later, to herself, she reflects that her afternoon lover will go back to his wife and "piece by piece repair the damage because damage was not destruction and was not meant to be." She, on the other hand, knows that finally her own marriage is over. For nine years the love remained, "not a comfort, too intense for that." But she will tell her husband she's leaving, and she surmises it will come as no shock nor even a surprise. He will understand: "The best that love could do was not enough."

Friends

Plato considered friendship the ultimate human bond—it is chosen freely, is sustained only through mutual consent, and is often based on genuine affinities unadulterated by family obligation or sexual desire. Our friendships often sustain us, especially when our relationships with lovers or families are problematic. Who is your character's best friend, oldest friend? Are they the same? Why or why not? Is there a friend he's lost touch with whom he misses deeply? Is there a friend he wishes he could get rid of?

One of the great tales of friendship, Flaubert's *Bouvard et Pecuchet*, revolves around the peculiar bond formed by two copy clerks who come into a modest inheritance.

Convinced, largely due to the groundless encouragement each receives from the other, that they can do as able a job as any academic in examining the day's intellectual conundrums, they launch themselves into a series of farcical misadventures, falling prey to their own blind prejudices and limitations, returning in the end to where they started, as simple—and humbled—friends.

James Dickey's *Deliverance* is not merely a cautionary tale about what can happen when suburban adventurers wander off into an unknown wilderness; it's also a piercing examination of the competitive insecurities at the heart of male friendship. The long-simmering tensions among the three men underscore how ill-prepared they are for their ordeal, and how lucky the two survivors are to come out alive.

With the possible exception of family, no other relationship provides more grist for the situation comedy mill than friendship. From Laverne and Shirley to Leonard and Sheldon on *The Big Bang Theory*, friendship comprises one of the great bonds of affection and antagonism, acceptance and competition, resentment and forgiveness. It's brotherhood in all but blood.

Do not shy away from friendships that cross the gender line. Perhaps it's true that a man and woman cannot truly be friends, and that any such bond is the result of one or the other being gay or married, or that the connection between them is either a stifled romance or a sibling relationship lacking its genetic excuse. But all of that only underscores how interesting such friendships are, and thus fertile ground for storytelling.

Jane Austen was a master at depicting friendship, though many of her male-female examples are marriages-in-waiting. And yet for all the heartsick floundering that takes place in their own lives and the lives of everyone around them, the friendship between Elinor Dashwood and Colonel Brandon in *Sense and Sensibility* remains one of the great pleasures of the novel.

Sometimes such friendships are in fact merely chaste romances, and the story revolves around how the sexual tension is controlled—whether through Victorian rectitude, as between Charlie Allnutt and Rose Sayer in C. S. Forester's *The African Queen*, or a nun's vows, as between Sister Angela and Corporal Allison in Charles Shaw's *Heaven Knows, Mr. Allison*.

And there is of course the case when the desire flows in only one direction, as it does between Scottie Ferguson and his onetime fiancée, Midge, in Alfred Hitchcock's *Vertigo*.

Sadly, male-female friendships inspire far less storytelling than their frequency in real life would seem to warrant. The novel *The Chess Player* by Bertina Heinrichs, adapted for the film *Queen to Play*, is an all-too-rare example. It's about the cerebrally intimate, sexually charged, but ultimately Platonic bond that develops between Hélène, a Corsican maid, and her American widower chess tutor. The sexual tension is there from the start—Hélène's first glimpse of chess takes place as she's cleaning the room of a honeymoon couple playing a game on the deck, and the man and woman clearly share an intriguing intimacy. Hélène's own marriage has reached a kind of habitual acceptance, and this sets the stage for a possible affair.

But something far more interesting happens. Hélène becomes intrigued with chess for reasons she cannot explain, and reveals an innate gift for the game that cannot be taught. And Professor Kröger, her tutor, remains haunted by grief; though he has lovers, he sees in Hélène someone more like his late wife—a gifted woman who struggles to embrace her talent. His fondness for Hélène is tragic, tender, and genuine, and she for the first time pursues something that is not for the sake of others—her employers, her husband, her daughter—but is hers alone.

The workplace generates a great many cross-gender friendships, in both life and fiction, but there again the issue of repressed sexual tension arises due to the frequency of office romance. The introduction of women into police forces has been particularly generous in this regard, inspiring a whole new onslaught of buddy story lines, with men and women fighting crime shoulder to shoulder: Mulder and Scully of *The X-Files*, David and Maddie in *Moonlighting*. Of course, both these pairings ended up in romance, to the fatal detriment of both shows.

A similar but far more interesting example can be found in Tana French's *In the Woods*. The friendship between Dublin homicide detectives Rob Ryan and Cassie Maddox begins with the former remarking, "I had no problem with the idea of Cassie Maddox." First, he disdains the "New Neanderthal" competitive locker-room overtones of the job, and he in general prefers women to men. Second, she's not his preferred type physically—she's boyish, slim, square-shouldered, where he's always preferred girly, bird-boned blondes. He becomes vaguely attracted and lets it slip out backhandedly in a feeble attempt at banter, to which she responds that she's always dreamed of being rescued by a white knight, only in her imaginings he was always good-looking. This snaps Rob out of his dog-on-the-hunt thinking, and he "stopped falling in love with her and began liking her immensely." It's a friendship developed deeply and satisfactorily throughout the book, until the inevitable night together near the end, when the sexual tension breaks and they make the awful mistake of, as Pinter might say, "going at it." Things are never the same, and it is a testament to the hunger we have for such connections that we feel this shipwreck of affection viscerally, as the great loss it is meant to be.

Name

Call a player "Sycamore Flynn" or "Melbourne Trench" and something begins to happen. He shrinks or grows, stretches out or puts on muscle. Sprays singles to all fields or belts them over the wall.

—Robert Coover, *The Universal Baseball Association, Inc., J. Henry Waugh, Prop.*

Like the body to which it refers, a name abides over time and provides a certain sense of coherence and continuity to a character. And yet, a name is a fundamentally social phenomenon. Whether your given name, surname, or a nickname, it's given to you by someone else, and reflects your identity *among others*.

The choice of a character's name is one of the most critical decisions to be made, precisely because of the sense of consistency it provides. Once you know the character's name, once you can picture her vividly enough to know that a certain name suits her—or better yet, is intrinsic to her—you are very close to seeing her whole.

The name can often substitute for a description if chosen wisely—consider, for example, some of the names from the TV series *The Wire*: Jimmy McNulty, Stringer Bell, "Proposition Joe" Stewart, Snoop Pearson, Bunny Colvin, Cutty Wise, Bunk Moreland, Bubbles.

Novelist Richard Price (who wrote for *The Wire*) also uses aptly suggestive names in his novels: Rocco Klein, Strike Dunham, André the Giant—and Buddha Hat, the name of a feared drug enforcer.

Other memorable character names: Chili Palmer (*Get Shorty*), Baby Suggs (*Beloved*), Nurse Ratched (*One Flew Over the Cuckoo's Nest*), Ree Dolly (*Winter's Bone*), Brian Remy (*The Zero*), Rooster Cogburn (*True Grit*), Quentin, Caddy, and Benjy Compson (*The Sound and the Fury*). Hemingway notoriously avoided suggestive names, except in his secondary characters, but even names as seemingly unremarkable as Robert Jordan, Jake Barnes, or Nick Carter convey precisely what their author was after.

The point: Try to choose a memorable name with a strong sound that in some way, at least to you, conjures a clear mental image or solid emotional impression of your character. That image or impression will provide a touchstone every time it appears on the page, a touchstone that mimics the sense of coherence and continuity that names provide in the real world.

That said, there's an intriguing challenge in a seemingly lackluster name—Jim Williams, Jane Smith, John Harris. Such names, by denying you a unique visual image, force you to remember that the character can't be confined to such an image. He's more than that. And he's going to change, even as his name doesn't.

Class

This tends to get overlooked in the United States, as we like to believe we are largely a classless society. And yet we all know there are those both above and below us on the economic and social ladders, and we either secretly or overtly hope that life permits us to take a place among the former, not the latter. These divides are enforced by barriers, some less subtle than others.

Know your character's relative place in his community with respect to income and social connections. What opportunities does this present, and which does it foreclose? Is he among the favored or the shunned? If middle-class, is he blue-collar or a professional? Are his circumstances stable, improving, backsliding?

Most important: How does your character interact with those of lower or higher social or economic standing? Is he comfortable? Resentful? Does he feel judged? Is he invited in or kept out? Is he getting ahead, trying to maintain, helplessly falling behind, hoping to get out altogether?

All of these tensions cry out for scenic understanding: the argument you could no longer avoid with a condescending, socially connected colleague; the moment when a friendship came apart because one of the pair at last got a chance to better her prospects; the awful embarrassment of being found lacking by someone you deeply hoped to impress—a professor, a famous author, a date.

The 2010 film *The Town* (based on Chuck Hogan's *Prince of Thieves*) used the insular blue-collar solidarity of Charlestown natives known as Townies—and their resentment of the upwardly mobile newcomers in the enclave, derided as Toonies—as a thematic substrate in its portrayal of a gang of bank robbers. Doug MacRay (played by Ben Affleck) feels sympathy for a woman bank manager taken hostage when the film's opening heist goes wrong. She represents the escape Doug wishes for himself, not just from crime but from the anchor of old allegiances holding him back, dragging him down, demanding loyalty above all else. All of this drives the dramatic tension between Doug and his accomplices, especially the murderous Jamie Coughlin and the sociopathic crime boss Fergie Colm, who refuse to indulge Doug's reckless, ungrateful wish for something better.

Crime stories in general may be the last refuge for tales of class tension. From the appearance of films such as *Little Caesar* (1931), *The Public Enemy* (1931), and *Scarface* (1932), as well as in the contemporaneous pulp stories of Dashiell Hammett, Cornell Woolrich, and Horace McCoy among others; through the 1940s crime films of European expatriates such as Fritz Lang, Robert Siodmak, and Jacques

Tourneur and their American protégés; paperback noir in the 1950s from writers such as Charles Willeford, Jim Thompson, and David Goodis; and the resurgence of American crime writing with a social conscience from such American writers as Don Winslow, James Elroy, Dennis Lehane, Laura Lippmann, and George Pelecanos—spurred by the increasing popularity of Irish, UK, and Scandinavian crime writers who bring a distinctly dystopian form of social commentary to their work—the gangster, crime, and noir genres have specialized in showing the brutal effects of economic inequality, class envy, and the unintended consequences of freewheeling capitalism.

Work

The actress and educator Stella Adler once said that you can ask no more important question of a character than what work he does: Is he a lawyer, a mechanic, an inventor, a cop? Each job requires a certain set of personality traits for dealing with one's bosses and subordinates, customers and competitors, government officials—other people.

How good is your character at her job? How secure is she that her job will be there tomorrow or the next day? Who could take her job away?

Is it her vocation or just something she fell into? Does it allow her the economic stability and freedom she desires? If not, what if anything is she doing to change that?

Take time to explore this, picture it with specificity—and in the scenes you envision, picture her challenged by someone, a superior, a client, a coworker. How does she respond?

In the film *Up in the Air*, Ryan Bingham's work as a corporate hatchet man underscores his resistance to commitment of any kind; he fires people—nobody fires him.

In Joe Connelly's *Bringing Out the Dead*, Frank Pierce's power to save lives as a paramedic has warped his sense of responsibility, and he's trying to find some way to forgive himself for the death of a young girl he was unable to rescue. But the technical expertise he brings to the various tasks at hand also help make Frank linger in the mind—reconnecting the Ambu-bag and squeezing, searching the patient's arm for blood pressure, hanging the IV bags, re-attaching the EKG wires: "The machine beeped out a record of the heart's stubborn knocking, a perverse cable from the pale-blue face whose open eyes pointed blankly at the ceiling. Twice I tried to close them, but the lids rolled back."

In David Benioff's *The 25th Hour*, two secondary characters are brought quickly and vividly to life by showing them at work. Frank Slattery, a former college wrestler, works as a bond trader on Wall Street. He's maxed out on his trade limit and waiting for the unemployment numbers that will tell him whether he's a genius or a fool. The job feeds his edgy competitive hunger, his need for respect and fantasies of revenge, his addiction to risk, and his obsession with never going back to Brooklyn. In contrast, Jakob Elinsky sits grading papers in the faculty lounge of the prep school where he teaches English, overshadowed by a rakish colleague, mocked and browbeaten by a female student on whom he has a secret crush.

Education

Knowing whether your character finished high school is all well and good, but from a dramatic point of view the more important factor is: Were there any teachers, administrators, or classmates who inspired her, built up her confidence—or contrarily, tore it down?

If education is important to your character, picture vividly the teachers who played a major role. Elementary school teachers spend almost as much time with us during our waking hours as our families, and high school teachers can ease or impede the transition to adulthood.

Goodbye, Mr. Chips and *The Prime of Miss Jean Brodie*, along with their more modern avatars such as *The Paper Chase, The Dead Poets Society, Mr. Holland's Opus,* and *An Education,* all testify to the enduring effect teachers have, for good and ill.

Education also defines how high your character can climb the economic ladder. How comfortable is your character in dealing with people of lower or higher educational accomplishment? What jokes does she tell, and do her friends understand them? Who does she consider her peers, her betters, her inferiors? Who's smarter, who's not? What does she reasonably believe she can accomplish in the work world given her educational accomplishments? Has she reached her potential? If not, why not? If so, what lies ahead?

Geography

Where your character was raised and where he's chosen to live as an adult indelibly shape his sense of place and even home. Place often dictates community, and community defines what's permissible, what's expected, what gets laughed at. Like family, it's crucial in shaping one's interior life and moral compass.

Explore the effects of where your character grew up, where she has relocated, how the regional values, urban or suburban or rural, have shaped her and her expectations.

Slumdog Millionaire relies heavily on its setting within the slums of Mumbai. In contrast, *Up in the Air* exists largely in airports and hotels; it's Ryan's aversion to any one place that defines his character. *Precious* calls poverty her home, and her story could be told in any major city where housing projects exist.

I've already discussed how Charlestown serves as a key thematic metaphor in *The Town*. Philadelphia serves as a similar backdrop for *God's Pocket* (named for one of the city's toughest neighborhoods). Scott Phillips's *The Ice Harvest* could take place nowhere else but in Wichita, Kansas (on Christmas Eve, 1979). Similarly essential are Boston in Mark Costello's *Bag Men*, New York in the work of Colin Harrison, Nottingham in John Harvey's Charlie Resnick novels. The list is seemingly endless. If a particular place figures heavily in your story, you owe it to yourself to inquire of people who have lived there, or research memoirs or other first-person sources, concerning the specific effects that place had on them and others who lived there.

No one can travel everywhere, so we have to rely on research at times for what we need to know about how regional considerations affect our characters. Two areas of inquiry one should never neglect are food and music. The television series *Treme*, based in New Orleans, relies on these two areas more than any other to capture the city's unique culture. Regional cuisine can often define home and hearth for someone, and music can help inform a sense of what kinds of cues trigger emotion. Someone raised on Patsy Cline will have a different aural and emotional palette, and perhaps even a different inner rhythm or sense of time, than someone who heard Tito Puente, Erykah Badu, or Beethoven growing up.

Home

Unlike with geography, here we're not simply asking how the places where our character has lived have affected him; we're asking where he feels he belongs.

When doing the initial sketches of your character, ask: Does he live in the place he considers home, or is he an outcast or exile in his own community? How do others view him because of this background—hick, city slicker, arriviste, bumpkin, boor?

What of his home lingers in his values, dialect, ambitions, prejudices?

If home is elsewhere, does he long to go back? *Can* he go back? Or has something happened—a scandal, a tragedy, a loss—that bars that road back forever? Has he made peace with his new home, made it his own, or is there something lacking about it? How long did it take him to get here? What price did he pay?

In *Up in the Air* Ryan's discomfort anywhere but on the road is key to understanding who he is; his ultimate turn to wanting something else, a genuine home, lies at the heart of his story.

In Richard Price's *Samaritan*, ex-teacher Ray Mitchell loses his job writing for TV and returns to his New Jersey hometown. He begins to settle in, get comfortable, but the old home ground has more than consolations. It has se-crets, and one catches up with him when he's beaten sense-less in his apartment.

Quoyle in *The Shipping News* was "born in Brooklyn and raised in a shuffle of dreary upstate towns," ending up in a nowhere called Mockingburg. Then his faithless wife, Petal, breaks her neck in a car crash. Desperate for some sort of solid ground, he uproots his two daughters and heads for ancestral property on the Newfoundland coast, and through the unwitting intervention of the locals does indeed begin to feel as close to home as he's capable.

When Frodo returns from the War of the Ring, his ordeal has rendered him so emotionally and physically spent he no longer feels at peace in the Shire. Instead, within two years, he departs with Gandalf, Elrond, and Galadriel across the sea, leaving Middle Earth forever.

To What "Tribe" Does My Character Belong?

All of these sociological considerations point toward a spe-cific question: What is your character's "tribe"? Is there a group of individuals with whom your character identifies, and in whose company she's learned, acquired, and prac-ticed what she considers her moral, social, political, spiri-tual, practical, even dietary norms?

Often, such tribes are formed at work (another reason this area is of such importance).

The power of the tribe can be subtle or stifling, inspir-ing or insidious. Anyone who has experienced corporate or country-club culture knows how conformist it can be—individual expression is encouraged only to a degree. But the same is also true of most college campuses.

Police forces are notorious cauldrons of a unique culture, even though it could best be typified as a "pack of lone wolves." Individuality and initiative are often prized and fiercely defended, and infighting can be brutal, but the group closes ranks when attacked from outside. In contrast, firefighters spend a great deal of time together and they respond to calls as a group. This is not a trivial distinction. Both jobs may foster heroism, but they attract heroes of distinctly different temperaments.

Soldiers who've endured combat often remark that no other bond in their lives ever can equal the affection, respect, interdependence, and loyalty engendered by that experience. But mothers at a playground can form a unique and tightly monitored tribe, too, as observed by Tom Perrotta in his novel *Little Children*.

And what are political parties other than tribes? There may be principles that define the party's core beliefs, but it is far more likely there is simply a recognition of fellowship among the party's members, a sense of belonging, a way to tell that someone is "one of us," even if the terms of that fellowship seem to an outsider as hopelessly vague or fluid. (As the comedian Will Rogers once remarked: "I don't belong to an organized party. I'm a Democrat.")

If your character belongs to a tribe, ask how far she's willing to stray from it. What would cause her to betray, defy, or even leave the tribe? To what degree are her ties to the tribe tested by the dramatic action of your story?

Remember, in answering the questions raised in this and the preceding two chapters, picture the scene in the character's life that poses the answer. You're not trying to accumulate data for an encyclopedia entry. You're trying to imagine the incidents in your character's life that shaped the behavior and inner life that arises in the course of your story—no more, no less.

Few characterizations will require detailed exploration of all the issues raised. A balance must be struck between what the story requires, what the character's role in the story is, and how much the areas you're exploring reflect on the action within that story. But each of the questions posed can open a window onto the soul of a character, and may provide you with an insight that takes your story in an interesting, unforeseen direction, or provides your character with newfound depth. The limits to that exploration are ultimately up to you alone.

Exercises

1. Take two characters from a piece you're currently writing and explore as discussed in this chapter each of the following sociological relationships or areas of social engagement:

Family

    (a) Father

    (b) Mother

    (c) Grandparents

    (d) Siblings

    (e) Children

    (f) Spouse

Friends
Name
Class
Work
Education
Geography
Home
"Tribe"

Has this work inspired any additional scenes, or suggested changes in scenes you've already written. If so, how? If not, why?

Chapter Fifteen
Picking a Fight: Politics

This subject could have been covered in either of the preceding chapters, as it touches on both psychology and sociology, but given the rancorous sniping that routinely typifies political discourse, it seemed appropriate to reserve a special section for this topic alone.

It's often said that if you want to avoid discord at a party, don't bring up sex, religion, or politics. This may be sound social advice but it's a disastrous approach for writers.

If Henry Brooks Adams is correct in characterizing politics as the systematic organization of hatreds, then ignoring it is but another lost opportunity. As with religious beliefs, political convictions often speak to the very core values we cherish. And as with sex, they often address key vulnerabilities, as many of our deepest ideals, hopes, fears, and suspicions find expression in our political inclinations.

The reason, I believe, that authors routinely avoid explicit mention of politics is twofold.

One, we often unconsciously avoid the confrontational edginess and rancor that makes life unpleasant but fiction interesting.

Two, we're afraid of falling into bombast or diatribe. This is a reasonable concern, especially given how often we're blinded by our own political allegiances. It's difficult to address politics without falling into clichéd thinking, cartoonish simplification, caricature—or just the comfy rut of preconceived notions.

The problem isn't politics. The problem is our own inability to discuss or even think about politics without plunging headlong into recrimination. Other than religion and sibling rivalry, nothing brings out the sanctimonious capacity for blame more intensely than politics.

It needn't be so. Conservatives outnumber liberals by far in my family. Tensions persist. Grievances fester. But we remain a family.

Don't judge your characters. This is especially true of their politics. You should be able to defend—and dare I say love—a character whose political convictions are opposed to your own. This is your responsibility as an artist. It doesn't mean you should excuse what you consider wrong, misguided, or evil. But you need to be able to get into the hearts and minds of people whose worldview is diametrically opposed to your own. Otherwise, you're revealing not just your political biases, but a certain small-heartedness as well.

Perhaps even more important, you need to step back from your own convictions and see them objectively. It's gratifying to believe that *but for those idiots* you and your kind would make the world a better, safer, saner place. It's also self-serving. The world is not the way it is because one camp or the other has lacked its fair chance to improve it.

Politics, like religion, is about how to live and with whom. It's about right versus wrong and us against them. Nothing could be more fundamental about people, and thus characterization. Controversial issues—abortion, gay rights, the death penalty, terrorism, poverty, law and order, torture, taxes, racial inequality, welfare, military spending, free enterprise—are exactly the topics that, if broached by your character, will very likely provoke a sympathetic nod or a vein-popping argument with other characters. Used wisely, this can open your characters up in illuminating ways. But if the reader senses that it's you, not the characters talking, you risk alienating, infuriating, or just boring her.

Politicized art descends into screed precisely because it roots itself in ideas instead of character. We get sermons, not scenes. The political drama *The West Wing* was revolutionary in many ways, despite its liberal leanings, principally because it showed true believers getting truly tested. At its best, its characters challenged, badgered, doubted, even undermined each other. At its worst, its conservative characters were contrarian props with all the oomph of a ventriloquist's dummy.

Political convictions are an expression of a want—a desire for a certain way of life. Dramatize the desire, the resulting conflict, make it personal not ideological, and don't stack the deck in favor of your own convictions. The only person you're apt to fool is yourself.

One of the more useful approaches to this territory, at least from a writer's point of view, is George Lakoff's *Moral Politics: How Liberals and Conservatives Think*. Lakoff's premise is that political beliefs are framed around a metaphor, that of the nation as a family, with the government as parent.*

Lakoff argues that conservatives largely adhere to a Strict Father model, where the world is a dangerous place; competition fosters discipline and moral strength; and legitimate authority—authority that encourages self-reliance and responsibility—should be obeyed, not questioned, for questioning legitimate authority only creates disorder.

On the other hand, liberals tend to ascribe to a Nurturing Parent model, which maintains that the world is not inherently dangerous; the best way to determine safety from danger is through dialog—establishing fact through questioning and answering—not ideological prejudgment; obedience is premised on respect, which is earned, not absolute; and fairness and cooperation provide a better path to the social good than individual moral strength.

These are tendencies, not straitjackets. Not even fire-breathing ideologues so tidily conform to type. But even given that caveat, it's not so difficult to see why liberals and conservatives often disagree so profoundly. Like Calvinists and Quakers, they inhabit distinct moral universes. This perhaps explains why they tend to congregate in dif-

---

* Lakoff isn't alone in thinking this way. The creators of the TV political satire *Parks and Recreation* have stated their guiding premise is that when citizens want a mom, they vote liberal, and when they want a dad, they vote conservative.

ferent professions: liberals in teaching, the arts, and health care; conservatives in law enforcement, business, and the military. But again, that's an oversimplification. There are conservative doctors and artists just as there are liberal cops and entrepreneurs, and recognizing that can spare you from cliché.

In truth, the contrasting belief systems are neither mutually exclusive nor irreconcilable, no matter what more extreme partisans might tell you. Due to our being schooled by the culture at large, we all share in the same stew of moral values. What we tend to emphasize differs depending on what moral system we embrace, how and by whom we were raised, and what our experiences have been. It's often quipped that a conservative is a liberal who's been mugged, or who's had to make a payroll. It could just as easily be said that a liberal is a conservative who at one time or another has needed a helping hand, or who again has been mugged—by her boss.

This way of looking at things shouldn't be used to create more elaborate cartoons. Instead, let it open your eyes to people who normally baffle, annoy, or even disturb you. If you're liberal, create a character who embraces strength, self-discipline, obedience to authority, decisiveness, self-reliance. If you're conservative, create a character who believes in communication, self-fulfillment, nurturance, empathy. Trust me, it won't kill you. It just might make you stronger.

Sometimes it's wiser to look at how your character engages with politics at the local rather than the national level: Is she a member of the Chamber of Commerce crowd, the Save the Waterfront crowd, those supporting the proposed Walmart, those rallying against it, those who join the neighborhood watch group, those who get their politics from the pulpit? Such collectives are far more diverse than ideology can explain, which makes them much more interesting than simply having an R or a D next to one's name at the local polling place.

People feel local issues far more viscerally, for they can affect property values, the quality of their children's schools, the safety of the neighborhood. How a character does or doesn't engage with that says a lot about him: Is he a rabble-rouser or a hermit, the town crank, the perpetual volunteer, the guy who ends up being in charge of every group he joins?

It's often here at the local level that the political impulse reveals its shadow side most insidiously. Politics is power, and there's a reason we use the phrase "lust for power." In Jess Walter's *Citizen Vince*, a young woman's attendance at a Spokane rally for Ronald Reagan during the 1980 presidential campaign isn't inspired simply by a sense of civic engagement. It provides her the opportunity to be with her married lover, a candidate for local office. She's sincere and supportive and stupid. Sooner or later the tryst will end, in heartbreak at least, which will gratify some dark impulse that was there all along in each of them: the need for attention, the need to be punished, the sneaky craving for a juicy secret. Both of them are jeopardizing their standing with a group of people they know well and rely upon. It's folly, but that's part of the thrill. The political angle isn't incidental—it amplifies the stakes. Political paramours betray more than just a marriage.

Exercises

1. Take two characters without any overt political affiliation from a book or film or TV program you've enjoyed. Look at how they address issues such as initiative, responsibility, discipline, danger, authority, communication, self-fulfillment, fairness. Can you discern a political inclination even though none is stated? Why or why not?

2. In the same way as in exercise 1, explore the politics of the characters in a piece you've recently written. Did you unwittingly make them all vaguely of the same political stripe? What would happen if you changed one of the left-leaning characters rightward, or vice versa?

3. Craft a character whose political convictions oppose your own. How successful is the result? Don't decide for yourself; let others read the work and judge for themselves.

Chapter Sixteen
Quirks, Tics, and Bad Habits

As we conclude this portion of the book, it's time to consider something a bit more whimsical—but no less valuable for characterization.

Much of what we've been discussing helps us understand a character's inner life—her psyche, her values, her hopes and fears—or involves her conscious engagement with others. What we'll explore now will feel a little more external and mindless, for they are behaviors of which the character herself is largely unaware, and may in many ways seem inconsequential, but nonetheless are so curious, odd, unexpected, or hard to explain that they automatically provide a vivid, impressionistic image and thus help the character come alive.

They can be helpless physical expressions—like a honking laugh, an anxious fluttering of the eyelids when feeling shy, a jerky twitch in the shoulder when anxious. They might take the form of vaguely conscious compulsions—

checking one's hair, makeup, or teeth in the rearview mirror; tapping one's pen against a desktop. Or they may be deliberate, even practiced eccentricities or affectations— quoting proverbs to summarize the "meaning" of what's just been said, or using French words or phrases *sans ironie*.

The list can go on and on. I sometimes visit cafés and shops to observe people, watching for just these kinds of traits or other unique, offhand, distinguishing behaviors. Other examples include:

- Slapping the arm of a listener to punctuate a thought

- Reaming one's ear, then inspecting the fingertip for wax

- Smoothing one's hair obsessively when nervous

- Jiggling one's foot while sitting, or dangling a shoe off the heel

- Running one's necklace over the lips or chin while reading or talking on the phone

- Wagging one's hands when in animated discussion

- Closing one's eyes, or fluttering one's eyelids, when laughing

- Tucking an unlit cigarette behind the ear

- Running one's tongue along the lips when concentrating

- Giving voice to a pet's imagined thoughts (pet ventriloquism)

In Robert Altman's *3 Women*, Millie Lammoreaux (Shelly Duvall) habitually catches her skirt in her car door. In Jess Walter's *The Zero*, an old woman wears her makeup slightly off center, so she looks like "a hastily painted figurine, or a foosball goalie." The guard at the Our Lady of Mercy emergency room in Joe Connelly's *Bringing Out the Dead* wears sunglasses at all hours so that, when anyone threatens to rage against the long wait, he can loom over them, arms crossed against his massive chest, and growl menacingly, "Don't make me take my glasses off." In David Benioff's *City of Thieves*, the redheaded Antokolsky twins had only one known talent, the ability to fart in harmony.

The risk in using such traits is their tendency to create an essentially comic effect. This can diminish a protagonist or an opponent, which is why one more often sees this technique used with secondary characters. This needn't be the case; it's a question of approach. Since the behaviors are largely unconscious, they can suggest a kind of helplessness, and elicit empathy. They can also echo other aspects of the character's nature and thus create complexity, not just idiosyncrasy.

In Richard Price's *Lush Life*, Detective Matty Clark has narrow eyes that squint all the more when he's asked a question, as though speaking and perhaps even thinking is painful. This gives people the impression that he's on the slow side, or inwardly seething, but he's neither. He in fact uses both false impressions to his advantage, and feels no particular compulsion to explain himself or express his thoughts to anyone. And in *Clockers*, also by Price, Rocco Klein tries to keep a handle on his drinking by permitting himself a slug from the vodka bottle in his freezer, but only for as long as it takes him to read the pledge of excellence on the side of a carton of Breyer's ice cream.

Even in secondary characters, these effects needn't be merely superficial. Uriah Heep in *David Copperfield* obsessively protests, "I'm so 'umble," which is part of an obsequious, unctuous mask meant to hide his scheming vanity and a bottomless contempt for his betters.

In *One Flew Over the Cuckoo's Nest*, Billy Bibbitt's stammer isn't merely a bit of stage business; it's a symptom of deep-seated sexual guilt centered around the puritanical harpy whose womb once engulfed him.

And Pope Cody, part of the criminal family at the center of the film *Animal Kingdom*, approaches his brothers with the seemingly benevolent offer to listen if there's anything they want to get off their chests. "You can talk to me, I'm here for you," is said so often, so earnestly, and to so many different siblings it almost seems like a running gag—until it becomes clear just what a sociopath Pope is. His seeming concern for his brothers is motivated by a desire to know their secrets and weaknesses, the better to use their confidences against them.

If a trip to your favorite people-watching haunt isn't practicable, try one of these prompts, or come up with your own:

- What irritates him? Phone solicitors, barking dogs, loud cars, fat people, rude people, boorish people, stupid people, people who go on and on . . . ? (Irritation is uniquely valuable in characterization because it lies beyond conscious control, and thus reveals a kind of vulnerability.)

- What food or drink or activity can she not resist? (Is it an addiction, an obsession, a disorder? Or just a nagging itch?)

- Is there a childhood pleasure in which he still indulges as an adult (a favorite cereal or dessert or comfort food, flannel PJs, campy horror flicks, a favorite sports team, saltines and milk before bed, afternoon naps)?

- What's the oldest thing in the refrigerator? What food invariably disappears first?

- What's beneath the bed? At the back of the closet?

- What's her favorite joke—is it risqué, raunchy, suitable for the vicar?

- Does he have a favorite pet? Is it still alive? If not, has he clung to telltale memorabilia?

- What's the worst thing she's ever said behind someone's back?

- What curse word or odd phrase does she utter when frustrated? (Be imaginative. I once worked with a woman who, whenever something went wrong, sighed darkly and said, "Oh, bother.")

- Does he have some other verbal tic? One of the characters in *Do They Know I'm Running?*, a Palestinian Iraqi with a serviceable if clunky command of English, announces his insecurity by beginning many of his sentences with a bombastic "Let me tell you something . . ." Another tic one encounters often in both real life and fiction is the serial interrogative: "Mrs. Robiskie? You know that errand you wanted me to run? Down to the store?" Other verbal tic phrases include "Swear to God"; "I'm tellin' ya"; "Boy oh boy"; "Know what I mean?" And few people are as irritating as the one who cuts off others before they have a chance to finish a thought.

- What's her favorite article of clothing, something slinky and elegant or something she can't throw away no matter how threadbare? (A friend of mine in high school had what she called "happy socks," a pair of striped knee-highs so distinctly ugly—fuzzy, itchy wool in muddy shades of green, brown, and gray—they always made her laugh when she had them on, and so she always wore them when she was feeling depressed.)

- What was the last movie that made him cry? Put him to sleep? Made him walk out?

- What was the last book he loaned to someone, saying, "You *have* to read this. It's *your kind of book*"?

The deeper you connect such an effect to the character's uniqueness, the more it will conjure his solitary nature, echoing with the afflictions or consolations of his loneliness or with the inescapable, baffling helplessness he feels toward life and his own behavior. In that way it will rise above the level of mere accent and feel more like a crucial detail.

Exercises

1. Take a trip to any local spot where a variety of people mingle. Make notes of intriguing, odd, or vivid touches of seemingly inadvertent behavior. Then take two characters from a piece you're working on and add one of these quirks, tics, or mindless habits to each. Does it feel organic or simply slathered on? What could you do to make it feel more natural?

2. Do the same with another two characters, this time using one of the examples discussed in this chapter or one of the interrogative prompts. Again—does the result enhance the characterization or feel forced? How can you tell?

PART III

Roles

Chapter Seventeen
Meaning and Its Messenger:
The Protagonist and the Premise

Choosing the Protagonist

So, you've found your inspiration for your characters from any of a number of sources—real people, art, nature, the unconscious, your story idea—and begun sketching crucial scenes that flesh out the characters' wants, adaptations, secrets, contradictions, vulnerabilities. You've thought up even more scenes while deepening your understanding of the characters' physical, psychological, and sociological natures. The material begins to gel into a more fully realized narrative arc. You see the characters enmeshed in meaningful conflict, and as that conflict intensifies—as the characters collide, cooperate, interact, responding to the frustration of their desires by digging deeper, redoubling their efforts, enlisting allies, confronting those who stand in their way, changing tactics, improvising cleverly or recklessly, crossing moral lines—it all begins to point toward some sort of crisis and resolution, even if it's not entirely clear yet what form that climactic event might take.

It's now time to figure out who the main characters are. This is sometimes an easier problem to state than to solve.

Some stories revolve around a decisive event and how it impacts a number of people, with the various plotlines tracking how each of the characters deals with the consequences of that event. It's not just disaster sagas that follow this approach: Boccaccio's *Decameron*, Thornton Wilder's *The Bridge at San Luis Rey*, Isak Dinesen's novella "The Deluge at Norderney," Ann Patchett's *Bel Canto*, and Jane Smiley's *Ten Days in the Hills* all conform to the pattern.

Sometimes two characters—siblings, friends, lovers, a married couple—rise above the fray and stand out because the story's events profoundly affect their bond. Returning to *Bel Canto*, the love that grows between the soprano Roxanne Coss and the Japanese businessman Katsumi Hosokawa elevates them above the other characters who nonetheless still compel our interest and affection. In Jennifer Egan's *A Visit from the Goon Squad*, Bennie Salazar and Sasha remain preeminent despite the intriguing misadventures of their various friends, associates, and hangers-on over the years.

Robert Stone often structures his novels on three main characters moving along parallel story lines, all of which revolve around a central event. In *Dog Soldiers*, the ex-marine Ray Hicks, the journalist John Converse, and his wife Marge all hold center stage at varying times as Hicks, at Converse's behest and with Marge's complicity, tries to salvage a misbegotten heroin deal. In *A Flag for Sunrise*, the anthropologist Frank Holliwell, Pablo the Coast Guard deserter, and Sister Justin Feeney all set course for a brutal collision as revolution breaks out in a Central American backwater.

But in the vast majority of stories, one character takes center stage, doing so because, in one or more of the following ways, he or she:

- Responds most deliberately to the inciting incident that changes the world as it exists when the story begins

- Feels the deepest impetus to action

- Has the greatest at stake in the story

- Arouses the deepest empathy in the reader or audience

- Serves as the focus of the story's moral premise

This character is the protagonist or hero. I prefer the former term because of its neutrality. The term "hero" has a lot of traction in some quarters, but it also carries a lot of baggage—ideological, political, semantic—that I find cumbersome and misleading. The character, for example, is often compelled to act in ways—or reveals himself to be, at heart—somewhat less than classically heroic. TV has recently featured a number of such protagonists, from Walter White in *Breaking Bad* to Don Draper in *Mad Men*— not to mention Tony Soprano. But each of these characters arouses our empathy because of the depth of his want, the vulnerability he reveals, the risks he faces, the manner in which he ultimately embraces those risks, and the strength of his response to conflict.

Beginning writers in particular are well advised to accept the discipline of focusing on one main character as the protagonist. It helps simplify the story and clarify its moral themes, it makes structuring the story more straightforward, and it helps engage the reader by identifying who the story concerns most profoundly. They may root for him or not, but they have to care what happens to him.

The protagonist is in fact so crucial to the nature and structure of story that I devote this and the next two chapters to exploring this character's role and purpose, for very often understanding your protagonist goes to the heart of what you're hoping to dramatize.

Summoning the Will

Whatever the protagonist wants, it must be wanted with her whole body and soul, so that losing it will be tantamount to death. This reflects recognition of the need for meaning in the face of the utter annihilation our mortality represents. The search for that meaning, when properly understood, demands our complete engagement.

In dramatic terms, the search for meaning lies in the pursuit of an overarching need, want, ambition, or goal—even if the pursuit is forced upon the protagonist by exterior events. In stories, wants are not mere cravings. They reflect a deeper hunger—for love, for significance, for understanding, for the welcoming safety of home. And when a character's desire for these things is thwarted, denied, opposed, threatened with destruction, it should evoke within her the full engagement of her being. The stakes, if properly perceived, are ultimate. The cost of being denied is devastation—if not existentially, then emotionally, socially, or psychologically.

When a protagonist fails to engage the reader or audience, the problem is almost always rooted in the writer's failure to properly understand the stakes—what it is the character wants, why he wants it, and the moral and emotional risk he's willing to take to get it. If, when reviewing a draft of your work, a reader or editor remarks that she "can't get into the protagonist," or doesn't find him compelling, look first to those three issues.

Framing the Conflict—
the Protagonist and the Premise

To dramatize the stakes for the protagonist effectively you need to frame the conflict properly—put something so formidable between him and what he wants that his success remains in doubt until the very end.

Lajos Egri calls this battle between conflicting, irreconcilable desires the Unity of Opposites. Great drama is created when two opposing forces go head-to-head, with the end result requiring the vanquishing of one or the other. Compromise is not an option.

But the dramatic staging of conflict requires more than just a proper understanding of what the protagonist wants and what prevents him from getting it. A story is a moral enterprise. Characters make choices in pursuit of a goal, inspired by a way of life they hope to obtain, preserve, or defend. In so doing they suffer the consequences and shoulder the responsibility of those choices. When a story gels it's because the actions give rise to an emotionally affecting climax that provides a moral revelation, for the reader and audience if not the characters.

What the Unity of Opposites provides is equal and opposing moral justifications—one for the protagonist, the other for whatever person(s) or power(s) oppose him. In every scene, each side is fighting for survival and supremacy. Each attack is met by a counterattack, and the counterattack must be stronger than the preceding attack or else the dramatic action fails to build. If the implications of "attack" and "counterattack" seem overly gladiatorial for your story, find terms that suit your purpose: action and reaction, perhaps, or even yin and yang. The point is to focus on the opposition, for it's that opposition that generates the conflict.

Whoever loses in a given scene comes back in the next even harder, trying to regain the advantage, and this escalation continues until the final, climactic confrontation, in which either the protagonist or the forces that oppose him prevail, with an understanding that no further conflict is possible. The reader or the audience feels that no more back-and-forth can occur. The matter is decided.

The protagonist is the character who conveys that moral revelation, even if she herself refuses to accept it or remains unaware of it. As such, the protagonist is the messenger most responsible for bringing the meaning of your story to the reader and audience.

By "meaning," I'm not referring to the tidy little moral we're supposed to take away from the story, as we do from a fable by Aesop—or the hectoring epithet William Bennett attached to each of the cautionary tales he compiled in his *Book of Virtues*. A story's meaning is felt in the body before it crystallizes in the mind. Its fundamental nature is dramatic, not intellectual. We discern the meaning as the scenes unfold, on a visceral, emotional, or intuitive level.

Understanding your story, therefore, requires not just understanding the protagonist's core desire and its relentless opposition—the Unity of Opposites—that generate the seesaw battle embodied in the action. It requires comprehending the moral, emotional, and thematic resonance you intuit from that action.

The key word is "moral." The more deeply you immerse yourself in the choices your characters make and the dramatic impact of those choices, the more you will discern a moral conjecture the drama asserts, or "proves." This moral statement is typically referred to as the premise, and the premise focuses most intently on the protagonist.

Premise is often confused with theme—and, as we'll see later, the more generally a premise is stated, the more likely this is to be true. Due to its generality, a theme normally feels static, whereas what one is after in a premise is a combination of a moral consequence with the factors that cause it within the story. The premise should identify the virtue or vice that resonates most deeply with your ending, and identify as well the reasons why that virtue or vice prevails or is vanquished. I'd add that it should apply uniquely to the characters who prove it, as the following discussion, on moving from the abstract to the specific, should make clear. The premise identifies What and Who and Why, leaving the How to the dramatic action of your story.

I can't know my premise until I know my ending. I may well select one only to discard or refine it as I continue revising. It's a working hypothesis embedded in the unfolding action of the story, which is built scene by scene, sequence by sequence, chapter by chapter, act by act. That dramatic action has to satisfy my own need to be both gratified and surprised. If I rig the result, the contrivance will be a secret to no one.

Once I know my ending I can use the premise during the revision stage to tighten the flow of scenes and enhance the rising dramatic action. And it's the rising dramatic action, not the premise, that's the point.

A premise is only as good as the action and the characters that prove it—especially the protagonist. There's no point trying to shoehorn meaning into the drama, or marshaling characters and scenes to fit a preconceived profundity. That's propaganda, not drama. Instead, I infer my meaning from what I've intuitively recognized as the story's best form. This can't be fudged or manufactured. It requires thinking and feeling deeply about the characters I've created, the compelling scenes in which I've placed them, and the rising conflict those scenes ultimately embody.

Working Backward—Conceiving the Premise from the Abstract to the Specific

Often a premise will be worded in the following way:

- Ruthless ambition leads to its own destruction. (*Macbeth*)

- Great love triumphs over even intractable hatred. (*Romeo and Juliet*)

- Belligerent vanity destroys the capacity to rule. (*Coriolanus*)

The use of Shakespearean examples is not accidental. The belief that premises automatically trivialize what one's writing often vanishes, or should, when they're recognized in the work of the greatest playwright in the English language.

Citing three more modern examples:

- Romantic love must be sacrificed to the fight against tyranny. (*Casablanca*)

- Even acts of compassion can kill when we don't know what's really going on. (*Chinatown*)

- Only by demanding responsibility from ourselves and others can we earn back our self-respect. (*Michael Clayton*)

The premise isn't proven through virtuous march step to a foregone conclusion. It's proven through a contest to the limit between antithetical moral views, the protagonist's on the one hand, and an opposing force or character(s) on the other. That's why each premise implicitly suggests a counterpremise that embodies the opposing action in the story:

- Those devoted to justice can defeat the heedlessly ambitious. (*Macbeth*)

- Family honor comes before all, including romantic love. (*Romeo and Juliet*)

- The people will rise up against arrogant tyranny. (*Coriolanus*)

- Fascism isolates its enemies and crushes their will to resist one by one. (*Casablanca*)

- Excessive wealth and unchecked power create confusion to escape culpability. (*Chinatown*)

- The duty of the professional class is to enforce the impunity of privilege, even to the point of murder. (*Michael Clayton*)

When worded this way, even a compelling premise or counterpremise can feel every bit as clumsy and simplistic as Aesop's and Bennett's pithy "morals to the story." They're themes, not premises. That said, distilling your premise in this way can still serve a useful purpose, if only in clarifying the moral conflict at the heart of the story.

But remember that it's not slogans that are battling the matter out, but characters with distinct and irreconcilable views of life—which is why each premise and counterpremise expresses both a *moral stance* and *an action*. The premise takes the form of an assertion in which two opposing moral visions clash, with only one prevailing, with a suggestion as to why.

The most compelling drama is always good versus good—two equally acceptable suitors vying for the loved one, or two equally admirable boxers hammering it out for the championship. Such stories ennoble us by giving us credit for realizing that loss is inevitable, merit and fortitude don't solve everything, and all too often the struggle is its own reward.

More often, however, stories revolve around some form of virtue versus vice: Either a virtue gets tested but ultimately overcomes a powerful or insidious vice, or a vice succeeds in destroying, undermining, or sapping the promise from a virtue. This needn't be as simplistic as it sounds, and we all carry a secret hope that virtue in the end does stand for something.

By virtue and vice I don't mean an abstraction; I mean a moral or existential condition, a situation that is lived, the way of life the protagonist or his adversaries embrace. That's why I personally find premises like the ones I proposed just now only preliminarily useful. I start there, but in any morally complex and thus interesting story, each of the characters is fighting to defend or save a certain manner of living that defines who he is.

- Macbeth embraces a world where the throne belongs to the man bold enough to seize it by any means necessary. He's undone by his guilt and his misjudgments of how fiercely men who believe in lawful and orderly succession will oppose him.

- Romeo and Juliet stand for a world where romantic love is the supreme good, which means little to their families, who are consumed with blood vengeance.

- Coriolanus believes in a world where fate and honor define preeminence, and thus the right to rule. The people sense in him a cruel and unyielding dictator, drunk on his own pride, and refuse to grant him the consulship.

- Rick understands that romantic love would be meaningless under fascism, which the Nazis confirm through the ruthless exercise of power.

- Jake believes in a world where the little guy has a shot and things make sense. His adversary, Noah Cross, believes in a world where the powerful make the rules—so they needn't bother with obeying them themselves—and create confusion to obscure their machinations.

- Michael Clayton ultimately embraces the world he sees in his son's eyes, a world where people may be lost, alone, and confused but they fight the good fight. Until then he's trapped in the world of institutionalized impunity, where the powerful get bilked by the billable hour to do as they please.

Seeing the story as a conflict between ways of life or worldviews can spare you the clumsy, overgeneralized way in which premises are often worded. They are not meant to be universal, indisputable truths, like Euclidean theorems. They are moral assertions that your *particular characters* and your *particular story* embody.

This is why I often take it one step further. I state my premise not in terms of principles but in the humble, specific beliefs and desires of my characters themselves.

Returning to our examples:

- A man with Macbeth's conscience will undermine his own murderous schemes, weakening his ability to withstand the resistance his ambition creates.

- Romeo and Juliet in their innocence would rather die than be apart, and thus see past the worldly hatreds of their families and truly love.

- A man pampered by his mother and yet forged by war like Coriolanus will never be able to submit to the people, whom he considers his inferiors—meaning he will never rule as he believes is his fate, because the people will defy him.

- Once Rick realizes how much Ilsa truly loves him, he can forgive her and thus see the bigger picture—she has to stay with Victor Laszlo, and he (Rick) has to return to the fight against fascism.

- Jake's intention to avenge himself and rescue Evelyn is doomed because he's blind to the full insidious power of the corruption he faces, and the constraints of his own limited understanding.

- Michael Clayton needs a madman and a child to remind him of what's truly important, and he owes it to both of them to stand up against the evil he's helped empower.

I create from my character work a number of scenes that begin to suggest a conflict with ultimate stakes for the characters—specifically, the protagonist—and a story with a clear moral spine. I generally see the more general conception of the premise first, in some version of good versus good, virtue versus virtue, good versus evil, virtue versus vice. Then I work backward, first taking that somewhat simplified and abstract view of the morality of my story and embodying it in competing ways of life, so I can see not just the morality at issue but the way that morality takes form in the lifestyles of the characters, their desires, fears, hopes, joys. Finally, I embody those competing ways of life in the specific actions of my characters, crystallizing what is most central to how they're defending that manner of living in this particular story.

This allows me in each scene to determine whether the action of the protagonist brings him closer or pushes him further from realization of the moral end he's seeking, the way of life he's trying to serve.

Every scene in the story has a moral and emotional weight, and resolves in a state of affairs, an imbalance of power, a personal setback or success, a victory or defeat of a certain virtue or value, that creates the circumstances— the setup—for the following scene in that plotline. This continues with escalating stakes, escalating conflict, scene by scene, sequence by sequence, act by act. The stakes escalate because the force or forces opposing the protagonist are as committed to prevailing as he is, and push back against his successes at every turn. The premise is proved when the protagonist fails or prevails, and what he lives for—emotionally, morally, spiritually—is vindicated or vanquished for good.

The embodiment of the premise in the actions of a particular group of characters in a particular story brings up one of the fundamental ironies of literature: *The universal is best conveyed through the specific.* The reason for this is because in providing the reader or audience crucial, telling details you evoke empathy for your characters: Rick's bitter insistence that Sam play "As Time Goes By" when the two men are alone, saying, "If she can stand it, I can"; Jake's doffing his hat as flashbulbs pop at the doorway to the morgue, spelling his name for the reporters as he hustles Evelyn Mulwray to safety; the helpless, wistful longing in Michael Clayton's gaze as he watches his son run to class. It's empathy, created in detailed moments like this, that creates universality. The more specifically real you make your characters, the deeper the kinship the audience can feel with them, and the broader that audience will be.

The Personal Nature of the Premise

The choice of a premise is personal. It reflects not just the moral viewpoint of the protagonist but the moral vision of the person who frames it and is obliged to work with it: you.

Trying to gear yourself up to propound a theme you only halfheartedly believe will deliver you straight into the hands of the trite, the overblown, the heavy-handed: cliché. You'll be trying to convince yourself instead of involving your reader or audience.

I often encourage students to draw up a list of scenes from books and films and TV programs that particularly move them: scare them, enrage them, excite them, disgust them, bring them to tears (especially this). Don't just study those scenes for craft. Accept that what they have to say touches you deeply: the importance of home, the solace of friendship, the redemption of an outcast though a selfless act of courage, the vindicating power (or destructive illusion) of romantic love. I call the content of such scenes a *personal theme*, and it's important to recognize those themes that touch you most profoundly. It's part of understanding your strengths as a creative artist, and defines at least part of your individual gift. Your protagonists will carry the banner for those themes in your stories.

In an age that prizes ironic detachment, deeply caring about something and allowing yourself to be profoundly moved can often feel like bad form. But you can't create meaningfully without caring deeply. The "detachment" comes into play as you craft your scenes, drawing back from portraying too much in order to lure the reader and audience in.

Even then, however, your protagonist must sooner or later, at one level or another, care with all her heart, and commit herself with the full force of her will. Anything less is unacceptable—not just for her, but for you.

Exercises

1. Take three films or books you especially prize and identify the main characters. Who if any of them stands out as the protagonist? Why? What's at stake for him or her?

2. Do the same as in exercise 1 for a piece you're currently writing.

3. Take three films or books you especially prize and try to discern the premise in each. Formulate it first as an abstract conjecture with a moral cause and an action, with either one good prevailing over another, a virtue overcoming a vice, or a vice defeating a virtue. Next, with these same three sources, outline the ways of life that are in opposition in the story. What does the

protagonist consider the good life at the beginning of the story? What does he recognize as the good life at the end? What's happened in between? If there's an opponent or villain, what way of life is he defending or trying to preserve? Last, formulate the premises in terms of the individual characters themselves, their wants, their moral convictions, their struggles, their adversaries. Which formulation of the premise feels most natural to you? Which inspires you the most, engages you most?

4. Do the same as in exercise 3 with a piece you're currently writing. Which formulation of the premise feels not just most natural, but lends itself most readily to your work, returns you to the desire to write?

5. Draw up a list of ten scenes from books or films that have moved you deeply. Identify what it is in each scene that you find so compelling. Do you detect in some of these scenes a certain thread of thematic similarity? Can you identify a set of personal themes you can use to guide your own writing?

Chapter Eighteen
The Challenge of Change:
Three Protagonist Questions

The Mysterious Necessity of Change

In Jim Harrison's novella *The Man Who Gave Up His Name*, the narrator remarks at one point: "The most vexing thing in the life of a man who wishes to change is the improbability of change." And yet Nordstrom, the protagonist, does indeed evolve bit by bit through seesaw crisis and reflection from a Lutheran capitalist to a short-order cook in the Florida Keys. And yet Harrison had his fingers on something subtle and significant: Change is a mysterious business.

The current disdain for plot in some quarters arises from a belief that action is inherently misconceived—man is a stranger to himself and his motives—and life is ultimately meaningless. Structure, in this way of thinking, is a human invention imposed on the chaos of experience. And so story is a presumption, an illusion, even a trap. Worse, a cliché. Death isn't the climactic resolution of a life, it's simply the end point. And so if your tale points toward some sort of climactic resolution, it's inherently false. Life is endured moment by moment, with no objective structure or coherence.

I don't dispute that there's a great deal of truth to this view. I also think it's largely irrelevant. It's like finding fault with a desire for stillness because you can't escape the sound of your own breath.

For all intents and purposes, there is no such thing as the chaos of experience. We're meaning-making animals; we couldn't stop trying to make sense of things if we tried. Just because we're wrong sometimes doesn't imply the whole enterprise of trying to find coherence is inherently misbegotten. We just need to remind ourselves how easily we fall prey to habitual thinking, misguided assumptions, and errors. This is no less true of storytelling than it is of life.

The key element of story, which is a dramatic form, is that in a story *something changes*.

There are of course many "slice of life" short stories, which aspire to a more poetic, descriptive effect. Even in these, however, matters almost always conclude with a revelation—for the reader or audience if not the characters.

A number of modernist novels seemingly defy plot, such as *Hopscotch*, *The Sun Also Rises*, and *Finnegans Wake*, and the latter half of the twentieth century saw a number of antiplot or nonplot films such as *Last Year at Marienbad*, *The Discreet Charm of the Bourgeoisie*, *Shortcuts*, *Naked*, and *Leaving Las Vegas*. But even here, a dramatic build often takes place toward a definitive insight, decision, action, or impasse that creates the emotional, moral, or philosophical takeaway from the work.

For all its picaresque violence and reckless sexuality, *Naked* careens toward a touching moment between Johnny and Louise in which the audience learns that, when the two lived together in Manchester, she aborted their child. This revelation provides insight into Johnny's bitterness and rage, if stopping short of actually explaining it. And *Leaving Las Vegas* similarly moves inexorably toward Ben's death while making love to Sera—which, as with Johnny and Louise, serves as an ironic act of tenderness.

Even in narratives where nothing changes, something happens. Often, stories that seem static, philosophical, or poetic at first glance in fact conclude with a revelation— Aristotle's *anagnorisis*. And even if this revelation is experienced solely by the reader or audience, not the characters themselves (as in *Naked* and *Leaving Las Vegas*), something dramatic has occurred, a change in attitude, perception, emotion, or understanding—or a *refusal* to change—that the dramatic force of the story has suggested, created, or necessitated.

Change remains one of the most baffling aspects of our existence. The mind, so entranced by images and ideas and names, naturally seeks to anchor itself in some notion of solidity. But the stuff of life won't hold still.

Stories that capture this tension—between the desire for meaning and the endlessly shifting ground beneath our feet—strike at a key truth of our existence. In the Arthurian legends, King Arthur tries to preserve the egalitarian self-sacrifice and equality embodied in the Round

Table, only to see it destroyed by the sexual passions unleashed by the betrayal of Guinevere and Lancelot. In the bildungsroman, the growth into adult awareness is often undesired but always inevitable, for the one essential aspect of innocence is that it will be lost. Crime stories at their most fundamental concern the attempt to reconcile the desire for order with the inevitability of change, specifically violent change, prompted by human want. And love stories can't exist absent movement—toward connection, separation, estrangement, reconciliation.

The more a story is rooted in life—rather than an idea of life—the more it will by necessity concern itself with change. Characterization is the portrayal of individuals making the decisions, suffering the insights, taking the actions, and enduring the ramifications obligated by such change. And the character most deeply affected by that change is usually the protagonist.

What of the So-Called Steadfast Character?

Lajos Egri famously remarked that the only place where characters defy natural law and fail to change is in the realm of bad writing:

> No man ever lived who could remain the same through a series of conflicts which affected his way of living. Of necessity he must change, and alter his attitude toward life.

It's one of those grandly confident pronouncements one can't help but believe—and yet, is it true?

For example, what of the so-called Steadfast Character, whose dramatic arc is premised precisely on his refusal
to change—usually by refusing to sacrifice an ideal or give
up on a goal he believes he cannot live without—despite
the onslaught of ordeals to which he's subjected?

Examples of such characters seemingly include Antigone, Romeo, Jake Barnes in *The Sun Also Rises*, Dr. Richard
Kimble in *The Fugitive*——and an army of other mystery and thriller heroes. In each case, it would seem that the
character in question is defined precisely by a refusal to
surrender his or her core goal, moral stance, or personal
commitment.

But this notion of "steadfast" glances past a key point,
as a closer reading of Egri's statement makes clear. Though
it might be said that the motives or behavior of such characters don't appreciably change, their *emotions*, *insight*, or
attitude toward life does by story's end. If not, that *refusal* to
embrace the opportunity for change is felt by the reader or
audience (and perhaps by the character herself), and the
emotional jolt or deflation of that refusal is the dramatic
payoff.

Antigone struggles with her choice, for she understands the merit of both obeying Creon, who has ordered
death to anyone who buries any of the Theban rebels, and
upholding her love for her brother Polynices, whose body
she's obliged by ritual to entomb. Both options have profound moral weight. But she has to choose. And a choice
always means change, for every option but one is eliminated. As she accepts the death her choice obliges, she and
the audience all feel deeply the increased depth of under-

standing she undergoes, even though, outwardly, her behavior does not change. She remains faithful to Polynices.

One might say that Romeo's *love* is steadfast, but as the
stakes change, so does his appreciation and acceptance of
what that love requires of him.

In *The Sun Also Rises*, Jake and Brett, like Ben and Sera
in *Leaving Las Vegas* and Johnny and Louise in *Naked*, experience a moment of ironic tenderness in the end. They
don't change because they refuse the opportunity that's
presented. Change isn't impossible, it's forsaken—meaning
a decision *not to change* has been made.

And *a decision is inherently dramatic.*

Distinguishing Growth from Transformation

Even in stories where the characters do change, some dramatize a more fundamental metamorphosis than others.
Lightning-bolt conversions such as Paul's on the road to
Damascus seldom work in drama; on the stage or on the
page, such shattering changes must be earned.

But there are stories that do involve a devastating transformation, and they usually involve a core epiphany—
sometimes referred to as a Change-or-Die Moment, or a
Crisis of Insight—in which the character, due to the shattering struggles she has endured, recognizes an error or a
mistake or a limitation in her previous conception of herself or her life, and that recognition provides her the insight
necessary to forge a new path.

Precious and Joe Buck exemplify such change through
insight. Ironically, so does Brett in *The Sun Also Rises*, but
she refuses to sacrifice her sexuality, even as she realizes

Jake, rendered impotent by his war wound, is the man she really loves.

Growth, however, suggests a change that is less abrupt or discontinuous, and less inspired by a dark night of the soul. Growth arises in those stories in which the protagonist, through conflict, gains in confidence, strength, courage, selflessness, or some other virtue or collection of virtues, without necessarily addressing a previous error, mistake, or limitation of character.

This kind of protagonist can be a youth who matures, an Everyman faced with a crisis not of his own choosing, or a gladiator thrown into the arena. He grows in awareness and self-assurance as events proceed and the conflict escalates. Think of a recruit in boot camp, learning to rely upon reservoirs of grit, strength, and endurance he never dreamed he possessed. His prowess, mettle, skill, and determination grow—or bit by bit are worn down and he's defeated.

A protagonist who grows usually strengthens something that already exists within her; one who is transformed normally removes a layer of denial, subterfuge, or deceit that has kept something within her hidden or stunted. It's a question of emphasis: A character that grows relies increasingly on her will. A character that transforms does so through insight.

Put differently, in growth, the hero digs deeper. In transformation, he tears down a wall.

Or: In growth, the hero accelerates. In transformation, he turns.

A protagonist may both dig and tear down, of course, or both accelerate and turn, and a transformed character, once he's suffered his devastating insight, may well react with greater determination or will. This is why distinguishing between growth and transformation can sometimes seem like belaboring a distinction without a difference. It is therefore often more fruitful not to think of growth and transformation as distinct and separate boxes, but as intersecting circles, as in a Venn diagram, with any particular protagonist's arc falling within one or the other or both.

Whether a protagonist experiences growth or transformation or some combination of the two can often be discerned by the type of question the story asks of him. Such questions typically fall into three categories:

- Can I get what I want?

- Who am I?

- What do I have to change about myself to get what I want?

We'll now focus on each of those questions in turn.

Can I Get What I Want?

Consider the film *Slumdog Millionaire*. Eighteen-year-old Jamal Malik from the Juhu slum of Mumbai is a contestant on the Indian version of the TV game show *Who Wants to Be a Millionaire?* Jamal is one question away from the grand prize, but before he's allowed to answer, the police detain and interrogate him. He's suspected of cheating: How else could a "slumdog" possibly know all the answers he's already provided on his triumphal march to the final gong?

In the course of his interrogation, Jamal recounts

through flashbacks the improbable incidents in his madcap life that, ironically, have provided him with each winning answer. These flashbacks tell the story of Jamal, his brother Salim, and the beautiful Latika, Jamal's enduring love. The three meet during their escapades as children in the Mumbai slums. Though Salim is initially resistant to having Latika join them, Jamal convinces him, saying she will be the third musketeer, even though none of them can remember that character's name.

Jamal is orphaned early in the story when his mother dies, and he survives as a cagey beggar and petty thief, with occasional stretches of honest work, growing from a confused urchin to a savvy, resolute knockabout, the one constant in his life being his undying love for Latika—whom, as a teenager, he is forced to abandon at gunpoint to his treacherous brother Salim.

As we finally reach the present, Latika is a virtual prisoner of the crime lord now employing Salim. When Jamal tracks them down, Salim hopes for a reconciliation, but Jamal wants only Latika. She tells him to forget her, but knowing she is a devotee of the gaudiest of game shows, he vows to get on her favorite program and win so they can run away together.

The police find his tale "bizarrely plausible" and let him return to the program. Though disdained by its sniffy emcee, Jamal takes his position for the final question. Salim, plagued with guilt, gives his car keys and cell phone to Latika, telling her to go to Jamal, even though it means certain death for Salim. His boss hopes to make a princely sum by selling Latika, who remains a virgin, to a wealthy buyer.

The final question asked of Jamal is: What was the

name of the third musketeer?—something he never knew. He asks to call a friend (a standard device for the program), and calls his brother, only to reach Latika. She tells him she doesn't know the answer, either, but it doesn't matter, she's been set free, she loves him, and they will finally be together. Thrilled, he hazards a guess at the answer— Aramis—learns he's correct, and wins the grand prize! His brother Salim, sitting symbolically in a bathtub stuffed with cash, kills his crime-boss employer but is murdered by the gangster's underlings, suffering the reformed criminal's traditional death of redemptive honor. Jamal and Latika escape into a final lavish orgasmic dance.

Although this story has elements of the Bollywood musical, its roots are in the Romantic and Victorian novel: a whirlwind of tragedy, comedy, and melodrama, spiked with coincidence, rich in setting, with narrow escapes, harrowing betrayals, wrenching separations, joyous reunions, and cumulative triumphs. The story's narrative thrust owes its momentum to the key question: Will Jamal reunite with Latika? That is Jamal's overriding goal, his quest, his heart's desire. Everything is premised on answering that question.

Never is he forced to ponder whether his desires are folly, only if they're attainable. And the change he undergoes is one of growth, becoming stronger and more certain in his pursuit, rather than transformation. There is no need for inner change because the conflict doesn't come from within himself, it comes from outside forces. Jamal triumphs by summoning greater will, not by correcting some undermining flaw.

The moral theme that lies at the heart of most stories

of this kind is that with sufficient determination, fortitude, and skill, we can ultimately realize our dreams, survive the terrible ordeal, slay the beast, solve the mystery, win the bet, obtain justice, and so on.

This sort of story has its roots in heroic sagas and the chivalric romance, a form that's proved remarkably resilient, enjoying a resurgence in the nineteenth century with writers like Dumas and Dickens, and it's a perpetual favorite at the Cineplex—it seems to make the popcorn taste better. Examples include virtually any romantic comedy, adventure story, buddy flick, mystery, action movie, or disaster saga one can name—from *The Count of Monte Cristo* (a tale of gratifying and morally justified revenge) to *Pride and Prejudice* (Jane Austen's immortal tale of the Bennet sisters' equally gratifying and justified pursuit of marriage); from the thriller *Taken* (about a former CIA agent forced to rescue his daughter from Albanian sex traffickers) to the stoner comedy *Pineapple Express* (about a process server and his pot dealer forced to rescue themselves from the murderous intentions of, well, murderers); from *The Silence of the Lambs* (in which the heroine slays a monster while refusing to become a monster herself) to *Around the World in Eighty Days* (in which a gentleman adventurer wins a wager that he can circumnavigate the globe in the allotted time). It is overwhelmingly the most popular and prevalent form of story on the map.

Of course, due to the essential role of conflict in all stories, a price is paid for the achievement of the goal. Structurally, the full extent of that cost is normally discovered in a scene often referred to as the *crucible*, when the protagonist finds herself on the brink of failure, but somehow musters the will, perceives the crucial insight, or enjoys the turn of fate that pivots the action toward the final series of tests, battles, or reversals that ultimately result in the climactic confrontation with the opponent or the core problem.

The message is almost always that, despite the costs or losses incurred, the effort was worth it. However, if the price paid begins to seem larger than the value of the goal—or worse, the prize, once attained, is found to be worthless—the answer to the underlying question *Can I get what I want?* seems less like a clear-cut *yes* than a more qualified, even cautionary *yes but*. . . . The misgiving only increases when the answer is *no*.

Stories of combat can be divided into prowar and anti-war largely on the basis of whether they fall on one side or the other of that line, where the costs of battle are measured against the value of the victory—or the devastation of the defeat. Most prowar stories answer the question *Can I get what I want?* with a *yes, but* . . . that suggests whatever price was paid, it was either worth it or unavoidable. Anti-war stories will answer with a *yes, but* . . . that finds any victory achieved conspicuously hollow, outweighed by the cost in flesh and blood paid for the triumph. Or it may just answer with an outright *no*.

Virtually every crime story that can be categorized as a caper or noir also answers this question concerning our ability to achieve our desires with a cautionary *no*—from *The Postman Always Rings Twice* to *Asphalt Jungle* to *Dog Day Afternoon* to *No Country for Old Men*. Grabbing the brass ring is an existential wake-up call, reminding us of how many of our wants reduce to vanity or worse. But this is also the form of tragedy, where a protagonist's limited understanding of himself or his world leads to destruction.

There is in every failure a tendency toward self-examination (in fiction, anyway). The character who fails is obliged to ask: What happened? Which easily translates into: Who am I kidding? What do I really want? Do I deserve it? These questions reflect an understanding that man is often mistaken or self-deceived, and stories of this kind routinely play in a minor mode. Regardless, this premise of searching for or blundering into a deeper understanding of oneself lies at the heart of the next story form we'll examine.

Who Am I?

Consider the character Ryan Bingham, played by George Clooney, in the film *Up in the Air*. At the beginning of the story, he embraces a gypsy life of interminable travel, shuns family and other lasting attachments, and feels more at home in airports and hotels than in the featureless apartment where, at least a few days a year, he's obliged to stay put. He likens himself to a shark. This is unsurprising, given his work: He's a corporate hatchet man, traveling city to city to fire employees from jobs they've held for years. And yet he does not do so heartlessly; he feels for the people he's destroying. Think Shiva with a heart of gold.

Enter Alex Goran (Vera Farmiga), a female version of Ryan. They meet in an airport hotel bar and share insider tips on club cards, mileage rewards, and the car rental companies most likely to grovel for their patronage. They also very shortly share a bed—or, more correctly, a night together, since they make love everywhere in the hotel room *except* in bed.

They make plans to meet up again when their cross-country itineraries intersect. The liaison works perfectly, suiting their peripatetic lifestyles. And yet finding a soul mate has its perils. Ryan, obliged to attend his sister's wedding, invites Alex along. He shows her the hometown where he grew up, and begins to reveal a side of himself he's shown no one in years. He's fallen in love. And he realizes that *for this woman* he's ready to give up the travel, to give up the move-or-die ethos, and for the first time in his life put down roots.

He is, of course, tragically mistaken: He has simply seen a reflection of himself in her, and thus erroneously believes she wants what he wants—a committed relationship. But that desire on her part is met by her family, which she has kept a secret from him; she has expertly compartmentalized her life, which she refers to as "being an adult."

As the movie ends, we see Ryan once again eyeing the Arrival and Destination boards at an airport, as we have seen him before—but there's a fundamental difference. The life he once embraced seems hopelessly empty. He finds himself in the same position in which he's placed so many others—he's been "fired," and just as he's counseled so many others to do, he's obliged to regard this cusp of change as an opportunity, even though it feels like a kick in the teeth.

He's been exposed in a fundamental way, and he will never look at himself, his heart, or the world in quite the same way. There will be no return to his old ways, not merely because he sees *their* foolishness, but rather he sees *his own* foolishness. And yet where will he go? In the center of an airport, with nothing but destinations displayed before him, he's stuck.

The key question this story asks is: *Who am I?* This may not at first seem certain. Doesn't Ryan, as in our first example, ask whether he can get what he wants—true love? In a sense, yes. But the answer to the question is *no*. And the reason he can't have the love he wants is because he *presumes* he can. The action of the story reveals the consequences of that presumption. He believes he knows his world and who he is. He's constructed his entire life around that illusion. When it catastrophically fails, he's obliged to ask himself: Who am I really? What do I truly know about myself, my life, and what I want? The *form* of the narrative is that of pursuing a desire, but the *thematic intent* is to ask a fundamental question about human nature.*

The drama concludes soon or immediately after the shock of recognition, with no time to correct or solve the problem. The ending doesn't point toward a solution or a victory but rather to a state of awareness caused by error, ignorance, deceit, denial, or blunder.

In all its varieties, this kind of story explores human identity and nature, and examples of the form reach back to antiquity and continue into modern times:

---

* As noted more than once, virtually every story concerns pursuing a desire. What distinguishes these three types of stories is the nature of the price paid or the insight gained in the attempt to gratify that desire.

- When Oedipus learns that the Oracle's decree is true—that he did slay his father and did bed his mother—he realizes everything he believed about himself was a lie, and tears out his eyes (a recurrent metaphor within *Oedipus the King* equates blindness with knowledge, sight with ignorance). In the story's modern incarnation, *Chinatown*, Jake Gittes's failure to understand the full nature of the corruption he faces leads to the death of the woman he was trying to save—and she is shot through the eye.

- In *Richard II*, when the ineffectual king is deposed by his rivals at the play's end, he at last wakes up to his own role in his fate, and faces death with courage and dignity.

- In George Orwell's *1984*, Winston Smith tries to resist the overwhelming power of Big Brother, only to be arrested, secluded, tortured, and terrorized until his personality is destroyed. He emerges from his ordeal transformed into exactly what he previously despised, a man who loves Big Brother, exemplifying the power of totalitarian states to crush not just individuals but the very notion of the self.

- In Ang Lee's *Lust, Caution*, Chia Chi is a female drama student during the Japanese occupation in World War II. Enlisted by the Chinese resistance, she is recruited into a plot to assassinate the collaborator Mr. Yee, chief of the secret police in Shanghai for the puppet government, and is assigned the task of seducing him. The scheme drags on for years due to Yee's extremely cautious nature, and Chia Chi, obliged to convincingly feign sexual attraction to him, finds herself developing a bond of sympathy and affection. Finally, just before her compatriots are about to spring their trap and murder Yee, Chia Chi warns him, foiling the assassination, thus condemning all the members of her cell, including herself, to death.

In all of these stories we feel the underlying warning that we at best imperfectly know ourselves, and the cost of that ignorance can be shattering, even fatal.

Sometimes the protagonist gains his self-revelation in time to renounce the ambition he's finally fulfilled (or is about to fulfill), as in the film noir classic *Force of Evil* or the more recent *Rain Man*, *The Limey*, and *Changing Lanes*.

A great deal of fiction plows this same ground, with the cautionary theme "Be careful what you wish for": B. Traven's *The Treasure of the Sierra Madre*, Jim Harrison's *A Good Day to Die*, Andre Dubus's "Killings" (made into the film *In the Bedroom*), Richard Price's *Samaritan*, Robert Stone's *Dog Soldiers*. Here again, as with *Up in the Air*, the form is that of pursuing a desire, but the theme is to reveal the folly, error, or corruption inherent in the wanting.

Sometimes the revelation results from the protagonist being forced by circumstances to forsake his original desire for another. In *The Godfather*, Michael Corleone assures his fiancée Kay that he is different than his family. But then one brutal killing after another forces his hand. He forsakes forever his outsider status and embraces with singular ruthlessness the devotion to blood loyalty that in the end defines him. He has at last discovered who he truly is—his father's heir. The Godfather.

Comedy frequently employs this form of story question as well, but here the consequences are not so dire. Again, the hero pursues some farcical or misbegotten want, only to fail miserably, or to find that his Grail was something less than he'd bargained for. The comic hero is almost always hoping to prove there is more to him than meets the eye, and he suffers for his vanity. But once the mask of grandiosity is given up, he's usually saved by love, family, community, or the eternal consolations of merriment. The message: Joy, despite our inherent foolishness, remains possible if we are suitably humble.

What Do I Have to Change About Myself to Get What I Want?

Think of this sort of story as lying somewhere on the continuum between the previous two. It's also a relatively recent arrival in the annals of storytelling, at least in its present form.

In *Precious: Based on the Novel "Push" by Sapphire*, Claireece "Precious" Jones is an obese, illiterate African American sixteen-year-old who discovers she's pregnant. She has already given birth to another child, whom Precious has derisively nicknamed Mongo, as in Mongoloid, i.e., he has Down syndrome. A grandmother raises Mongo, while Precious's mother claims the boy is hers so she can receive welfare checks for the child's support. To call Precious's life loveless is beyond understatement; her mother is a harpy of disdain and abuse.

Precious's school principal, sensing the girl is at risk, refers her to an alternative school. Precious's mother resists this fiercely, fearing the scrutiny that such a change would incur, possibly jeopardizing the welfare stipend she receives. But the transfer goes forward, and Precious meets with a teacher, Ms. Rain, and shortly after that a social worker, Mrs. Weiss, who combine to provide a crucial caring presence in Precious's life. For the first time, she admits that Mongo is hers. Not just that—the child was delivered by Precious herself on her kitchen floor, and the man who got her pregnant was her father.

Mrs. Weiss and Ms. Rain redouble their commitment to help her, and Precious responds with increasing skills and growing self-esteem. She resolves to keep the child she is carrying, to reclaim Mongo from her grandmother, and to see that both receive the education she was denied until recently.

After she delivers her second child, she returns home with it, but her mother throws the infant down violently and hurls a glass at Precious, saying the girl's ruined everything by confessing who Mongo's real mother is—the welfare money's been cut off.

Precious flees with her newborn, breaks into the alternative school, and waits there until her teacher and the principal arrive. They find a halfway house where Precious and her child, whom she names Abdul, can live. Then Precious learns that her father has died of AIDS, and that he infected her when he raped her. Terrified, hopeless, she confronts Ms. Rain and Mrs. Weiss, saying love has never done anything but beat her down. They respond that she is loved by them, and her children love her. There is real love in her life if she'll embrace it.

But hoping to recover the welfare money she's lost, Precious's mother seeks reunification of the family. Confronted by Mrs. Weiss with the history of abuse, the mother admits she turned a blind eye to the years of molestation and rape because she feared Precious's father would leave if she made him stop. She brings in Mongo and begs for them all to be a family again, but Precious refuses. She intends to continue to improve herself and her circumstances, finish high school, go to college. Knowing the welfare office can help find her work, she plans to care for her two children and wants nothing to do with her mother. She leaves, carrying young Abdul, and walking with Mongo's hand in hers.

As with Jamal in *Slumdog Millionaire*, Precious pursues a cherished desire, but it's not entirely clear to her at first what that desire is. Her abusive life has numbed her to it. And like Ryan in *Up in the Air*, she faces a change-or-die moment, but it's not at the story's end; it's when she accepts the presence of genuine affection and concern in her life. Precious finally has a dream: to have a real home, where she can love and be loved. But she can't fulfill that dream unless she herself changes by admitting she is capable and worthy of love.

This type of story has its roots in tales of conversion by eminent saints, and it became more distinct in style with the novels of personal redemption of the early eighteenth century, a form epitomized by Daniel Defoe's *Moll Flanders*. These were followed by romances and novels of self-improvement during the late eighteenth and early nineteenth centuries.

The advent of psychoanalysis gave this sort of story a shot in the arm, providing a whole new language and methodology for plumbing the aspects of the personality that limit our capabilities and inhibit intimacy. Characters were not paralyzed by fate as in Greek tragedy; insight pointed a way out.

A great many modern love stories have this same basic form, due to the fact that what's keeping the couple apart is some sort of fear of intimacy or other psychological or emotional limitation on the part of one person or the other.

The coming-of-age story or bildungsroman can also conform to this story type. In the film *An Education* (screenplay by Nick Hornby), seventeen-year-old Jenny Mellor attends a private girls' school and is focused on getting into Oxford, circumstances that oblige tireless study and strap her middle-class parents. Along comes David, a globe-trotting sophisticate nearly twice her age who shows her a lifestyle she's only dreamed of. She begins to see the life she previously planned—that of an educated woman in early 1960s England—as hopelessly, even bitterly constrained. She accepts David's call to adventure, even as she realizes that his means to wealth are less than legitimate. But the real epiphany comes when she learns David is married and has a family, living only blocks from her home. Shamed into self-awareness, Jenny is obliged to go back to the teachers she has denigrated as futureless spinsters and try to recoup what she can of her previous dream of attending Oxford.

The fact that a character undergoes a fundamental transformation does not necessarily mean it conforms to this basic story type, however. In *Michael Clayton*, the protagonist undergoes a profound change, forsaking his role as "bagman" and "janitor" and salvaging his integrity. But the change comes late in the story, just before the climax. The effect is one of self-definition, with Michael finally making a statement about his true nature. The fact the story's fundamental concern is identity should hardly come as a surprise, given the number of times in the course of the story other characters make statements such as: *Who is this guy? . . . If you're not the enemy, then who are you? . . . You've got everybody fooled but yourself—you know who you are.* The film's ending credit sequence, which serves as a kind of denouement, in which Michael disobeys his brother's instruction to stay close and instead gets into a cab and asks for "fifty dollars' worth," suggests that his change, though profound, is still being processed. He's dealing with the repercussions, which will now define his life. And, of course, the film's title is the protagonist's name.

The distinctions I'm making may suggest solid categories into which every conceivable tale can be neatly, uniquely, and conclusively placed. If only. Reality is messy, stories wander the landscape, and artists are magpies—they use anything they find interesting for their purposes.

There are conceivably stories that conform to none of the three modes of narrative I'm outlining here. And often a slight shift in perspective can make a story of one type seem more indicative of another. It's therefore better to think of the three templates I'm proposing as *emphases*, with stories conforming more or less to one or the other based on the particular purpose you have in mind. The possibility of a mixed marriage is not just possible but likely.

For example, any all-consuming battle will in some sense define who we are. But are you trying to show how we can overcome even seemingly insurmountable obstacles to achieve victory? Or do you hope to reveal how we need to develop insight into our intrinsic fallibility, for only then can we correct the flaws of character that impede our defeating the invaders? Or do you intend to portray instead an existential reckoning, in which we discover the painful truth about ourselves just as we face our decisive showdown? This choice of theme will point you toward a certain protagonist question, and thus a certain way of structuring your story, and framing the primary conflict from within or without.

As you write and rewrite your story, take a moment to reflect on which thematic question you wish to pose. Each one suggests a different moral perspective, resolves with a different reflection on who we are as human beings, and consequently obliges a different structure.

Exercises

1. Take the same three examples you selected for exercise 1 in the preceding chapter: Does the protagonist in each story exhibit growth or does he exhibit transformation? How can you tell? Does he exert greater will, suffer a life-changing insight, or both?

2. Ask the same question of the protagonist in a novel, story, or script you're working on.

3. For each of the examples used in exercise 1, what is the question for each protagonist? If there's a moment of transformative insight, where is it located relative to the climax? What dramatic effect does this create at the story's end? Has the character had time to use the insight to his own advantage and change his behavior? Or is the insight the climactic event of the story?

4. Ask these same questions for the protagonist you used in your response to exercise 2. How profoundly would the story change, and in what specific way, if you were to pose the protagonist question differently?

Chapter Nineteen
Ciphers, Stiffs, and Sleepwalkers: Protagonist Problems

<hr/>

If you catch them in an unguarded moment, many writers will confess that villains and secondary characters are much easier to write than protagonists. And one sees the problem in not a few books, some of them famous. Why are so many heroes—from Gulliver to Candide to Oliver Twist to Jonathan Harker—the blandest character in the book?

More often than not, as I noted in chapter 17, a lackluster protagonist normally results from the writer's failure to properly understand the stakes—what the character wants, why, and what he's willing to risk to get it. It can also result from a poor formulation of the premise or weak identification of the question at the root of the story. But there are several other reasons the protagonist might not engage the reader or audience as much as she should, and we'll cover some of them now.

When the Protagonist's Struggle
Is Fundamentally Internal

In stories centered on the protagonist's battle to overcome guilt, cowardice, mistaken ideals, addiction, or even madness, there may not be an opponent per se. And this normally results in a premise and a counterpremise that both center on the actions of the same character—the protagonist.

There may (and should) be a revenant, or more than one—a character type I defined in chapter 7 and which I'll address further in chapter 21 in our discussion of secondary characters. The revenant helps or forces the protagonist to confront and resolve his inner conflicts. But the role of opponent is embodied in the protagonist himself.

To dramatize the conflict it's useful to see that a choice lies at the heart of the character's problem. By anchoring each option of the choice in something concrete—optimally, another character or a goal—you give the protagonist the opportunity to play out his conflict in scenes.

Returning once more to *Midnight Cowboy*: What Joe Buck wants is intimacy, but his history of abandonment and betrayal have created a profound mistrust of others. And so he has assumed the role of the hustler to protect himself from the pain he associates with desire and closeness. The premise of the story is: *Only by opening himself to the pain of loss can Joe obtain the love he so deeply wants.* The counterpremise could be worded as *Only by using people as he's been used can Joe protect himself from further humiliation and heartbreak.* Joe doesn't have an opponent embodying that counterpremise. He's his own adversary, at war with himself.

Joe's dilemma can be seen as *a choice*: to open himself to pain or not. And each option of that choice is embodied in a character: If Joe chooses to remain closed to pain and hold on to his hustler mask, he can spend his life with women such as the well-to-do Shirley, who would pay him for sex and even enjoy his company, but never be a true companion; or he can open himself to pain and loss and care for his dying friend, Rizzo.

The genius of *Midnight Cowboy* resides in the unsentimental staging of Joe's dilemma. One could easily see him choosing the path suggested by Shirley: She's bright, witty, attractive, well-off financially. She exhibits a genuine and nonjudgmental if businesslike concern for Joe. In contrast, Rizzo is a gutter rat, physically repulsive—something particularly repellent to Joe, who fashions himself a lady-killer—as well as crippled, penniless, dishonest, and ill-tempered. He carps at Joe for being stupid and fantasizes about pimping him once they reach Miami. Why does Joe hesitate for even a second? Because when he was in need, Rizzo took him in. And through the privations they've shared, they've forged both a grudging respect and an abiding fondness. Joe cannot abandon Rizzo, especially given how sick he is. But the price is high, much higher than many might be willing to pay, which is what makes Joe such a compelling hero.

A great many love stories have a similar setup, being premised on the protagonist's inability to break through some inhibition and open his heart. Again the protagonist's situation lacks an opponent, and can be reduced to a question: Will he find a way to put aside his fear of betrayal, rejection, humiliation, abandonment or not? Stage the conflict through characters—the problematic and terror-inducing loved one versus any number of others who provide solace, pleasure, companionship, but not the deep connection the protagonist craves—and fears.

Recovery narratives observe a similar logic. In tales of this type, from 1945's *Lost Weekend* (alcoholism) to 2011's *Shame* (sex addiction), the protagonist and opponent are sadly one and the same. The stories succeed best when the battle for sobriety is embodied in characters who reflect the protagonist's various options and offer opportunities for him to act them out: punitive guilt, reckless excess, sentimental self-pity, angry denial, manipulative bargaining, responsible insight, and so on.

Caution: Whenever staging internal battles between health and pathology, rigging the game so that the best choice is obvious only guarantees moralizing banality. Absent a tangible, detailed grasp of what in the character's past explains why she clings to her defenses against rejection and shame, or why he helplessly succumbs to obsessive pleasure—even to the point of letting the abyss not just sing to him, but swallow him whole—such tales routinely become the stuff of waiting-room pamphlets.

Dramatizing the battle with madness obliges the same concerns. One of the greatest examples of how to do this well is Ingmar Bergman's *Through a Glass Darkly*. Karin battles latent schizophrenia, and the various forces working on her from the outside are embodied in her father, her brother, and her husband, but none is a stick figure representing judgmental scorn, solicitous concern, envious resentment, and the like. Each character is fully realized and unique, and their interactions play out in accordance with their singular personalities, not some psychological pantomime.

The common element in all the foregoing examples is the lack of a character serving as opponent. The problem this creates normally involves trying to avoid long passages of meandering rumination, and an inability to stage the conflict in a compelling way. The solution lies in formulating the protagonist's conflict as a question, and staging the drama through characters who represent in varying degrees one answer to the question or another.

When the Protagonist Doesn't Know or Is Confused by What She Wants, or Is Afraid to Want It

A great many protagonists begin their stories being unclear, confused, or fearful of what they want, something addressed in some depth in chapter 5. The problem is solved in much the same way as when the conflict is internal: Anchor the character's various wants, both true and mistaken, in something concrete, preferably a character.

In particular, give the protagonist a misbegotten objective, something she *thinks* she wants, either because she's fooling herself, is in denial, or is otherwise resistant to accepting the real object of desire. Then have her repeated failures to achieve real happiness clue her in bit by bit to her error. Don't select the misbegotten object of desire arbitrarily. It must reflect the thing the protagonist has clung to rather than face the truth. As such, it reveals as much about him as what he ultimately realizes he's truly wanted all along.

Precious Jones is numb to her desire for love. Instead she tries as best she can to placate her shrewish mother.

The futility of that becomes increasingly apparent as Precious interacts with people who truly have her best interests at heart.

When the Protagonist Faces a Problem, an Enigma, or a Disaster Instead of an Opponent

A middle-aged schoolteacher in a small southern town is trapped in a loveless, sexless existence, caring for her clueless, acidly sweet, impossible-to-please mother. (*Rachel, Rachel*, screenplay by Stewart Stern, based on the novel by Margaret Laurence.)

A young man wakes up one morning and finds himself transformed into a cockroach. (*The Metamorphosis*, by Franz Kafka.)

A father and son must navigate a postapocalyptic landscape in an attempt to find some kind of refuge. (*The Road*, by Cormac McCarthy.)

Each of these stories presents the protagonist not with an overwhelming opponent but with an intractable situation or problem. As always, the protagonist's desired way of life provides his ultimate goal, but there isn't another character standing in his path. Instead the question goes deeper, addressing whether that way of life is even possible. The problem the protagonist faces often goes to the heart of who he is, addressing what it means for him to live his life—even what it means to be human.

It's one of the oldest story forms in existence, and examples range from *The Odyssey* and *Jude the Obscure* to *The Time Machine*, *Heart of Darkness*, *Bel Canto*, and *Bringing Out the Dead*, to name a scant few.

The problem is not just difficult but seemingly

unsolvable—so unsolvable it's easy for the writer to get stuck, spinning wheels in the sand of speculation. Or else the hero gets lost in the situational specifics of this particular emergency, that particular encounter, losing track of the larger thematic issues that make the story something more than just "one damn thing after another."

The solution lies again in seeing the question at the heart of the protagonist's dilemma: Can I reclaim my own life before my mother dies? Will my family still love and help me despite my being an insect? Will my son and I still be recognizably human if we manage to survive? Once the question is identified, anchor the real answer and various false ones in different goals, situations, or characters, and force the protagonist to confront one alternative or another at every step of the action.

Such stories often give rise to *situational opponents*, who stand in the way of the protagonist in this or that section of the story. But the overarching problem is far greater than any of these minor skirmishes, and remains the underlying issue, like a thorn in the heart, until the very end.

Rachel Cameron is the aging sister left behind to look after her difficult mother. She remarks to her best friend, "I'm in the exact middle of my life," by which she means from this point forward her days will consist of one long slide into death. Her struggles to find love—from her mother, from her friend (a closeted lesbian who confesses a secret crush), from the holy rollers at the friend's church service, and most poignantly from a childhood neighbor, Nick Kazlik, who comes back to town for a few weeks that summer—are all desperate attempts to make that long slide mean something.

In *The Metamorphosis*, Gregor Samsa faces a series of harrowing situations, all premised on the question *How do I reconcile my strange condition with my life among other people?* And though in any given scene, one or another character may stand in the way or actively oppose Gregor's goal or want, it's his condition that frames his essential conflict, which is metaphorically that of man: our freedom and the alienation it causes on the one hand, our need for society and the self-camouflage it obliges on the other. Only death can resolve that tension.

In Cormac McCarthy's *The Road*, the father grapples with how to retain human decency in the midst of a living nightmare. It's that moral question and not just the brutalized landscape or the scarred people who inhabit it that defines the conflict. Even if the cannibals, looters, and brigands vanished, the father would still have to wrestle with his moral qualms, for it is the devastation that has undone the others, and might still undo him.

A more commercial variation on the same dramatic setup is the British film *28 Days Later*. Inadvertent release of a deadly virus from an animal research lab raided by well-intentioned fools has decimated London, producing rage-intoxicated cannibals who ravage the landscape. But the underlying moral question—What value is survival if I become unrecognizable to myself?—necessitates more than a mano a mano bloodbath between the Survivors and the Infected (though there's plenty of that). The key dramatic turn is when the protagonist Survivors, Jim, Selena, and Hannah, reach a British military garrison near Manchester broadcasting that they possess "the answer to infection," only to discover that the soldiers' solution to the plague is to wait for the Infected to die of starvation, then repopulate the island through forced intercourse with Hannah and Selena, who are now reduced to slaves. The individual adversaries change even as the fundamental moral problem remains the same.

To keep the situational emergencies from creating dramatic chaos, or the thematic dilemma from dragging things to a ruminative halt, it's sometimes wise to give the protagonist one clear-cut outer goal to strive for—to reach the ocean in *The Road*, for example. This keeps the action from seeming merely episodic, while at the same time allowing you to frame the action so the overall moral theme echoes that strategic goal. The survival of each minor section, by pushing the protagonist closer to or further from his outer ambition, partially answers the overarching question *How did what I needed to do to withstand that crisis reinforce or undermine the life I hope to live?*

When the Interconnection Between Outer Goal and Inner Need Is Insufficiently Realized

As noted in the last section, it's necessary to maintain a link between the protagonist's outer goal and his inner need, to the extent that they're not identical. Failure to do this normally represents an incomplete grasp of the stakes.

Whatever the hero is trying to achieve in the outer world—rescue the hostage, marry the soul mate, survive the cataclysm, escape prison, return home—the goal and the effort to achieve it speak to some inner need that the character often does not even recognize until the events within the story expose it. The outer goal represents the specific way of life the protagonist hopes to defend. The inner need represents the reason that way of life is so meaningful to him. This relationship is the machine that creates the protagonist's growth or transformation.

In the film *The Secret in Their Eyes*, Benjamin Esposito returns to the attorney general's office in Buenos Aires where he once worked as an investigator to show his former boss, Irene Menéndez Hastings, the novel he's written about a murder case they worked on many years before. The case was unsatisfactorily resolved—just like the romance between Benjamin and Irene. Benjamin, from a lower social class, believed himself unworthy of Irene, and was blind to her interest in him. Irene reads his novel and makes the obvious point: It lacks an ending. The comment is almost a dare, and works on both levels, that of the murder and the romance. Benjamin's quest to discover what actually happened so he can finish his book also serves his need to see if there remains any chance with Irene. The three story lines—how the investigation and romance proceeded in the past, how Benjamin tries to wrap up loose ends in the present, and how he hopes to see if he still has a chance with Irene—all reinforce and reflect on one another.

Joe Connelly's *Bringing Out the Dead* would be a manic litany of well-crafted, expertly detailed, beautifully written emergency calls—in other words, a reasonably good book—without the crisis eating away at the protagonist's soul, which turns it into a great one. Each call echoes Frank's aching need to forgive himself for the one patient he couldn't save, a girl named Rose, who literally haunts him, visiting him when he's alone, appearing in the corner of his eye as he makes one mad dash to the rescue after another. The climax resolves both his obsessive need to be the hero and his guilt, as he finally codes a patient and lets him die, accepting both his fallibility and the inevitability of death, and at last making peace with Rose.

There are some writers, such as Lee Child, who arch an eyebrow at the "bullet in the heart" hero, one whose deep-seated psychological wound moves him to act. Lee considers the setup contrived, fabricated by writers overly obsessed with meaning. Whether the protagonist is a sniper, a lawyer, or a nurse, more times than not his motivation to achieve any particular end reduces to the simple fact that it's his job. To the extent there's an inner need, it's the professional's desire to do the thing well.

There are indeed times when a writer creates an inner need so hackneyed it actually undermines the story. Then again, as in the two examples I cited here, the difference between an acceptable story and an unforgettable one often depends on the writer's ability to see the thematic interconnections between the protagonist's outer and inner journeys, and to weave them together seamlessly.

When the Protagonist Is Conceived as a Vessel of Virtue (or the Myth of the Likable Hero)

The legacy of the New Testament Jesus has not been sanguine for drama. Though he is considered by many, like Buddha, the consummate hero, his divine serenity creates an impression not of stoic strength but supernatural calm—worse, sanctimonious indifference—even as he's enduring the terrible cruelties of his passion and death. He comes most alive in moments of uncustomary weakness: when his temper flares at the money-changers; when he suffers doubt in the Garden of Gethsemane; when he utters the cry of dereliction from the cross: *Lord, Lord, Why hast thou forsaken me?*

In contrast, the stubborn, cowardly, hot-tempered, doubt-afflicted Peter—who denies even knowing Jesus only hours after cutting off a man's ear to protect him—comes across as vividly solid. At the risk of blasphemy, I'll admit that for my money, Peter is the most interesting character in the Gospels. Not even Mary Magdalene can compete.

Unfortunately, it was the serene savior who became reincarnated in chivalric heroes such as Galahad. Noble, brave, pure of heart—not even his exploits can spare him a cipher's existence. Strip him of his horse and sword and you get Everyman, the nameless nobody who sleepwalked through the medieval period's morality plays. Not surprisingly, audiences responded with far more enthusiasm to the Vices that afflicted him.

The legacy of the Everyman survives in characters such as Candide, Justine, Gulliver, and Dickensian heroes such as Pip, Oliver Twist, and David Copperfield, who invariably pale beside the scurrilous, earthy, villainous scene-stealers around them, plodding through the story aglow with virtue like a night-light—and generating just as little heat. Meanwhile the secondary characters and antagonists around them act foolishly, aggressively, wickedly—that is, interestingly. This is particularly the case when the opponent drives the action, creating the circumstances compelling the protagonist to (merely) react.

As mentioned earlier, part of the problem in such cases is that the protagonist's wants are insufficiently realized;

THE ART OF CHARACTER

the character resembles a pawn being nudged across the chessboard on its way to being queened.

And if the protagonist is forced over and over into a reactive posture because the opponent is the one taking the initiative, you've misconceived the conflict. Deprive the protagonist the right not just to defend herself but to attack, and all you have is a noble victim, perhaps the most uninteresting character known to man.*

But it's not just the protagonist's wants that so often remain vague. Where are the *contradictions* that would conjure depth and complexity? Specifically, where are the less-than-stellar characteristics—the venality, the cynicism, the impatience, the lust—that we all share, but for some unfounded reason feel are inappropriate in our heroes?

One of the emotions writers seem particularly loath to grant their protagonists is hatred—not for a character who rightly deserves it, or more generally for evil or injustice or the harsh treatment of puppies, but simply for another character who drives the protagonist up the wall. The irrationality of contempt, embodied in the person who through some black magic knows just how to push your buttons, provides one of the more unsettling mysteries of existence. Such people often reflect back to us aspects of ourselves we'd just as soon not admit. Unless you're a bodhisattva, there is someone somewhere who just bugs you to death, to the point you fantasize about ripping him a new one, as they

---

* See chapter 5, page 58, for the earlier discussion of *Little Bird of Heaven* by Joyce Carol Oates. The protagonist, Zoe Kruller, faces a situation to bemoan but no objective to pursue; a potentially compelling drama gets reduced to a 400-page lament.

quaintly say—insulting him, mocking him, torturing him. It's not flattering to recognize this in oneself. And yet what could be more human?

Absent the grim, bitchy, perverse sides of their natures, characters can't help but ring false—or fall flat. Blanche DuBois, one of the greatest protagonists in American drama, is petty, dishonest, and manipulative, which is what makes her relentless ferocity so compelling. Yossarian in *Catch-22* exhibits none of the physical courage and valor we associate with the warrior in the Galahad tradition, but he's grimly dogged in his desire to survive his combat missions: "He had decided to live forever or die in the attempt." Clarice Starling in *The Silence of the Lambs* embodies law-enforcement rectitude and small-town good manners, but Hannibal Lecter sniffs out her cunning ambition.

The inclination to confine protagonists in a prison of virtue typically traces back to the often-heard demand that they be likable. It's true that in a novel or film you're asking the reader or audience to spend a great deal of time with a character, and no one wants to spend hours with an annoying, wheedling, sniveling piss pot. But neither do they want to waste an afternoon with a Boy Scout's shadow.

It's far more important that we empathize with a character than like her—which is just as true of villains as heroes. And empathy is created by a well-drawn character taking on a convincing dramatic problem, in which compelling wants are at stake in the face of potentially overwhelming opposition. We feel for such a character, even if she's imperfect, for we all understand that necessity compels us to act as we must, not as we should.

In fact, a great many stories are premised on the protagonist's painful discovery of his blindness to the suffering, injustice, or hypocrisy he's been party to through unconscious, reflexive, or reckless acts. It's precisely through acting in conflict with her ideals that she creates the moral revelation at the heart of the story. She finds out firsthand the values she can't live without, because she has tried to live outside of them and created nothing but failure, disaster, and pain.

Taking three examples we discussed in the previous chapter:

- In *Casablanca*, Rick Blaine takes the letters of transit from Ugarte, then stands by idly as the police kill him; he cruelly insults Ilsa and insinuates she'll betray her husband, Victor Laszlo; he rejects Laszlo's request to buy the letters of transit and tells him to ask Ilsa why, hoping to undermine or destroy the bond between them.

- In *Chinatown*, Jake Gittes betrays his own savvy self-image by getting duped by a conspicuously fake Evelyn Mulwray; to find out who set him up, Jake employs all the ethically dubious tricks of his trade—lying to the police, trespassing, destruction of public property (the County Recorder plat books)—and even resorts to violence against a helpless woman, the real Evelyn Mulwray.

- In *Michael Clayton*, the hero's entire career is premised on letting the guilty off the hook; but he also engages a Mob-connected loan shark for financing on a restaurant; he short-shrifts his son who clearly wants to engage with him; he betrays his troubled friend, preferring to believe his rants are entirely due to his bipolar disorder instead of being rooted at least partially in the truth; he violates a crime scene; he accepts a check for $80,000 in exchange for his silence, sealing his culpability, then returns to gambling like the addict he is.

Each of these litanies of bad acts leads to a crisis that forces the protagonist to look at himself, his actions, and his life in a more objective way. It's precisely this all-too-human willingness to act immorally in the service of what the character tells himself are justifiable ends that creates the complexity that will help you steer clear of sermonizing. It also once again reveals the *contradiction* between the virtues we tell ourselves we live by and those we actually act upon. Most important, by prompting failure, it creates the squeeze that forces the character to look at his behavior honestly.

If you remain concerned that the less right-minded traits you've given your protagonist jeopardize the ability of the reader or audience to feel empathy for her, consider using insight, regret, or humor as counterpoint. We are often willing to forgive a great deal when we can sense that the character possesses a capacity for reflection and even doubt. Why? They suggest *vulnerability*. And a bracing or earthy wit has rescued many a dubious character from scorn. Humor suggests again a certain self-awareness, but also an appreciation and even enjoyment of life despite its less pleasant episodes. Tony Soprano's ability to fascinate audiences despite being a sociopath largely resulted from his lusty appetites and his sneaky wit.

And even as potentially repulsive a character as Humbert Humbert, the pedophile protagonist of Nabokov's *Lolita*, gains our sympathy through a simple device—the withholding of the gratification of his want. It's also why we find Yossarian's seeming lack of patriotism or even cowardice acceptable—his aching desire to be relieved from duty is consistently denied. We readily sympathize with the frustration of a desperate want. Keep this trick near at hand—it not only can help you render compellingly a less-than-lovable character, it can add concern and drama for one who's already nicked our hearts.

When the Protagonist Is a Thinly Veiled Stand-in for the Author

Once again, problems arise here more through execution than conception. Every writer to some extent uses herself or her life as inspiration if not material. No one personifies this inclination more perfectly than Franz Kafka, though he vehemently denied any autobiographical intent or inspiration in his work. But not everyone is capable of such exacting, pitiless objectification. And without that emotional distance, you risk unconsciously sparing the character the pain and scrutiny that will make her compelling.

It is perhaps an unfortunate truth that we are far more likely to torment our creations than ourselves, and sparing a character the full impact of the conflict the story requires is a recipe for lukewarm or even insipid drama.

We also seldom have the same kinds of blind spots for a character's behavior as we do for our own. The tendency is to let ourselves off the hook, and if extended to the protagonist, this can all too often lead to a certain blandness.

If you're truly capable of being not just fair but pitiless with yourself, by all means have at it. If not, do everyone a favor and pick on someone else.

Choosing the Wrong Character as the Protagonist

As mentioned in chapter 17, in choosing what character should serve as protagonist, remember that the reader's or audience's empathy naturally gravitates toward the character with the most at stake, especially if what that character has to lose is something we all can understand.

In the film *Blade Runner*, the protagonist, Rick Deckard (Harrison Ford), is a former "blade runner," a police officer tasked with "retiring" (murdering) replicants—organically engineered robots who are virtually indistinguishable from humans. They are banned on Earth, but four of them, led by the charismatic Roy (Rutger Hauer), have returned, seeking to extend their life spans. Deckard is coerced out of retirement to track down the renegades and kill them.

Several narrative choices conspire to turn the audience's empathy away from Deckard and toward Roy. First, Deckard's task is to kill, and he has to be threatened into accepting it. His reluctance is palpable and never really vanishes, making his actions seem more mercenary than just. In contrast, Roy wants to live—something even nonreplicants can identify with—and though he admits to doing "terrible

268) THE ART OF CHARACTER

things," some of which we witness, he expresses convincing regret. He is after all a manufactured creature, his impulses have been created by someone else, and he feels a certain sorrowful puzzlement at the pain he has caused. This again renders him eminently "human." Despite the fact that so much of the film is visually arresting and conceptually intriguing, the drama is inherently ambivalent, dividing our sympathies and rendering the conclusion puzzlingly ironic, not as though by design, but as though the creative team behind the script wasn't entirely sure how else to wrap things up.

Multiple Protagonists

A similar division of sympathy and blurring of focus can occur in stories with intersecting or parallel story lines, each with its own protagonist, or point-of-view character. In inexperienced hands, this is often the result of not understanding where the moral and dramatic focus of the story should be, or being devoted to scenes that seemingly exclude one main character or another. The latter problem can usually be solved by creatively reimagining who needs to be in the scene and why. The former problem is more serious.

The dramatic and emotional impact the audience wants to feel in the story's climax results from empathic identification with the main character in it. Ask the reader or audience to divide their sympathies during that climactic scene, or leave out a character with a key stake in what happens, and the result can't help but leave the audience wanting.

As a result, when there are multiple main characters, most writers will choose one to be the standard-bearer for

the main dramatic action, effectively serving as protagonist. The other characters will be secondary, even if only
slightly so.

An example is *Dog Soldiers* by Robert Stone. Even
though the dramatic action—the horribly misconceived
plan to bring a shipment of heroin from Vietnam into the
United States—is launched by John Converse, deemed
"the world's most frightened man" by one of the other
characters, he ultimately delivers the package to the far
more competent Ray Hicks, who is supposed to deliver the
heroin to Converse's wife, Marge, in Berkeley. Although
Converse, Marge, and Hicks all receive significant narrative focus, the main action is driven by Hicks and is seen
through his eyes, and his death provides the climactic action of the story, with Converse and Marge providing a
sort of coda in the denouement.

An alternative approach is to have parallel stories that
have their own arcs and conclude independently, such as in
Quentin Tarantino's *Pulp Fiction*. To provide the climactic
sense of conclusion to the film as a whole that the audience
expects, the final sequence includes the character of Jules
Winnfield (Samuel L. Jackson), who with his butchered
biblical quotations and tortured reflections has served as a
kind of conscience for the film, even though he has only
appeared up until the end in his own subplot. The coming
together of his story line with another that initiated the
film as a whole provides the gratifying sense of dramatic
finality we want (even if we're too hip to admit it).

When the Narrator and Protagonist Differ, but Both Are Characters in the Story

Although we'll have more to say on this subject in the chapter on point of view, here we want to simply address the potential problem, again, of divided focus.

In chapter 5, while discussing characters who can't own up to their real wants, it was suggested that such characters be given an obsession or mania to serve as the outer drive as they secretly or unconsciously pursue their hidden or unconscious desires.

Examples of such characters are Captain Ahab and Jay Gatsby—and both *Moby-Dick* and *The Great Gatsby* are narrated by characters other than the protagonists. Given the obsessive and essentially self-deceived natures of Ahab and Gatsby, having them narrate their own tales would result in a markedly skewed point of view—above and beyond the minor problematic detail that both characters die. But since both narrators also participate in the action of the stories, there is a potential for the reader to invest in the moral and dramatic roles they play.

The problem in each case is solved by restricting the dramatic role of the narrator largely to one of observer, a role underscored by the relative outsider status of both Ishmael and Nick Carraway. Ishmael is named for the son of Abraham sent away upon the birth of Isaac and obliged to wander in the desert with his mother, Hagar—an archetypal outlander. And he's a relative newcomer to the *Pequod*'s crew, which motivates the curiosity and attention to detail he demonstrates in his account of events aboard the ship. Nick Carraway is a midwesterner who looks upon the events at Gatsby's mansion with the staid circumspection of his breed. Thus the capacity for scene-stealing by either narrator is limited. Next to the larger-than-life protagonists whose stories they tell, they're conspicuously minor players.

Exercises

1. Return to the three protagonists you selected in response to exercise 1 in chapter 17. What risks does the protagonist take to achieve her main objective? Does her behavior, motivation, or resolve change as the conflict intensifies? How?

2. In these same three examples, are any of the protagonists unaware, unclear, or frightened of their true desires at the outset of the story? When does their awareness crystallize? What action obliges that recognition? What is the dramatic effect of that insight?

3. Take an event from your own life and dramatize it, with the protagonist based on yourself. What personal flaws, shortcomings, or limitations do you find most difficult to portray? How does the story require them? (If the event you've chosen doesn't require depiction of a personal flaw or shortcoming, choose another.) Pay close attention to the feeling that arises as you discern the shortcomings in the character based on yourself: Are there any other characters you've created that have affected you in a similar way? Can you think of ways to improve their depiction now that you recognize their similarity to you?

272 } THE ART OF CHARACTER

4. Consider a story with multiple main characters or story lines. Is there a character who provides the principal focus to the story—i.e., who effectively serves as protagonist? How can you tell? What happens in the climax of the story? Who is present? Who is most profoundly affected? What happens to the other characters in the climax and the denouement?

5. Consider a story in which the narrator differs from the protagonist but also takes part in the action of the story. Does the focus of the story shift from narrator to protagonist at any time? Does this cause a division of sympathy, or a diffusion of dramatic effect? Why or why not?

Chapter Twenty
The Character of Conflict: The Opponent

> Let me but remark that the Evil One, with his
> single passion of satanic pride for the only
> motive, is yet, on a larger, modern view, allowed
> to be not quite so black as he used to be painted.
> With what greater latitude, then, should we
> appraise the exact shade of mere mortal man,
> with his many passions and his miserable
> ingenuity in error, always dazzled by the base
> glitter of mixed motives, everlastingly betrayed
> by a short-sighted wisdom.
>
> —Joseph Conrad, *Under Western Eyes*

Justifying the Opponent

The opponent is the character with the ultimate power to deny, destroy, take away, or claim for himself what the protagonist wants. The opponent's goal is equal and opposite to the protagonist's, and his motivation is embodied in the counterpremise.* Since the protagonist is measured by the conflict he overcomes, an ambivalent, facile, cartoonish, or otherwise unconvincing opponent can only diminish

---

* See chapter 17, "Meaning and Its Messenger: The Protagonist and the Premise."

THE ART OF CHARACTER

whatever success the hero achieves. The opponent forces the protagonist to rise above himself, to excavate from the depths of his will the fortitude he needs to not merely endure but also to prevail, or to stare into the dark mirror of his soul and suffer the transformative insight that will turn him toward decisive change.

Because human nature is what it is—we all too often assume that what we want is valid or at least understandable—and because the hero symbolically stands in for us, we tend to view the opponent in a negative light. But as I mentioned in chapter 17, the most compelling drama is always good versus good, so the more you cannot just defend and justify but embrace the opponent's point of view, the more compelling the drama will be. The stakes are automatically raised when we understand not just that one side of the conflict is condemned to lose, but that we are as morally and emotionally invested in that character as we are in her adversary.

There may never come a time when serial killers, Nazis, terrorists, child molesters, monsters from the muck, aliens from space, mad scientists, brutal fathers, shrewish mothers, selfish children, greedy landlords, godless savages, heartless dognappers, and all other embodiments of consummate evil will surrender the field and leave drama to the less conspicuously loathsome. As gratifying as it may be to hiss the villain's entrance, it makes little difference if you're snoring by the time the credits roll.

This doesn't mean avoiding stories where one side is clearly pursuing something you or your audience would most likely consider wrong—or even when both sides are morally compromised. But it does mean submerging your-self in the wrongdoer's world and finding the justification that permits him to see his actions as not merely advanta-geous, but morally just and logically correct.

Even war and crime stories, where it's often easiest to succumb to the good-versus-evil temptation, needn't be reduced to moralistic simplicities, and the best are not.

Arguably the greatest battle in all of literature doesn't pit Michael the Archangel against Lucifer, Saint George against the dragon, Beowulf against Grendel, Uncle Sam against Hitler, or concern any other contest where only a deviant would root for the wrong side. It's Achilles' combat with Hector outside the walls of Troy. Neither warrior elic-its our complete allegiance or enmity, though Hector prob-ably earns the sympathy nod. Both, however, inspire us with their courage and skill. And when Achilles slays Hector, then desecrates his body, tying it to his chariot and drag-ging it around the city's walls so all the Trojans can bear witness, he reminds us that the Greeks are not unqualified heroes. War honors not just valor but viciousness and hate.

Richard Price's *Clockers* has forever raised the bar for crime writers not just because of its realism, its pitch-perfect dialog, or the vividness of its details, but because its two adversaries, the drug dealer Strike Dunham and the detective Rocco Klein, are permitted equal moral footing. We fully inhabit both their worlds, and root for each of them, though in distinctly different ways.

Nurse Ratched in *One Flew Over the Cuckoo's Nest* doesn't pursue her quasi-fascistic obsession with order purely out of cussed meanness. She truly, deeply believes that absent order, the patients under her care will suffer; chaos can only exacerbate their symptoms. This puts her on a collision course with McMurphy, who equates sanity with self-expression, freedom: fun. He's also reckless and violent. In a clash of these two temperaments, only one can win.

And yet (I hear you cry), doesn't the audience deserve its catharsis? How can that come off if the climactic battle leaves us ambivalent, wondering if we didn't misplace our allegiance?

This misunderstands the moral significance of regret. There are a great many things we must do even if we'd prefer to have done otherwise. A protagonist who defeats an opponent for whom we do not lack sympathy merely reminds us that every battle involves another human being. It's not such a terrible truth to remember.

When the Opponent Is Genuinely Evil

There are of course situations when the opponent represents what can only be considered evil. Crime fiction in particular deals with greed, violence, corruption, the lust for unquestioned power, the indifference to misery, the seduction of cruelty. How can any of that be considered good? And there's not enough lipstick in the world, no matter how thickly slathered, that can tart up the pig of rape or genocide or lynching.

But the redneck lawmen and good old boys who terrorized southern blacks; the SS troops who rooted out Bolsheviks, gypsies, homosexuals, and Jews; even the skulking nobody who terrorizes women—they all have mothers, as the saying goes. They often can explain and justify what they do, even if it repulses you. They enjoy a warm bed and a hot meal; they can feel the spring air on their skin and smell the fresh-cut grass.

A police officer friend once confided that he never believed the criminals he arrested were that much different than him; the biggest difference was that he knew he had a future, and could imagine his life years in the distance, whereas most of the young men he put in jail looked at most only a couple of hours ahead. The most terrifying thing about evil is not that it's monstrous, but that it's so recognizably human.

Just as many beginning writers fail or refuse to see the darker, unflattering sides of the protagonist, rendering him superficially likable, so they also too often fail to show the redeeming aspects of their opponents, rendering them banally wicked.

The more you can understand how your opponent has come to justify the wrong he commits, why it is essential to his view of himself in the world, and why he chose this path instead of another one, the more convincing and dramatically effective he will be. Noah Cross in *Chinatown* represents the corruption inherent in unchecked power, but he certainly doesn't see it that way. He says it himself: He stands for the future. And the future ain't cheap.

Even if the opponent takes conspicuous pleasure in the suffering, betrayal, and even torture of others—like Richard of Gloucester in Shakespeare's *Richard III*—he may see this as the natural way of the world to which others, especially the weak and sentimental, are blind; he may consider his sadism, selfishness, and brute indifference the true mark of human nobility and enlightenment. (If so, he won't be the first.)

He may find the example of the rebel Lucifer far more compelling than that of the loyal archangel Michael—and we can all identify with standing up to an authority figure we consider unjust. He may have witnessed combat—or prison—and come to believe this experience was the true essence of life, and that anything else is just a socially acceptable form of gutlessness.

Or he may exhibit what the philosopher Simone Weil calls *affliction*. This goes beyond suffering, in that there is a social dimension to the torment, not just physical or psychological. Slavery is a form of affliction, as is rape, child abuse, torture; the victims have not just endured great and puzzling pain, they've been shamed or ostracized by it.

According to Weil, affliction plunges a soul into darkness where there is no one and nothing to love, not even oneself—especially not oneself. The person who's suffered affliction has retained at best half his soul. If, once plunged into this loveless darkness, the afflicted one gives up his belief that love will ever again be a possibility, the entire soul is lost. An example is Captain Ahab, who is based on the biblical character of Job—without the upbeat ending.

But there are smaller, all-too-human afflictions that nonetheless have deadly consequences. The character of Tristan Acevedo in Richard Price's *Lush Life* has been so brutalized by his drunk, mercurial father and the generalized humiliation of being poor that his sudden, seemingly unmotivated shooting of a defiant yuppie who refuses to hand over his wallet during a robbery seems more the result of punk stupidity and indifference than anything worthy of understanding, let alone respect. But as we see more and more of his daily life, we comprehend the dead end that his existence represents. This doesn't justify his act, but it does contextualize it. And that context provides the moral and social resonance when he is finally apprehended. Here, the hero (Detective Matty Clark) has not slain a dragon or overcome a monster; he has navigated the chaos of modern New York and found the sad, ironic, and tragic cause—the human cause—of a senseless act of deadly violence.

Given the number of excellent, relevant memoirs available, there really isn't much excuse for thinly characterized opponents. From *The Labyrinth: Memoirs of Hitler's Chief of Counterintelligence* by Walter Schellenberg to Jimmy Lerner's *You Got Nothing Coming: Notes from a Prison Fish* or *Eight Ball Chicks: A Year in the Violent World of Girl Gangs* by Gini Sikes, the sources are there.

But if both the protagonist and opponent are equally justifiable in their actions, don't they become too similar to be dramatically interesting? Without sharply drawn contrast, doesn't the conflict dissolve into one big grayish blur? Not if you remember that these two characters are equally, obsessively devoted to opposite ways of life. Flesh out their conflicting notions of what makes life worth living, populate that way of life with friends, family, subordinates, superiors, ask what defines home, where they go to get away—their distinctions will soon emerge.

In *Michael Clayton*, both adversaries are lawyers—a profession not known for high contrast. But one is male, one is female. One is intuitive and a gambler, the other is compulsively tidy, detail-oriented, a control freak. One dresses in black and white, the other in earth tones. One is comfortable in his skin, the other seems constantly to be walking on eggshells. The opponent needn't be shrill with villainy to stand apart from the hero.

Just as you should understand what or whom the protagonist hates, you should also determine what or whom your opponent loves. And making the love noble—his children, his family, his honor, his way of life—increases the weight of the character and makes him more compelling. As with the protagonist's hatred, the opponent's love creates both a contradiction and a vulnerability, something he has to defend. Once again, Noah Cross: He truly believes his daughter Evelyn is disturbed (though he accepts no blame for her being that way), and that she can only make an unfit mother. In the remaining time he has in this life, he wants to protect and share the only daughter he has left to him. This is not cynical doublespeak or transparent hypocrisy. It's conviction. That's what makes it haunting.

When the Opponent Is Offstage for Long Periods of Time—Clues and Underlings

In stories involving a mystery, where the protagonist must find out what has happened or who is responsible—find the killer, in the most prosaic example—the initial stages of the narrative may have only foreshadowing hints or clues. Though the opponent is ultimately revealed to be the source of the trouble—or the problem, the enigma— he's as yet unidentified. If he has made an appearance, his true involvement in events is as yet unknown.

A similar setup occurs in stories where the hero must

travel to a faraway place to perform some arduous task, normally in the lair of the mountain king or one of his fictional stand-ins. In such cases, the opponent is seen only through his effects or the barriers he's erected, and his resistance to the efforts of the protagonist is often performed at a distance, or conducted secondhand through underlings or proxies.

In mysteries, the opponent's presence is often inferred not through surrogates but through the nature of the clues: Is he brutish or surgical in his violence? Is the evidence simply the natural detritus of the crime or a well-crafted message? Was the weapon something readily at hand, a specialty item only an expert would use, or a curious rarity that only a unique mind would possess—or create? The clues, like clothing or class or education, reflect the opponent's character, and should be devised with equal care.

When staging such scenarios, remember you have a choice as to whether the subordinates or surrogates reinforce or contradict the opponent's character. A monster unleashing other monsters—or a Nazi dispatching a faceless troop of Wehrmacht infantrymen—seldom serves the interests of dramatic surprise. The shambling sluggard Mulvihill and the sadistic dandy Midget in *Chinatown* couldn't resemble each other less, but they echo contrasting sides of Noah Cross, whom they serve: Mulvihill resonates with Cross's humble, folksy affectations; the Midget with the wealthy man's taste for finer things. This contrast and counterpoint provide variety, pique our interest, reinforce the opponent's character, and enhance suspense.

In contrast, the underlings in *Michael Clayton* resemble each other so closely—they're almost identical, like two versions of the same character, just ten years apart—that another effect is created: the eerie homogeneity of drones. If there were more than two of them the effect would be undermined, even silly; it's the fact they're a perfect pair—evil golf buddies—that makes it click. Their being ex-military only enhances the impression of stamp-press conformity—but it also provides a specific skill set that creates their uniqueness. Though in their own way they're as precise with detail as Karen Crowder, the lawyer who enlists them, there's no denying that the two men and their female employer inhabit different worlds. She wouldn't need their unique services if that weren't true. Not only do they go where she won't go, she won't even acknowledge their destination exists. This creates a fascinating tension, as the audience wonders if Ms. Crowder knows exactly what breed of dog she's unleashed, or wants to know.

In short, think the problem through, consider what effect you're after, and what would best serve the story and the need for variety and surprise.

Can the Opponent Change?

The "rule" that the opponent never changes basically reflects the routine use of this character as the embodiment of evil—a villain. And all too often villains are conceived as psychopaths or sociopaths, which is to say people with rigid personality disorders that by their nature resist change. But the opponent can and often does change, especially in dramas where the conflict is motivated meaningfully on both sides, as when good is pitted against good.

This comes with a caveat: If the opponent has the

psychological complexity and capacity to change, she may well detract attention from the protagonist. This, is however, merely a caution, not a prohibition.

Even in a standard western like *3:10 to Yuma*, based on a story by Elmore Leonard, the so-called villain is permitted to change. This is rare in action-based dramas, but that is precisely why they often feel wanting, and one reason this one succeeds where others don't. Here the outlaw Ben Wade grows as the story progresses, never surrendering his outlaw nature—that would be clichéd and feel forced—but gradually coming to admire the fatherly protectiveness and steely determination of the ex-soldier and luckless farmer Dan Evans. But it isn't just his feelings that change. The transformation prompts a redirection of behavior that crucially affects the ending of the story.

Exercises

1. Choose three novels or films with a clear-cut opponent. What are the qualities that spare him from being, to quote Conrad, "quite so black"? Does he change?

2. Using the same examples, does he have stand-ins, proxies, underlings that do his bidding before his appearance in the story? How does the character of each of these surrogates compare or contrast with that of the opponent? How does any such contrast create suspense or surprise within the story? Ask these same questions of the opponent in a piece you're currently writing.

How Secondary Is a Secondary Character?

E. M. Forster, in his *Aspects of the Novel*, first presented the concept of "round" versus "flat" characters, stating that the former were always preferable to the latter because they were more fully realized. In his collection of critical essays on the novel, *How Fiction Works*, James Wood took issue with both Forster's metaphor and his reasoning.

Wood prefers to think of characters as "transparent" or "opaque," distinguishing characters who do not reveal themselves totally in a glance from those that do. And he argues that transparent characters, despite the facility with which they present themselves, nonetheless serve many valid and important fictional purposes. The novels of Dickens abound with them: Uriah Heep, Daniel Peggotty, Mr. Micawber, and Jeremiah Flintwinch are some of them. Such characters are limited with respect to their more "opaque" companions, but they still can serve as compelling individuals on the page, as long as they don't become cartoonish.

What Wood was getting at is that transparent characters are often a type, and as such frequently serve a certain role. How transparent to make them is largely determined by how much their function defines their presence in the story.

The roles we'll explore in this chapter—ghost, revenant, crucial ally,* and so on—all serve a certain dramatic function. They provide a means to dramatize your main characters' needs, fears, hopes, regrets, ideals, qualms of conscience, strengths, vulnerabilities. They help flesh out the way of life and the morality your main characters cherish and intend to protect.

The layers of complexity that make a protagonist or opponent interesting are best explored through interactions with subordinate characters. The secondary characters Michael Clayton engages with, for example—his son Henry, his detective brother Gene, his addict brother Timmy, the loan shark Gabe Zabel, the bipolar lawyer Arthur Edens, the law firm's lead partner Marty Bach, its hatchet man Barry Grissom—elicit different responses, emotions, needs, and attitudes, from fatherly affection and concern to competitive impatience to pitiless frustration to calculated gamesmanship to pleading desperation to misguided candor to open contempt. The hero comes alive in stages through these exchanges, showing us different facets, new variations, more complex connections.

Although serving a certain dramatic purpose, secondary characters have to rise above their roles to avoid cliché. The way to do that is to provide them the same uniqueness

---

* The term "crucial ally" is traditional. I owe the term "ghost" to John Truby, though his use is more general than mine. The terms "revenant" and "counterweight character" are my own.

of personality, emotional range, and capacity for freedom as your main characters, with the understanding that you'll need to exert control to guard against the threat all well-drawn secondary characters present: scene-stealing.

The functions secondary characters serve often—almost necessarily—overlap, precisely because the characters are not mere devices. A crucial ally may turn against the protagonist and become a betrayer, a counterweight character may suffer a change of heart and become an ally, and so on. This provides you with opportunities for both character development and surprise, and readers and audiences always respond well to characters who emerge from some limitation, exhibit insight, or otherwise prove to be more than they initially seemed.

Secondary characters are part of a long dramatic tradition, and thus create reader and audience expectations. The more you can see them in their unique individuality, the better you will be able to improvise upon, undermine, or even betray those expectations, and thus create surprise. These characters may serve a secondary purpose, but if they also demonstrate secondary effort on your part, the story will feel half realized and trite. They can, as Wood notes, remain transparent, revealing their personalities in a glance, as long as that personality is complex and unique enough to be interesting.

What follows is an analysis of a variety of roles. The list is hardly exhaustive*—the creativity of writers will

---

* A brief list of possible secondary characters, each a variation on one or more of the roles discussed in this chapter, would include: Fairy Godmother, Helpful Woodsman, Boy/Girl Next Door, Femme Fatale/ Black Widow, Seer/Sibyl, The Third Son, Whiz Kid, Absent-Minded

always race ahead of any list—but these character types are some of the most commonly found and the most dramatically useful, and deserve at least a passing word.

The Ghost

In chapter 6, while exploring adaptations, defense mechanisms, and pathological maneuvers, we first explored the roles of the ghost and the revenant. The ghost is a somewhat general term, and it can mean anything from the past that continues to create a moral, emotional, or psychological problem for the protagonist. Here, I'm speaking of the ghost not as a general condition but as a character, with the understanding that it's always best to embody the protagonist's moral, emotional, and psychological backstory in specific characters who have created the baggage he carries into the present.

Sometimes the ghost is really a spectral being, such as Rose in *Bringing Out the Dead*. She's the girl Frank, the paramedic protagonist, failed to rescue, and thus embodies

---

Professor, Mad Scientist, Bad Boy, Bad Girl, Gentleman Thief, Evil Twin, Quarrelsome Sibling, Perverted Old Man, Witch, Crone, Evil Clown, Reclusive Wizard, Magician, Divine Fool, Wise Child, Hooker with a Heart of Gold, Manic Pixie/Puck/Ariel, Warrior Monk, Cannon Fodder, Ingenue, Jailbait, Jewish Mother, Magical Negro, Monster-in-Law, Pompous Ass, Nerd, Snooty Servant, and Devoted Domestic. More can be found in the "moral types" of Theophrastus, a student of Aristotle's who compiled an entire catalog of characters premised on moral type—the flatterer, the coward, the newsmonger, the backbiter, the braggart, and so on. This typology helped form the comic characters of Theophrastus's student Menander, and a century later those of Terence, and its influence continued well into the eighteenth and nineteenth centuries. One sees Theophrastian characters in the work of Dickens and Thackeray in particular, both of whom saw great satiric potential in these exaggerated types.

his moral crisis over what it means to have the power to save—and also to lose—human life.

Similarly, in *Death of a Salesman*, Willy Loman's brother Ben, recently dead, haunts Willy's hallucinogenic daydreams, reminding him of his lifelong failure to succeed.

The ghost can be several characters, both living and dead, as in Joe Buck's case. His absentee mother, the town slut Crazy Annie, the various teenagers who enjoyed his body but seemed little concerned that he was inside it—though still alive they remain in Joe's life only in nagging memories. His grandmother Sally Buck is dead, but her death prompts one of the key turns in his journey, forcing him to admit that despite all her sentimental cooing she too never loved him. These characters flesh out the legacy of false affection, abandonment, and outright abuse that forms the crisis of soul he faces within the story.

The ghost can also be not only alive but present within the narrative. Parents and other family members often play this role, representing the ongoing burden of the past. The mother in *Rachel, Rachel* embodies the small-town rectitude and inescapable familial duty that chains her daughter to a loveless middle age. The mother in *Ordinary People*, the father in *I Never Sang for My Father*, the mother and crippled sister in *The Glass Menagerie* all in their own unique way play this same role.

The ghost is as complicated or as simple as the protagonist's problem with the past. The more nuanced or oppressive that history, the more detail you'll need to bring to the characterization.

The Revenant

The revenant is the character who deliberately or unwittingly forces the protagonist to work out the issues embodied in the ghost. The term covers a variety of different secondary characters, from love interests to sidekicks to clients to mentors and sometimes even opponents. A revenant usually proves most useful when teasing out the contrast between the conflict generated by the protagonist's pursuit of her outer goal and that created by the inner growth or transformation taking place simultaneously.

In *The Adventures of Huckleberry Finn*, Huck's understanding of what it means not just to be free but to be human would be impossible without the companionship and sacrifice of the runaway slave Jim—and Jim's generosity, courage, and devotion stand in stark contrast to the sheer mendacity inflicted by Huck's father. Jim is more than an ally. He's a mirror.

In George Eliot's *Silas Marner*, the young girl Eppie serves as revenant, teaching the embittered recluse Silas that happiness is never lost forever except by choice.

Tracking other examples we've used throughout the book: Evelyn Mulwray in *Chinatown* serves as both sidekick, assisting Jake solve the outer mystery of who set him up and why, and love interest, helping him deal with the inner cynicism and distrust that he uses to protect himself from his own guilt. In the climactic scene, the two story lines converge and Jake, Evelyn, and the opponent, Noah Cross, are all on-screen at the same time, staging that permits resolution of both levels of conflict at once.

In the film *Michael Clayton*, the bipolar attorney Arthur

290 }   THE ART OF CHARACTER

Edens, whose psychotic break creates an intractable outer problem, also triggers a crisis of conscience and identity. And as in *Chinatown*, the two threads of conflict converge and resolve in the climax. Arthur is not there physically at the end since he's been killed, but he's there in spirit, as Michael makes clear by several references to him in his confrontation with Karen Crowder, his adversary.

In the novel *City of Thieves*, Lev is dealing with both his fear of death and the shame of his virginity. The gallant charmer, Kolya, helps him deal with both these issues, teasing him, educating him, goading him on—and providing brotherly encouragement in the face of danger. Meanwhile the enigmatic sniper, Vika, serves dual duty as crucial ally, teaching Lev how to use his knife to kill, and love interest. Both Kolya and Vika not only provide crucial survival skills, thus serving as crucial allies, they also help him overcome his shyness and dread, thus reminding him of the essential truth of why the war is important—to protect the people one loves.

The revenant differs from other secondary characters in the depth and enduring nature of her influence on the protagonist. A hero may grow purely from the pressure of external events, but it's doubtful she can transform, moving beyond a previous flaw or limitation, without the challenging or supportive scrutiny of another person. We don't know ourselves by ourselves, as the saying goes, and it's no less true of fiction than real life.

The Counterweight Character

Where the revenant obliges the protagonist to deal with his inner issues in the service of insight or change, the counterweight character serves the interest of maintaining the status quo, or even dragging the hero back into some problem or trap he's not yet fully escaped. If the ghost appears within the story, he often serves this role as well.

The restrictive spouse, the poisonous old flame, the circle of misfit enablers, the unambitious friend, the manipulator who plays on the protagonist's guilt or generosity—all of these characters provide a kind of gravitational pull, checking the character's forward movement. The counterweight character is often in direct conflict with the revenant over who will exert the most long-lasting impact on the protagonist's struggle with his inner demons.

In *Prince of Thieves* (film adaptation, *The Town*), Doug McCray's circle of Townie cronies, from his accomplices and their pitiless boss to his ex-girlfriend Krista and even his imprisoned father, all make their claim on his soul, denigrating his faithless ambition for a better life, a life represented by the bank teller Claire.

The group of hangers-on who surround Jesse Pinkman in *Breaking Bad* all drag him back into the boredom, insecurity, guilt, and fear that trigger his relapse.

Sometimes the counterweight character is not entirely negative in her influence; she simply provides the emotional pull of tradition or normalcy, with the revenant, representing the possibility of change, exerting an equal and opposite attraction.

In the classic French film *Les Enfants du Paradis*, the mime Jean-Baptiste is torn between his longtime love interest, the stoic, manipulative, provincial Nathalie, who becomes his bride and the mother of his son, and the siren Garance, the actress who represents his dreams.

A similar dichotomy appears in Edith Wharton's *The*

Age of Innocence, with Newland Archer torn between domestic duty and bourgeois conformity on the one hand, represented by his wife, May, and erotic pleasure and bohemian freedom on the other, represented by the countess Ellen Olenska. Here especially the characters rise above their roles. May nobly offers Newland his freedom if he wants it, and later acknowledges how selflessly he gave up his opportunity for romance with the countess to honor his obligation to his family. Similarly, the countess refuses to cause May pain; despite an intense attraction she resists Newland's courtship.

The Crucial Ally

Like the revenant, the crucial ally comes in many forms: the mentor, the love interest, the sidekick, the expert, the fellow traveler, the trusted sibling, the faithful servant. At some point in the story, the protagonist comes to rely on the support, specific skill or expertise, sober judgment (the "voice of reason" countering a destructive passion), propensity for violence, ability to rally support, simple companionship, or some other talent or trait that the crucial ally provides. If some of that support, assistance, or expertise concerns matters that affect the protagonist's inner conflicts—such as with Evelyn Mulwray, Arthur Edens, Kolya, and Vika—the crucial ally also assumes the mantle of revenant, serving an essentially dual role.

Often this character contrasts sharply with the protagonist or acts as a foil, the better to depict in sharp relief the protagonist's strengths or weaknesses. This is particularly true when the crucial ally also serves as a mentor, where there is an aura of wisdom or even arcane knowledge to the assistance rendered. Often but not necessarily a difference in age, sex, class, ethnicity, or nationality between the two characters underscores the divide between what the protagonist knows and what he needs to learn.

In many writing guides, one reads that the crucial ally normally appears near the end of Act One or the beginning of Act Two, and then vanishes—or dies—at the beginning of Act Three, so the hero can achieve the climactic resolution solely on her own (or obtains sufficient motivation for vengeance, since the opponent is normally responsible for the ally's disappearance or death). Like all formulas, this is useful guidance until it becomes a trap. As you'll see from the examples that follow, many crucial allies survive Act Two quite nicely, thank you.

But when the crucial ally does die, it often provides one of the most affecting scenes in the story, and may even create one of its most lasting emotional impressions. This is especially true when the death results from an act of selfless courage or sacrifice—particularly if the ally has previously exhibited fear or doubt—or when shared conflict, born shoulder-to-shoulder with the protagonist, has forged a bond of profound respect, gratitude, and fondness. If depicted poignantly, the protagonist's (and by extension, the audience's) "encounter with death" may even be vicarious, experienced through the ally—as anyone who has shouted out a belief in fairies to spare the life of Tinkerbell can sheepishly attest.

In *Oliver Twist*, Oliver's tutelage with the Artful Dodger is one of the most gripping parts of the book. Oliver's almost annoying innocence is finally tempered by the street-savvy Dodger, who teaches him not just how to steal, work the streets, and play marks for fools, but how to win the attention and approval of both Fagan and, more important, Nancy. Without the Dodger, we might lose interest in Oliver, because innocence is seldom as compelling as experience.

In *Romeo and Juliet*, the friendship between the shy romantic Romeo and the worldly, quick-tempered Mercutio provides more than just an occasion for superb dialog. It's the major motivation for Romeo's vengeful murder of Tybalt, Juliet's cousin. It's difficult to see Romeo rising to the level of bloodlust this act of vengeance requires absent Mercutio's influence.

Sometimes the crucial ally is a spouse, as in Dashiell Hammett's *The Thin Man*. Nora may not offer Nick any particular skill, but she does goad his conscience, prodding him on to do what he does best: figure things out.

In crime novels, the hero is sometimes spared the more extreme deeds required of him. In the Spenser novels of Robert B. Parker, for example, as well as the Easy Rawlins novels of Walter Mosley and the Dave Robicheaux novels of James Lee Burke, the protagonist relies on a shadowy counterpart who lacks the hero's reluctance to kill without regret or even much deliberation. Spenser has Hawk. Easy has Mouse. Dave has Clete Purcell. What these murderous sidekicks permit is the hero's ability to battle a monster without becoming monstrous himself. The hero retains some sense of the moral upper hand, with the thematic understanding that when confronting evil, killing is often inescapable, and those who do it best are often those who lack any qualms about it. The hero, given the capacity for moral reflection, joins the reader in a sense of uneasiness and existential regret the killers themselves find superfluous, if not counterproductive. Put differently, the writer's use of a remorseless killer as a sidekick permits the reader to fully enjoy the cathartic vengeance meted out without feeling the hero has degraded himself by the ruthlessness everyone secretly agrees is not just called for but desired.

It's not just protagonists who have allies, of course. Just as heroes have their sidekicks, so villains have their underbosses, consiglieres, assassins, and crucial henchlings. One of the great joys of crime fiction, in fact, is the variety of such characters it affords, for they get to be far more colorful, rude, erudite, stupid, bumbling, sly, shaky, or just plain wicked than just about any other character, without the heavy lifting necessary to lend the opponent his gravitas.

Sometimes the henchling gets painted in less-extreme hues, with even a comic aspect, and this can humanize the opponent by association or demonize him in contrast—or both. He may serve the same role that Hawk and Mouse provide their protagonists—i.e., he can be the villain's excessively violent or remorseless emissary. He can be the opponent's genius, his driver, his brother, his priest. If he dies, that death may elicit vindication, pathos, even comic relief. At his best he provides critical assistance as the opponent pursues the counterobjective, while at the same time adding a unique and compelling shade to the opponent's emotional palette.

Main characters aren't limited to one crucial ally. Think of the array of skilled sidekicks Frodo acquires in *Lord of the Rings*, or the tight-knit crew of credible, distinct, eminently human henchlings who serve as Avon Barksdale's inner circle in the TV series *The Wire*, from strategist Striker Bell to chief enforcer Slim Charles to trusted soldier Wee-Bey Brice.

What an ally provides is a person with whom the protagonist or opponent can mentally or emotionally wrestle, or from whom he learns a necessary skill, or gains access to some new expertise or wisdom that either facilitates the achievement of his objective or highlights the reasons why he cannot or will not do so. Think of what outer conflicts the main character is undergoing, and discover those individuals who either come to his aid or rally to his side. Then make those characters real in their own right, not just plot puppets.

The Betrayer and the Sympathetic Heavy

The act of betrayal packs such a gut-wrenching emotional charge that any character guilty of it normally demands center stage: Brutus, Richard III, Madame Bovary. But betrayal also plays in the middle ground, and it creates an excellent opportunity for reversal in a story, so it's often an opportunity lost if a writer doesn't understand who in his cast of characters might flip allegiances.

To effectively dramatize betrayal you have to both establish trust and motivate the shift in loyalty, otherwise you telegraph or weaken the dramatic turn, which should register as a stunning shock, tinged with rage, disgust, or dread.

In *Sense and Sensibility*, John Willoughby's heartfelt wooing of Marianne wins over not just her but the entire Dashwood family. He encourages her public displays of affection and returns them. She discusses with him not just tender matters of the heart but their common ideals, mutual interests, and they visit together the house he expects to inherit. Without this elaborate demonstration of Willoughby's sincerity of affection we wouldn't feel the knife blade of his deceit so viscerally. Though he claims to have loved Marianne, he won't contemplate a life of poverty, and so he deserts her without warning, marries a rich woman in London, and insinuates publicly that Marianne must be deranged for ever inferring from his actions he felt anything for her at all. And when he's obliged to confess all this to her, he does what all weak men do—he claims he had no choice.

It's not just protagonists and allies who get betrayed. The term "sympathetic heavy" comes from crime fiction, but the nature of the role transcends genre. This character is affiliated with the opponent but befriends or takes pity on the protagonist. As such, he may provide the hero with some crucial bit of information or a needed insight into what exactly it is she's up against, and as such serves as a sort of crucial ally. And yes, he almost always dies or otherwise vanishes at the end of Act Two—his just deserts for betraying his kind. But his ethical terrain is almost always befogged, and that moral ambiguity, along with the glimmer of hope he provides the protagonist, is the key to his interest.

In Desmond Lowden's *Bellman & True*, the criminal arriviste Salto recruits Hiller, a former computer security wonk, as a crucial cog in his bank robbery scheme. Hiller gets in far over his head, and once the plot is handed off to a veteran crew for execution, Salto, at considerable risk, looks after Hiller and his son protectively, both of whom are now virtual captives.

But as I noted, this role need not be limited to crime stories. It's essentially that of an emissary or go-between for the opponent who develops sympathy or fondness for the protagonist: the guard at the POW camp who secretly provides extra rations for the prisoners; the assistant DA who develops a crush on the defendant; the antagonistic neighbor's wife who accepts a cup of coffee, grateful for someone who listens. The character provides a means for the protagonist to gain information about his adversary, and possibly plead his case by proxy. And the risk the character faces, of being seen as a betrayer, creates dramatic tension and suspense.

The Visitor and the Stranger

Both these characters provide an opportunity to reveal a perspective on the events of the story from outside the social and cultural norms of the main setting. They are similar to the outsiders Ishmael and Nick Carraway, except they do not step up into the role of narrator. Their perspective remains at eye level, and it presents a challenge—and sometimes an advantage—to the protagonist in her efforts to understand the circumstances she faces.

In *To Kill a Mockingbird*, the summer visits of Dill Harris (based on Truman Capote, a childhood friend of the author, Harper Lee) provide Scout an opportunity to look with fresh eyes at what otherwise are the exasperatingly humdrum circumstances of her life in Maycomb County, Alabama. Dill's imagination by nature runs hot, nowhere more so than with respect to the recluse Boo Radley, and even though Dill fashions Boo a kind of hobgoblin, his insatiable curiosity emboldens Scout and her brother Jem to probe Boo's sanctuary, a move that unwittingly flushes him out of hiding and into Scout's life.

In the film *Rachel, Rachel*, thirty-five-year-old spinster Rachel Cameron is emotionally shaken to her core by the visits of two strangers to her small southern town: an itinerant preacher whose charismatic services raise more than the roof beams, and Nick Kazlik, a childhood friend who returns from his new home in the city and is looking for "a little action."

The Village

The distinct ways of life the protagonist and opponent are seeking to defend are not abstractions; they're populated with people who reflect the main characters' joys, consolations, secrets, morals, duties, entanglements, opportunities, regrets, and more. They include family, friends, neighbors, members of their church, coworkers, business associates, rivals, the bridge club, the poker crowd, the other parents at the playground or the PTA—the list is endless, which your cast of characters obviously can't be. Choices have to be made concerning who to include and who to leave out.

From the perspective of characterization, the important point is that these characters reflect the variety of countering allegiances and forces influencing the main characters in how they behave—specifically, how they go about pursuing their chief objectives in the story, which in one way or another serve to protect or beneficially change the way of life these other characters represent.

Whether they're the citizens of Bedford Falls in *It's a Wonderful Life*, the refugees stranded at Rick's in *Casablanca*, Jake's present associates Duffy and Walsh and his former associates Lieutenant Lou Escobar and Loach in *Chinatown*, the hostages and terrorists trapped inside the villa in Ann Patchett's *Bel Canto*, or the uniquely imagined barflies at Mahoney's in James Crumley's *The Wrong Case*—these characters don't reside within the story because they might be there but because they must be. They provide contrast or amplify the emotional or practical effects created by the other secondary characters. In the various exchanges they have with the more principal players—the demands they make, the promises they keep, the secrets they betray, the assistance they render, the jokes they repeat, the bargains they offer, the lies they get away with and those they don't—they reveal not just themselves but the weight of the world the main characters carry on their backs, and the stakes of buckling under.

Tony Soprano engaged audiences so completely because the multifaceted aspects of his character were fleshed out so well by the other characters around him, from the trusted curmudgeon Silvio Dante to the put-upon mama's boy Paulie Gaultieri, from the reluctant informant "Big Pussy" Bonpensiero to the sweet-natured killer Bobby Baccalieri, from the Camorra enforcer Furio Giunta to the trusted adviser Hesh Rabkin.

But his two children deserve particular mention, due to the insightful way they were used to tease out different aspects of their father's personality.

Meadow was the princess discovering her own mind. She fed her father's narcissism and yet also defied his power, one minute cooing flattery, the next spitting insults. She was smarter than her dad and possessed much of his strength, but she was a girl—her curse and her escape. She would never be a part of the world that defined him outside the family, a world she blithely pretended to understand with her brother and coyly denied to her friends. For Tony she elicited both pride and shame, protectiveness and powerlessness, and the scenes between them explored those dualities.

In contrast, where Meadow was the shining star, Anthony lived almost entirely within his father's shadow. Tony wanted a son, was proud to have one, and yet Anthony clearly lacked what it took to follow in his father's footsteps. And so that role was assumed by Christopher, Tony's nephew. Anthony obliged Tony to manage his disappointment, temper his outsized ego, muster patience in the face of frustration. But Anthony also elicited from his dad many of the childlike qualities that made Tony endearing; their connection was best when they were at play, eating, or watching TV. When Tony craved a cocoon, he sought out his son, then dealt with the ensuing sense of genetic letdown later.

Where a visitor or stranger provides an outside perspective on the main characters' worlds, the village is composed of insiders. They represent the bustle and bother of daily life, the moral barter of the world, and thus provide color, contrast, and depth to the more major characters. You'll discover which ones to include in your exploration of the main characters' psychological and especially sociological natures (chapters 13 and 14) and weigh which elements of that exploration bear most significantly on your story.

Exercises

1. Return to the novels or films you selected for the exercises in the previous two chapters on the protagonist and the opponent. Identify the most significant secondary characters:

- Is there a ghost—a character in the protagonist's backstory still exerting some troubling influence over the protagonist?

- Is there a revenant forcing the protagonist to deal with that influence in a positive way or to resolve the conflict it creates?

- Is there a counterweight character in the present time of the story impeding the protagonist's efforts at insight or change?

- How do these characters help the protagonist confront or resolve his inner conflicts? Analyze how this gets dramatized in specific scenes. What moments of agreement or discord externalize those conflicts and allow the protagonist to focus on them?

- Are there any crucial allies? What specific form do they take: Mentor? Love interest? Sidekick? Expert? Confidant? Faithful servant? Do they also serve as revenant? Again, analyze how these characters in specific scenes assist the protagonist or opponent in pursuing their goals, then help flesh out the complexity of the plan each has undertaken.

2. Ask the same questions as in exercise 1 for a piece you're currently writing.

3. Go through your bookshelf and your own work and find examples of each of the following types of secondary character:

- *The Betrayer*

- *The Sympathetic Heavy*

- *The Visitor*

- *The Stranger*

As before, with each example, analyze the scenes they share with the protagonist or opponent for how the main character's emotional complexity and depth is revealed, explored, and developed through their interactions with these characters.

4. In the works you selected for the previous three exercises, identify the most significant secondary characters beyond those already addressed in the previous exercises, and analyze how, in specific exchanges, they help flesh out the protagonist's and opponent's distinct ways of life. What would be lost if any of them were eliminated?

5. Return to the work you did in chapters 13 and 14 on the character's psychological and sociological nature. How did this work provide you with suggestions for necessary secondary characters? Which roles did those secondary characters assume? Which possible characters fell by the wayside? Why?

PART IV

―――

Technique

Chapter Twenty-two
The Clash of Character: Scenes

The Centrality of Scene

In exploring how secondary characters draw out the emotional complexity of the major characters, and how the main characters chisel it from one another, the invisible participant in the discussion is scene. It's through the dramatic action of scenes that characters engage each other and are forced to weigh options, make choices, take responsibility, and plow ahead. Scenes externalize the conflicting emotions, values, and ideas in each of the characters, and by making the characters act on those emotions, values, and ideas, scenes forge those aspects of inner life into something concrete.

Beginning writers often shy away from scene work because it obliges a stirring up of anxiety and dread and even more violent emotions they would rather keep under wraps, believing wrongly that the goal of writing is to make things aesthetically pleasing and understandable—less messy.

Clarity of course is necessary, as is control of one's craft.

But clarity and control are at the service of deeper emotional truths than everyday life routinely permits. Those truths are most engagingly, poignantly, and honestly portrayed through conflict, and conflict is most effectively, simply, and directly depicted in scenes.

In Arthur Miller's *The Price*, brothers Walter and Victor Franz face off after their father's death, battling over who made the right decision—and paid the most legitimate price—for the life he has chosen.

Walter stayed by the father's side and endured abject poverty for his loyalty. Victor launched off and made a success of himself, but at the cost of alienating himself from his family and home. Each brother embodies the doubts and uncertainties of the other. For Walter, Victor stands in for the nagging suspicion he erred in staying behind, having so little to show for his sacrifice now that the father is gone. For Victor, Walter represents the emotional solidity his success has never brought him. Rather than have soliloquies in which each brother ponders alone the choices he's made, Miller puts them face-to-face in a room, tearing away the masks and bits of moral disguise, fighting it out like boxers. The same point is made, but of the two options, self-reflection or scenic confrontation, the latter is inherently more interesting.

The reason that scenes strike us as more compelling and illuminating is that the conflict is overt, the emotions exposed. In *The Price*, we see the premise of the play, the costs of irreconcilable but equally justifiable moral choices, battled out right before our eyes. For each of the characters something crucial is at stake, someone stands to gain, someone stands to lose. How one withstands such a contest defines who he is.

Until our thoughts and emotions are acted upon, they remain mere possibilities. Once they exist in behavior and not just contemplation, they can't be taken back. Deeds commit us, forging a bond between inner life and outer experience, dragging us from our solitude into the arena of other people. Our actions anchor us once and for all, for better or worse, in the world.

The Mechanics of Scene

Structurally, each scene possesses three key elements:

- **The Setup:** This lays out the situation among the characters as the scene begins. It routinely poses a question, presents a dilemma, or otherwise sets out the groundwork for the conflict that defines the scene.

- **The Turning Point:** This is an unexpected turn of events—an action, decision, or revelation—that in some way forces a significant change among the characters.

- **The Payoff:** The climax of the scene, presenting the new state of affairs created by the Turning Point. This often creates the Setup for the following scene (or the next scene in this plotline).

Consider these examples:

Setup:
- A group of Basque separatists meets to plan the abduction of the American ambassador's teenage son in Madrid.

- A reporter attends a lavish party in Naples where, "across a crowded room," he spots a woman who instantly fascinates him.

- A burglar needs to crack open a wall safe in a Hamptons beach house before the vacation home's occupants return.

Turning Point:
- One of the conspirators, after weighing the risks and benefits and hearing the others out, refuses to agree to the kidnap plan.

- The reporter, while trying to charm his enchantress with small talk, is introduced to her husband, an admired painter much older than his wife and in poor health.

- The beach home's residents suddenly return home.

Payoff:
- The abduction plan's naysayer is appeased by the group's leader in such a way that he realizes he's been marked for assassination.

- Despite the risks, the reporter manages to get the painter's wife to agree to meet him again, alone.

- The burglar is forced to hide inside the house rather than flee.

From the viewpoint of character, another three elements are crucial:

Objective: What the character wants in the scene.

- The reluctant insurgent wants his companions to recognize the folly of their plan.

- The suitor wants some hope of getting together with the enchantress he's met.

- The burglar wants to get into the safe and out of the house undetected.

Obstacle: The force within the scene that stands between the character and his objective.

- The insurgent leader is in favor of the abduction, and his rank, plus the command he holds over the others, makes ratification of the plan all but certain.

- The woman with whom the reporter is smitten isn't just married; her husband is admirable and infirm, enhancing her devotion, at least outwardly.

- The burglar has only a small window of time before he risks being discovered.

Action: The tactic the character employs to overcome the obstacle and continue pursuing his objective.

- The reluctant conspirator tries to convince the group's leader that the kidnap plan is reckless, or barbaric, or politically unwise. He hopes at least to delay it, thinking secretly that time will prompt caution, reflection, and reconsideration.

- The reporter overcomes the wife's initial resistance by feigning that his interest is entirely innocent—by engaging the husband in energetic conversation, for example, then asking her to be his guide to the city, for her insights on Naples might be crucial for a piece he's writing. The wife remains circumspect. Ironically, it's her husband who urges her to agree.

- The burglar, guessing that the homeowner has not foreseen this option, sledges a hole in the wall above the vault and hatchets in from the top, circumventing the time-consuming combination problem altogether.* (This of course prevents him, when he's surprised by the return of one of the residents, from simply closing the safe door before he hides, and the damage to the wall will reveal what he's done, creating the setup for the next scene.)

A character may employ several actions within a scene in his continuing attempt to overcome the obstacle—each

---

* This was the strategy used by Ernie Mullins (Burt Reynolds) in the film *Breaking In*, script by John Sayles.

such action/reaction is called a *beat*—and each failed attempt represents another turn, until the dilemma or question posed by the setup is somehow fulfilled or answered (the payoff). More often than not, the scene concludes with the protagonist failing to accomplish his objective, or succeeding only partially, spurring him on to rethink his strategy or reassess his goal. In a sense, this failure is a success, because it forces the protagonist to look within, rise to the challenge his lack of success represents. This is how the protagonist becomes stronger, wiser, more resolute.

At the end of each scene, and at times within it— particularly as the character is reacting to what is happening, weighing his options—he will experience the emotional impact of what's happened, think through what to do, suffer an insight or a change of heart, and form a decision as to what to do next. In this way, emotion and thought are always in the service of action, and help move scenes forward through cause and effect, action and reaction.

Within the scene itself, it's often best not to dwell too long on the emotional responses or inner calculations of the characters, unless this slowing of the action serves your purposes. Often the emotional response and consideration of options is implicit in the actions the character makes and the way he goes about them.

For example, taking our reporter in Naples hoping to connect with the aging artist's wife: He first experiences the heat of attraction, then has to decide how he'll approach her. Should he just saunter over and introduce himself? Should he play it more cautiously, ask someone he knows at the party about her, get a little background? One way or another he learns her situation, and feels a minor jolt of disappointment—or the thrill of the contest. And then, in meeting the husband, he experiences envy, guilt—or disgust. Perhaps he shares in everyone else's admiration but sees an opportunity regardless. Perhaps he feels disdain for the old man, and considers the marriage a sham. Either way, he decides, she's wasting the best years of her life. She's trapped, her marriage is a sexless chore, she's just counting the days until death settles the matter. She needs someone to shake her out of her numbing routine.

Within the scene itself, you could describe all this deliberation overtly—at the risk of bogging down the action. Or you could let it serve as subtext and be conveyed in what the reporter says and does—and what he doesn't say or do—and the manner with which he goes about his business. The best option is usually to balance the two approaches, revealing *just enough* reflection to *suggest* how the character's thinking and feeling, then conveying the rest through dialog and action, allowing your readers or the audience to fill in the blanks, which enhances their investment in the story.

Beginning writers often fail to realize how much thought and emotion can be conveyed through attention to the surface of things, by which I mean not just appearances but what people say and do. It's a great exercise for any writer to try to strip a scene down to its pure exterior and see how much remains in the way of reflection, feeling, nuance, and the like. Prose is ironically far more poetic when deprived of access to the mind or heart, for the sheer order of words, the rhythm, the clatter of consonants, and the breath in every vowel counts for so much more.

The time for more deliberate exploration of emotion and thought is often after an extended scene or a sequence of linked scenes that end in some conclusive action, decision, or revelation, especially if the drama has been tense, violent, or rapidly paced. The reader or audience will need a breather, and the characters themselves will be at a juncture where time is needed to process the emotional impact of what's occurred, think through their options, and work out a plan for how to proceed from that point forward. Occasionally, for the sake of variety, this can be slipped into the scene itself, but it's best to keep such insertions brief. Even in sections where the emotion, thought, and decision stand alone, keeping it short is wise. Such sections can often devolve into labored explanations of what you've either already shown in the preceding scenes or are about to show in the ones to come. The first place to look for editorial trimming is where you attempt to justify what you've already established.

This respite section of emotion, thought, and decision is often called the *sequel*, and the rising conflict of your story will build through the alternation between scenes that emphasize dramatic action and sequels that process that action through a brief responsive episode of feeling, reflection, and determination of what to do next.

Balancing Action and Inner Life

In judging the relative weight of scenes and sequels—dramatic action on the one hand, emotion and thought on the other—we're seeking to balance exterior with interior, the crackle and snap of behavior against the softer echoes of inner life. Where and how to strike that balance will depend on your artistic intent.

Literary fiction often emphasizes the descriptive over the dramatic. The writing, in its rendering of events, often aims for the searing insight, or strives to reveal the incandescent in the ordinary, to make us aware of the wonder or the terror or the ineffable silence that always abides in the seemingly everyday. At times such writing seems to aspire to an iconic characterization of events that renders them frozen in time, as in poetry or paintings or sculpture. As lovely as such writing can be, it can also seem—especially when taken to excess—cool and less than lifelike, a beautiful corpse.

And yet the solution isn't to concatenate unreflective actions in a chain of jump-cut events that possess all the subtlety of a freight train hurtling toward a cliff. Once it's understood that thought and feeling are in service to action, that they provide response, reflection, and decision, the matter clarifies and becomes more manageable.

The first chapter of Kate Atkinson's *When Will There Be Good News?* ends in a heartbreaking crime. It's narrated from the point of view of a six-year-old girl named Joanna, the only survivor of an attack that claims her mother, her older sister Jessica, her baby brother, even the family dog. As in all of Atkinson's fiction, the character is rendered vividly in her moments of inner life, seemingly contradicting my emphasis on action. And at first glance, Joanna's thoughts may seem typical of the obsession with familial minutiae that children exhibit, and point toward nothing. But that obsession betrays the underlying action: The little girl is trying to determine what her mother's failed marriage means; she's faulting herself for not being as capable as Jessica. She's looking for her place in the family, the moment before that family is wiped off the earth forever.

In Richard Price's *Clockers*, homicide detective Rocco Klein comes home at two in the morning, lifts his sleepless but uncomplaining two-year-old from her crib, and carries her about the apartment, even as he grabs a nip from the vodka bottle kept in the freezer. As he bobs the girl in his arms, he not only internally recalls his own father's execrable parenting skills, he notices himself noticing how much he's making an effort to be a better dad, and fearing he's failing miserably. The self-consciousness reveals his cynicism, his disbelief in moral clarity, and yet also his vulnerability: He *wants* to be a good dad, he's even *trying* to be one, even as he suspects the best he can do is go through the motions and hope that's good enough. And yet, all the while, he's bobbing his daughter gently, trying to get her drowsy, and telling her to join him as he looks out the window at the sparkling cityscape, saying good night to the taxis and bridges, good night to the crackheads and werewolves.

In Richard Ford's *The Lay of the Land*, Frank Bascombe describes what he's wearing as he prepares for a tense reunion with his first wife, Ann—specifically his "tan barracuda jacket" that he fears will make him look like "some rube showing up for flying lessons." The entire passage is fraught with the uneasy peace Frank has made with aging, and every detail is weighed against the one key phrase: "I don't know what Ann will think." He's preparing to be appraised—he's a realtor, after all—and the touchstone of his evaluation is loss and death.

In each of these examples, the thoughts and emotions exhibit some inner struggle—moral, emotional, situational—that:

- Points toward an action, a decision, or a crucial event

- Comments ironically on the exterior action taking place within the same scene

- Expresses mentally what the character, for whatever reason, declines to say out loud

This tension between inner and outer is another form of drama, another conflict.

The tension between inner life and outer action also provides an opportunity to reveal *contradiction*: Let the reader know what a character thinks or feels, then have that character act or speak in a contrary manner. In Patricia Highsmith's *The Talented Mr. Ripley*, the contrast between Tom Ripley's inner monologues, characterized by derision and deceit tinged with fear, and the bland reasonableness of his actual statements creates the tension that compels the reader forward as Ripley perfects his ability to mimic those whose lives he envies and ultimately co-opts. And Rocco Klein acidly scrutinizes his parenting skills, even as he cradles his baby.

Exercises

1. Take a scene from a novel or film you've recently enjoyed and break it down: What are the objective, obstacle, and action for each major character in the scene? What are the setup, turning point, and payoff for the scene?

2. Do the same as in exercise 1 for a scene from a piece you're currently writing.

3. Consult a novel you've recently enjoyed and try to find a section that appears to be composed solely of a character's thoughts or feelings. Go back to the preceding scene and try to discern how its dramatic events led to the more descriptive section. In particular, does the passage provide an emotional response to the preceding action, or an analysis of options, or both? Is there a movement toward a decision or a change of heart in the character's reflections?

4. Taking the same novel or film chosen for exercise 1, can you identify any characters who embody or help externalize an inner conflict in the protagonist?

5. Again, taking the same novel or film chosen for exercise 1, find a section where inner life is contrasted with outer action. How is this accomplished? How well does it work—i.e., what is learned about the character from this contrast?

Chapter Twenty-three
The Personal in Perspective: Point of View

Choosing the Point of View: Three Key Questions

Novice writers often misjudge the importance of establishing and maintaining point of view, but giving the reader a sense of firm ground at the outset is crucial. Few things are as unsettling as a perspective that feels loose on deck, and readers gain comfort, and thus trust the story and you, the author, when they can rely on who is the viewpoint character in a scene, and how intimately or abstractly she'll depict events. If either of those things changes, it needs to be justified in a way that the reader can implicitly comprehend, rather than puzzle through.

You may select your point of view instinctively, finding it as intrinsic to the story as the characters and setting and events themselves. Or it may result from extensive trial and error, from troubling over which perspective conjures the greatest empathy, or objectivity, or irony. But whether it comes naturally or painfully, the point of view normally results, directly or not, from answering these three questions:

- Why is this story being told?
- Who has the authority to tell it?
- How should it be told?

In other words, granting the "what" (events and characters) and "where" (setting) of the story, point of view addresses the "why," the "who," and the "how" of *the telling*.

No specific point of view offers hard-and-fast answers to any of these questions, nor can one point of view offer categorically different answers than another. The distinctions are subtler than that, and the advantages and disadvantages of each approach never point conclusively one direction or the other. A choice always has to be made, meaning something is gained and something is lost no matter what you decide.

Why is this story being told? The question isn't asked at the level of the writing but on the plane of the story's events, and the answer lies with those characters most deeply moved, shocked, damaged, or transformed by what happens there. Whether the point-of-view characters tell the story themselves (first person), or the story is told about them (third person), or the story is told from the perspective of a nameless observer who implicitly understands all that's happened (omniscient), the person through whose eyes we see events isn't disinterested. In one way or another, she stands at a point of impact.

There is no such thing as an indifferent point of view. You can choose whatever perspective suits your purpose—the person with the most to lose or gain from what takes place, an otherwise interested party, or a hapless bystander. But though that character's involvement in *events* may well have been accidental, her engagement with *the telling* cannot be. She steps forward to lend her viewpoint because something matters to her.

Who has the authority to tell the story? The characters most profoundly changed or compelled to act in the course of the story, the ones with the most at risk—normally one of the main characters, usually the protagonist, perhaps a few additional principal actors—are the ones who have the best vantage on the key events and the greatest claim to authority. Some writing guides are more practical: The character in the most scenes, especially the most dramatic ones, should be your point-of-view character. The reader wants to experience these events, and relating them secondhand is guaranteed to disappoint.

In *To Kill a Mockingbird*, Scout narrates the story, but key sequences—the trial, the attempt to lynch Tom Robinson—focus on Atticus. The author had to find a way to get Scout into those scenes, and did so not just credibly but compellingly.

Perhaps the wisest advice is this: Whoever your point-of-view character is, she has to be in the climactic scene. If not, she has to have some meaningful stake in it to lend gravity and interest or at least irony to the fact she's reporting it secondhand.

Sometimes it's not the story's events or even their devastating effect that's the issue but rather their meaning, and the telling of the tale is intended to explore or unearth it. In most cases this suggests a narrator, one who's not just recounting events but simultaneously wrestling with their significance. If you accept the challenge of this approach, your narrator has to be fleshed out like any other character, with the same deep understanding of his wants, limitations, biases, secrets, wounds. Otherwise his reasons for narrating will feel uncertain and vague and undermine the story.

Regardless of whether the narrative point of view is that of a main character or a sideline observer, the constant requirement is an investment in the events, to either resolve uncertainty, quiet a moral qualm, understand what took place, or simply depict what happened from the catbird's seat. The question of authority is answered by the quality of that investment.

How should the story be told? Are you hoping for ironic detachment? Moral uncertainty? Emotional immediacy? Comic distance? Impact through understatement? Counterpoint through alternative perspectives? A rip-roaring yarn? Taking a moment to meaningfully examine what effect you're hoping to accomplish may suggest a point of view you've previously not considered, or reassure you that the one that came to you off the bat was the right one after all.

It may be that the "what" and "where" of your story largely dictate your point of view: Is the story intimate or in some other way contained (for which first person or close third person usually serves best), or does it sprawl across space and time (suggesting a multiple-third-person or an omniscient point of view)?

In determining your own approach, take a look at the last dozen books you've read that have moved you most

deeply or influenced you and examine the point of view.
You may find that there is an approach that intrigues you,
or a method that feels instinctive to you, and questioning
that is just a way to spin your wheels.

But if you are open to different approaches and want to
explore a variety of storytelling perspectives and effects,
remember that the entire issue of point of view is an attempt to answer those three key questions—why, who, and
how. It can help simplify your decision by framing it in a
manageable way.

Objective Versus Subjective Mode

Regardless of which point of view you select, you'll need to
decide how and to what degree you want to access the
point-of-view character's thoughts and feelings in the telling of your story. This decision may come first or last or
in-between, but I raise it here because it applies to all the
points of view we'll consider, and they become easier to
discuss with this issue already covered.

Objective focuses on the exterior, though not absolutely or exclusively. If thoughts and feelings are expressed,
they're described with a certain lack of engagement, as
though they're being observed, not experienced. Used
well, the detachment this mode evokes strangely enhances
the emotional impact of events by limiting explanation of
them. This echoes a point made in the preceding chapter:
The less you explain, the more powerful the impact, assuming you're not being unclear or enigmatic. Less is
more, unless it's not enough.

In general, the more inherently dramatic, intense, or

sensational the events being described, the better the objective mode works. Hemingway is the accepted master here, though other journalists who've turned to fiction, writers such as Joan Didion and Pete Dexter, routinely take this approach as well, and masterfully.

In contrast, the subjective mode provides ready access to the point-of-view character's thoughts and feelings, and its strength is the intimacy it provides. The risk is the temptation to overexplain or to get lost in mental states, analyzing the action instead of portraying it.

Subjective mode is sometimes referred to as "close" point of view. It feels, as is often said, as though we are "looking over the shoulder" of the character—or inhabiting his mind and body. We are "with" the character, rather than "looking at" her.

You're not stuck with an either/or proposition. There's no toggle at the narrative switch box that turns one mode on and the other off. You can move in and out, if you manage that movement with care. And, as noted, even thoughts and feelings can be depicted objectively, with a cool, analytical tone, and often to great effect.

As an example of how this is done well, consider the Hemingway story, "In Another Country." The narrator is an American being treated for his combat wounds at an Italian hospital. The majority of the story deals with his interactions with the optimistic medical staff and his less hopeful fellow patients, especially a major, once the national fencing champion, now the owner of a withered hand. The narration gets established in strict objective mode: surfaces, actions, dialog. Only briefly does the focus move inward on the narrator's inner life—his feelings about having medals he received only because he's an American, in contrast to the sacrifices the Italians suffered to earn theirs. But even these impressions are described with a cool touch, as the narrator remarks on how his fellow patients invariably withdraw once they realize his distinctions are a fraud. Then we return to the exterior, and the tone is devastating because what is being described is extreme: the mutilation of young men from combat, the savage loss of their futures, their hopeless attempts at rehabilitation, crowned by news that the major with the ruined hand has lost his wife to pneumonia.

The mode could have remained strictly objective, but by deftly entering the narrator's thoughts just long enough to suggest a poignant, shame-tinged distance between him and the men he describes, it crystallizes their suffering all the more, and intensifies the ultimate effect.

This works well because the movement from remote to close, objective to subjective, is rooted in the character. Whether in first person or third, a step back from the character's thoughts, once they're established, can feel like an authorial intrusion if mishandled. One second we're hovering in the character's mind, the next we're at some distance, exploring the setting, weighing the circumstances, explaining what everything means. Who, exactly, is saying all this? Such sloppiness is the mark of an inattentive writer. An omniscient narrator can get away with this, but that point of view is the most challenging to pull off well, something I'll address below.

First Person

This is often considered the most natural point of view, because it's how we tell stories about ourselves in everyday life. The author assumes the persona of someone within the story, normally the protagonist, or someone with a convincing justification for describing the events.

The advantages of this point of view are its naturalness and immediacy. By naturalness I mean the seemingly unforced quality of the storytelling. We use this technique effortlessly in everyday life:

> I visited Julia yesterday to let her know she can depend on me if James doesn't recover. She told me that's all well and good but she'll never forget that I kept James's secret about that horrible woman, and if I so much as show up at her door she'll scream.

The other allure of first person is its immediacy—we are there with the narrator. That comes with a qualification. Since the narrator is looking back at events, there can often be a lack of immediacy *in time*. This typically comes across in a tone of reflection, rather than direct action, and even the best writers can get caught unawares by this.

When you already know how the story turns out, it takes a skilled hand not to let that knowledge seep in and leech away tension and suspense. We know the narrator survived, for example, so that cat's out of the bag, to the degree it's relevant. The solution, as is often the case, lies in focusing on scenes rather than explanations.

In the hands of a great stylist, first person can be used to great effect. Think of Conrad with his narrator Marlowe, or more contemporary first-person virtuosos such as Marilynne Robinson or Andrew Sean Greer, comic novelists such as Jonathan Lethem and Gary Shteyngart, or crime novelists such as James Crumley and Lawrence Block. The detective novel in particular thrives because of its singular first-person narrators. It might even be argued that the gift of first person for the reader is the richness of voice, whether reflective, pragmatic, philosophical, or humorous.

First person has the additional advantage that there's no question that the thoughts, impressions, memories, and emotions of the narrator are accessible. Better yet, they're easily expressed and can flow together naturally, with no need for tags such as "he thought" or "she wondered."

But again, every garden has its serpent. A section narrated in first person possesses certain inherent structural limitations:

- You can have no scenes in that section that do not include the point-of-view character without recounting them secondhand—always a letdown, no matter how cleverly told.

- You cannot describe the narrator from the outside; the narrator can comment on how he believes he appears at any given moment—weary, pert, disheveled, neat—or you can resort to the tired trick of having him look in a mirror or some other reflective surface, but by and large you should embrace the narrator's lack of physical description as a creative challenge or even an advantage.

The challenge: You'll need to embody the character in his voice. The advantage: The lack of physical detail makes it easier for readers to project themselves onto the character, and thus personally invest in the story.

- Given that the events are told entirely in the first-person narrator's voice, you're restricted to his attitude and worldview in describing the people, events, and physical environment of the story. Authorial intrusions can be particularly glaring in this point of view.

- The story cannot reveal information the point-of-view character does not already possess. Just as you're restricted to his worldview, you're restricted to his knowledge. Violating this rule means the author has implicitly entered the story as a narrator, disrupting the fictive illusion and undermining the reader's suspension of disbelief.

Despite all these quibbles, first person still most closely approximates that intimate sense of wonder you felt when Uncle Ray arrived on Sunday in his Buick, dragged his bad leg up the porch steps, collapsed in the rocker, accepted a lemonade from your mother, petted the dog, rolled himself a cigarette, and then, after a shameless onslaught of begging, told you one of his stories.

The Special Case of the Unreliable Narrator

The use of this technique underscores the inescapable nature of our subjectivity, and provides a kind of subplot by creating uncertainty in the narration.

To a certain extent, every narrator is unreliable, if only because of youth, as with Scout in *To Kill a Mockingbird*, a feverish grudge, as with Charles Kinbote in Nabokov's *Pale Fire*, or a history of walled-off feeling, as in Julian Barnes's *The Sense of an Ending*.

The more distinctive the first-person narrator, the greater the likelihood that his perspective represents an inherent "distortion," the word so prized by Nick Carraway in *The Great Gatsby*. On page one, Nick unwittingly alerts us to his own blind spot by misinterpreting his father's advice to recognize his own advantages. Instead, he says he'll reserve judgment, while simultaneously blasting the people he describes with smug superiority—all except the enigmatic Gatsby, for whom he expresses contempt one moment, an almost boyish fascination the next. Fitzgerald isn't just telling us about Gatsby; he's dramatizing how a sheltered, self-righteous midwesterner can't help but miscomprehend the world he encounters on Long Island's North Shore.

The nameless English instructor who narrates Joseph Conrad's *Under Western Eyes* reports with excruciating specificity on the inner turmoil of the main character, Razumov. He claims authority to do this because of access to Razumov's diary, which has come into his possession, and his own personal acquaintance with several of the people in Razumov's circle. Still, we only know of Razumov's inner life through the narrator's "western" eyes. In the end, we wonder how much of Razumov's story can be comprehended by us or the narrator, what biases we share, and whether a great deal, perhaps even the most essential thing, has escaped us.

A narrator can be unreliable because of mental defect, as is the case with Chief Bromden in *One Flew Over the Cuckoo's Nest* and Hugh Boone in Peter Carey's *Theft*. He may be unreliable because of personal flaws, as in *Catcher in the Rye*, or a full-blown personality disorder, as in *Fight Club*. He may be unreliable because of drug use, as in *Fear and Loathing in Las Vegas*, or due to a self-serving perspective on himself and society, as in *A Clockwork Orange* and *The Collector*, or because of an extravagant need to justify the unjustifiable, as is the case with Humbert Humbert in Nabokov's *Lolita*, who remarks grandly, "You can always count on a murderer for a fancy prose style."

Regardless of why the point of view is suspect, the purpose of the approach is to put the reader on guard, to remind her that things are never quite as they seem. In each case, it's not that the text is entirely untrustworthy. Quite the opposite. There's always a great deal that rings true, at least enough for us to continue investing in the story, even as our suspicions increase. Readers who want to suspend disbelief may find this tiresome. But of all the approaches to point of view, none is more deeply enmeshed in character.

Other Special Cases:
Second Person and First Person Plural

These points of view—both, to my mind, stealthy or veiled uses of first person—are unique as well as rare.

The second person attempts to achieve one of two effects. One, it universalizes what's being portrayed, encouraging the reader to immerse herself in the action as a character:

> You enter the classroom hoping the professor will
> ignore you, at least until you've had a chance to
> glance at the syllabus and peek at a page or two of
> the text.

Here, the character tends to be generalized to the point of feeling vague, insubstantial.

The other use suggests a first-person narrator alienated from himself, and allows for more specificity of character:

> You enter the waiting room and take your place
> among the geriatric flotsam, the rheumy-eyed
> wheezers, the syphilitic toe-tappers.

This effect always draws attention to itself, and should be selected with care.

Authors of writing guides will forever be grateful to Brett Easton Ellis for penning *Bright Lights, Big City* so we could cite it as an example. Lorrie Moore's story collection *Self-Help* provides a more recent example, and a good one.

A more poignant usage—effective precisely because it's short—can be found in *The Brief Wondrous Life of Oscar Wao*, where the one chapter told from the viewpoint of Lola, Oscar's sister, begins in the second person:

This is how it all starts: with your mother calling you into the bathroom.

Belicia, naked from the waist up, her bra "slung about her waist like a torn sail," asks Lola to feel for a lump in her breast. The girl resists, but is goaded into obeying and finds the "knot just beneath the skin."

And at that moment, for reasons you will never quite understand, you are overcome by the feeling, the premonition, that something in your life is about to change.

The use of "you" by Lola instead of "I" under-scores not just a sense of out-of-body disbelief, the dread of what the lump foretells, but the pivoting transition be-tween her understanding of her life and herself before this moment and after. It provides a way for Lola to effectively split herself in two: the child she's been, the woman she'll become.

The first person plural, which serves as a kind of quasi-omniscient point of view, is used to brilliant effect in Jef-frey Eugenides's *The Virgin Suicides* and Kate Walbert's *Our Kind*. Both novels establish a sort of duplicitous, unwit-ting conformity, without feeling judgmental. The nameless narrators focus here and there on individual members of their groups, then recede to provide the communal per-spective, revealing the shared beliefs, wants, and misunder-standings that forged their collective point of view. The narrator needs to be uniquely realized while remaining con-cealed behind that tiny word: *we*.

Third Person

Anyone who has heard a fairy tale knows third-person point of view: *There once was a woodsman who lived deep in the forest.* You probably grasped third person in the context of story before you did first person, and it's used every day to discuss what's happened to other people:

> Jack got fired again yesterday, some fight with one of the other linemen, and Jill said she's had it, she's leaving, this time for good.

It's by far the most widely used point of view and is the easiest to control—and thus the wisest choice for beginning writers. But it's hardly a technique that mature writers outgrow. Novels employing the third person include Flaubert's *Madame Bovary*, George Eliot's *Middlemarch*, Jonathan Franzen's *The Corrections*, and Michael Ondaatje's *The English Patient*, to name but an illustrious few.

The advantages of third person include:

- The ability to describe the point-of-view character from the outside (not an unqualified advantage, as we discussed with respect to first person).

- The fact that you are not strictly limited to the point-of-view character's worldview. This advantage should be exploited with care, however. Authorial intrusions usually smack of sloppiness, a lack of authorial control, and should be avoided. Rather, if you want to pull back for a more objective or general view, try to retain some sense of the point-of-view character's perspective, sticking to his attitude and what he knows, and make the transition as seamless as possible.

- You can withhold crucial information to maintain suspense.

The disadvantages of third person are usually considered to be:

- A greater intuited distance between the point-of-view character and reader, though this can be mitigated by use of close or subjective modality.

- Less fluidity in transitioning among memories, thoughts, impressions, opinions, and other aspects of inner life. Third person often requires tags such as "he thought" and "she wondered," which call attention to themselves and can disturb the flow of the language. Mental and emotional impressions have to be rooted in a character or they risk being seen as authorial intrusions.

Normally, it's best to establish clearly the point-of-view

perspective in any given scene, section, or chapter, and not to shift or change to another character's point of view without providing a lucid transition.

It's not just transitions between characters that require care. Third person can embrace a subjective modality, conveying a character's thoughts and feelings with great intimacy, or a more objective one, describing events clinically and staying as much as possible with surfaces, dialog, and action. Problems arise when transitioning from one to the other. Unlike first person, there isn't a personal narrator to justify this movement from the immediacy of the scene to a more reflective distance. The reader often feels the writer's hand in such things, which disturbs her investment in the telling.

It's sometimes useful to think of the narrative perspective in third person as that of an invisible film crew that can move in and out at will, with the additional capability of recording thoughts and feelings. But just as overly frenetic editing can fracture a scene in a film, jumping around from subjective to objective, surfaces to interior, can seem arty in the worst meaning of the word. It's better to establish a certain perceived distance from the point-of-view character and maintain it throughout the scene, pulling out of it only for a momentary effect, if then, and minimizing such shifts as much as possible.

As an example of what I mean, consider the following passage concerning two characters, Roque and Mariko, from *Do They Know I'm Running?**

---

* I use examples from my own work for this and the following chapters because, often when analyzing technique, it's necessary to focus

Gently, he tugged the sheet from her sleep-warm shoulder. She'd want to be wakened before he gathered his clothes and slipped out. "This kind of thing isn't known for its shelf life," she'd told him once. "I want to make the most of my chances."

Twenty years separated them—practically a crime, given he was eighteen. He realized there were probably clinical terms to explain the thing, especially since he was motherless. In his own heart, though, it felt simple—they both were lonely, he liked her a lot, she seemed to like him back and he enjoyed getting his ashes hauled, an inclination she happily, at times rabidly indulged. The sex was always instructive, seldom routine, often kinky, especially once she cracked open that second bottle of wine. If any of that's a problem, he thought, let somebody else worry about it. Every important connection he'd ever had was with someone older than he was—musicians, librarians, a cop here and there—why should this be any different?

She had her back to him, sleeping on her side, pillow balled tight beneath her chin as she snored.

Here we start with third person close and subjective, from Roque's point of view. The specifics of the situation

not just on execution but on intent, and discussing another writer's intent always requires a certain level of presumption. In contrast, I know what I was meaning to do. Whether I pulled it off or not, of course, is another question entirely.

338)   THE ART OF CHARACTER

trigger a memory—Mariko's comment about wanting to make the most of her chances, since she knows their relationship won't last—which prompts Roque to pull back into reflection. The text makes explicit what he probably feels in a fleeting impression. The expansion is for the benefit of the reader, to provide context, and is, of course, provided by the writer. The trick, to the extent it works, is to express the more elaborate thoughts in a manner that still conveys the young man's voice. We still feel with the character, even though we've stepped back just a little to reflect on the relationship and how he feels about it. Then we're brought back to the present with the physical details of how she's sleeping.

The more you can ground insertions of context, backstory, and setting in character, the more the reader will experience the uninterrupted flow of the story. Keeping such intrusions as brief as possible, of course, is also wise.

Single Versus Multiple Points of View

A single point of view forges an intense bond between the reader and the point-of-view character, and provides a consistent narrative. The reader seldom feels lost, and never rues abandoning the perspective of someone with whom she's formed a feeling of trust or intimacy.

The limitation lies in its inability to portray scenes that don't include the point-of-view character. This restriction of perspective can facilitate surprise but inhibit foreshadowing or suspense, in that the single perspective can only see what's there in front of it, and the reader is similarly limited.

The advantage of multiple points of view is the ability to portray scenes in which one or more of the other main characters are absent. It can also provide a variety of perspectives on events, for the sake of contrast, foreshadowing, complexity, suspense, or irony. Each character should possess his or her own tone, expressed through voice, and that shift in tone can provide welcome variety.

Multiple first person provides a great opportunity for a stylist to strut, since the voices will have to be exquisitely distinct—as they are in Peter Carey's *Theft* and Ursula Le Guin's *The Left Hand of Darkness* (both of which use alternating first person), as well as Jake Arnott's *The Long Firm* and Faulkner's *The Sound and the Fury* (which combine multiple first person with third person).

Multiple third person is the point of view most commonly encountered in fiction. It's flexible and natural and provides a great opportunity for variety. It's normally wise to restrict the number of viewpoint characters. I typically try to stick to three, though isolated sections from a secondary character can sometimes provide an interesting element of surprise or contrast, as long as they're kept brief.

Omniscient

Many students confuse multiple-third-person with omniscient point of view. The difference is that multiple third person employs only one point of view at a time for a particular scene, section, or chapter. Omniscient has no such restriction, for the viewpoint is always that of the omniscient narrator, who can be all places at all times, including inside people's minds.

This was once the preferred mode of narration, and it

dominates many nineteenth-century novels. It particularly suited sweeping narratives such as those of Dickens and Tolstoy and Hardy, though it was also used to excellent effect in the less epic novels of George Eliot and Jane Austen, among dozens of others. More recent practitioners include Gabriel García Márquez, Salman Rushdie, and Ann Patchett in *Bel Canto*.

The omniscient narrator is an unnamed person who is knowledgeable about the events of the story, including the thoughts and feelings of the principal characters. He recounts the narrative as a kind of all-seeing, all-knowing eminence.

The strength of this point of view is its ability to be anywhere and everywhere, to tell all, and the assumption of reliability it routinely conveys. It works best when, despite the sweeping nature of the narrator's knowledge, he attends to the specific details of his characters, with both affection and circumspection, like a wise parent. The limitation is that it feels reflective and thus remote from the action, and by having access to so many minds and hearts it can actually serve to diminish the readers' empathy, because its focus is spread too thin.

The omniscient point of view requires a very strong narrative voice, and it's not an approach for beginners. It's most effective when it conveys a distinct sense of character without assuming the mantle of an identifiable "I," and is not just a way for the author to nudge his way anonymously onto the stage. Rather, the narrator should sound like an accomplished raconteur, and what intimacy the telling conveys will be in the sensitivity of that narrator, the humanity of her voice, and the specificity of her details.

Point of View in Film and TV

The camera analogy used above should make plain that cinema not only employs point of view but has had a profound effect on its usage. In film and TV, the director and his camera serve as a kind of omniscient narrator, moving in, dropping back, offering variations not just in perspective but tone and mood through the use of multiple camera angles in a single scene. The camera facilitates this fluidity of movement in ways that language cannot.

In this sense scripts are something of a crossbreed between a play and a story with an omniscient narrator. Scenes can vary not just with respect to who the principal character is but through whose perspective we're seeing the action.

But there remain limits on how many characters' viewpoints can be embraced before testing the audience's patience or understanding. In many cases, we follow one character, the protagonist, through the whole of the story, as happens in *Chinatown*. This was a deliberate choice by the screenwriter Robert Towne, who wanted to re-create the feel of the lone-wolf hero in many detective novels. But it's also true that every story relies on the hero, and it's best to remain with the protagonist's perspective as much as possible. This means that writing your script from an implicit third-person viewpoint is in most cases wise.

The usual manner in which first person occurs in film is through the use of overnarration. In the hands of a deft filmmaker—like Billy Wilder with *Sunset Boulevard*, or David Fincher with *Fight Club*—overnarration can produce the same kind of intimacy first person does in fiction, even though the point of view routinely shifts to a more omniscient perspective in scenes lacking the narrative voice-over. And its pitfalls are similar to those of fiction first person: the tendency to tell, not show.

Although a subjective camera can provide a sense similar to first person in prose, its effect soon begins to feel contrived. Had Humphrey Bogart in *Dark Passage* not gotten his face job, the audience would have wearied of the tunnel-vision effect produced by the subjective camera, and secretly yearned for Agnes Moorhead to steal the movie.

But camera placement is often more of a visual or contextual consideration than one involving character, and most producers and directors do not want screenwriters dictating camera angles. Point of view in the sense we've been discussing is instead determined by whose objective in the scene commands the greatest dramatic force. That's a function of where we are in the story or, more simply, which character is the focus of the scene's opening or most important image or action.

Exercises

1. Take three novels and ask the three key questions addressed at the outset of this chapter: Why is this story being told? Who has authority to tell it? What effect does the point of view achieve? How would the story be different if told from a different point of view?

2. Take a self-contained section from a piece you're currently writing and again ask those same three key questions. Have you chosen the point-of-view character wisely? Who else might step forward and assume

that role? How does that change alter the quality of the telling? What events are now difficult or impossible to narrate because the point-of-view character isn't in them?

3. Using the same work in progress as for exercise 2, change the point of view from third to first, or vice versa. What has changed? Does the difference improve anything, dull an effect, enhance it, create greater or lesser intimacy with the point-of-view character, evoke naturalness in the telling?

4. Take a section from a first-person story or novel and look for transitions from subjective to objective modality, or vice versa. How does the transition work, what is the tonal effect of the movement, how does the language change, if at all? Does it feel convincing or leave you puzzled? In either case, why? Do the same for a story or novel section in the third person.

5. Compare your results from exercise 4 for first and third person. Did you notice any particular difference in how transitions were handled? What were they? How did the distinct approaches to transition underscore the advantages or limitations of the point of view used?

6. Take a novel in the omniscient point of view—*Tess of the d'Urbervilles*, by Thomas Hardy, for example, or Jane Austen's *Sense and Sensibility*, or Ann Patchett's *Bel Canto*—and locate those sections that most conspicuously feel "omniscient," i.e., from the point of view of an all-knowing intelligence. How unique or

characteristic is the voice? How distinct is that voice from those of the characters? How could the omniscient point of view be rewritten as multiple third person? What would you miss?

7. Take a film or TV script and analyze its first five scenes from the perspective of point of view. How many points of view are there? Are there too many? Does the focus seem scattered or simply ambitious? What are the various ways point of view is established in the scenes—i.e., how do you know which character is the central focus of the scene?

Chapter Twenty-four
Language as Attitude: Voice

Establishing Authorial Voice

Voice forms perhaps the most mercurial of all the attributes
of writing. It's the hardest to get one's mind around, the most
elusive to develop in one's own writing, and the most difficult
to teach. It incorporates style (diction and rhythm), worldview
(choice of topic, time, setting, and approach to that subject
matter) and attitude (blithely comic, bitterly satiric, ironic,
tragic, nihilistic, fatalistic, philosophical, and so on). It's the
expression of your unique humanity through words.

Though voice is a subtle, sneaky, almost intangible
thing, specific to you and your writing, there are in fact
exercises that can help you develop it. One can be found in
James Frey's *How to Write a Damn Good Novel*, though I
originally learned of the technique from writer and ex-
boxer Floyd Salas.

Salas taught himself to write by typing out entire books,
including *Crime and Punishment*, and he did this back in the

day of the typewriter. The hammering rhythm of pounding out those words, those sentences, those pages helped him develop an internal sense of rhythm, style, and syntax that stayed with him when he composed his own work.

Frey's exercise is not quite so laborious, though it's essentially the same. He advises his students who feel their voice is vague or weak to take the writing of an author they admire—and over time, several such authors—and for a half hour every morning copy out a section from one of their stories or books. Frey states with no small amount of astonishment that he has seen students' command of voice blossom through use of this technique. Again, it's the combination of imitation followed by your own creative effort that gradually hones an inner sense of your own true voice.

Another way to go about it is to read a section from a cherished author, then go to your desk and try to re-create it from memory, with no glances at the original for reference. You will learn a great deal about not just your memory, but how you form your impressions, how you recall them, and what language you have at your disposal to portray and dramatize them.

These exercises create of a kind of golem in the mind, a stand-in for the author or authors whose work you admire. As you internalize their prose you embody them as a kind of internal critic or reader. Joseph Chaikin in *The Presence of the Actor* remarked on the importance of personalizing the audience, placing someone in the seats who was both supportive and demanding, inspiring your best work. He never went onstage without imagining Martin Luther King Jr. in attendance, for this always created a desire to give everything he had to his performance.

Chaikin likened this to Shakespeare's admission he wrote for kings, and Shaw's that he wrote for philosophers. When I'm rewriting, I often read a section from a favorite author before turning to my own pages, to make sure I rise to the level I believe I should—in essence, turning the other author into an imagined reader. As much as writers may claim to write for themselves, doing so risks shoddy work. Only by writing for others, by trying to make sure the story is told clearly and compellingly *to someone else*, especially someone we respect, do we avoid the kind of self-indulgent, dishonest, or just slipshod mistakes that typify mediocrity. As I've said elsewhere, you don't know yourself by yourself. This is no less true of writers than their characters.

Don't fear becoming imitative through efforts such as these. The risks of your being able to perfectly mimic someone else's writing are minimal unless you have a plagiarist's soul. The best writing advice I ever received came encapsulated in two words from Oakley Hall: *Steal wisely.* Part of the wisdom in this sort of theft is that you can't steal another's voice. You can only develop your own. Or not.

Although voice is less of a factor in film and TV than in fiction, it's hardly absent. It's what distinguishes *The Wire* from *The Shield*, *Breaking Bad* from *Modern Family*, or the film scripts of Tony Gilroy (*The Bourne Identity*, *Delores Claiborne*, *Michael Clayton*) from those of Diablo Cody (*Juno*, *Jennifer's Body*, *Young Adult*). The distinctions very much incorporate worldview and attitude, not just style, and that means voice. And using the same exercises as for fiction but with scripts instead of books you'll be able over time to see your own voice develop.

Voice in the Portrayal of Character

In discussing multiple third person in the previous chapter, I noted how it's important to craft the individual-point-of-view characters in such a way that they have distinct voices that the reader can identify, to help identify whose perspective commands the stage. This is akin to an orchestral composer with a distinctive compositional style crafting solos for particular instruments—the oboe, the trumpet, the violin—so that the soloists' efforts both stand out and yet never betray the tone of the piece as a whole. Sam Shepard once remarked that he crafted the roles in his plays by thinking of a jazz combo, with one character standing in for the piano, the other the sax, another the drums or the bass, and so forth.

I find the musical analogy helpful, and it's one I use in trying to make sure I keep my point-of-view characters distinct. But it's not just the sound of the words that makes a difference in distinguishing one character from another. Just as with authorial voice, style combines with worldview and attitude to make up the character's voice.

In particular, attitude is crucial. Often an "attitude adjustment"—making the character more opinionated, less patient, more forgiving, less dour—will instantly turn up the treble, ease back on the bass, fatten the middle, or even cast these qualities in a much different timbre. Giving the other characters, especially those sharing a scene, a similar attitude adjustment, so that their demeanors differ from the first character and each other, can help provide the combo effect I've described.

You can see this kind of variety in the following examples from *Do They Know I'm Running?* The characters, in order, are a nameless rancher on the Mexican border; Roque Montalvo, an eighteen-year-old Salvadoran American; and Godo, Roque's twenty-year-old brother, a badly wounded Iraq War vet. First the rancher:

> It was daybreak and the rancher, standing at his kitchen window, watched two silhouettes stagger forward through the desert scrub. One clutched the other but they both seemed hurt. The porch light, the rancher thought, that's the thing they been walking toward all night. See it for miles. All the way from the footpaths snaking through the mountains out of Mexico.

We're looking out the window with this man, we're even in his thoughts, and the clipped, laconic language of those thoughts is clearly his. And yet we feel a certain distance, not just because of the hardness of the language, the simple syntax, but due to the fact he's "the rancher," and does not possess a name. Despite the elements of closeness— his visual perspective, his thoughts—we remain at a slight remove, and this contributes to how we engage with him on the page.

Next, we have Roque:

> Roque sat up in the predawn stillness, startled awake by a nasty dream: menacing dog, desolate twilight, the sticky dampness of blood and a sense he was carrying some kind of treasure, something he'd have to

fight to keep. Rising on one elbow, he glanced past Mariko toward the bedside clock. Three-thirty, the hour of ghosts. Rubbing the sleep from his eyes, he told himself it was time to go.

In sharp contrast to the rancher's hardened shell, we see Roque on softer, more interior terms, in accordance with his grogginess, his dreams, his intimations of death.

Next, there's the young ex-marine:

What the whole thing gets down to, Godo thought, head tilted back, draining the last few drips from the can—the trick to it, as it were, the pissy little secret no one wants you to know? He crushed the empty and tossed it onto the floor where it clattered among the others, then belched, backhanding his scarred lips to wipe them dry. Figure it out, ca-brón: The whole thing gets down to knowing which guilt you can live with.

The cynical anger defines Godo in the same way the stoic directness defines the rancher and a dreamish, bad-boy sensuality defines Roque. Since they're half brothers, that bad-boy element is shared between Roque and Godo, but because Roque can still indulge it, he's not as bitter as the disfigured Godo.

The distinctiveness of voice extends to descriptions of the physical environment, since in each case we're evaluat-ing the scene from the point-of-view character's perspec-tive. Consider the following descriptions of setting, again from the rancher's, Roque's, and Godo's points of view, respectively:

> Rooster lurched at the end of his chain, hackles up, that snarl in his bark, trying to warn the strangers off. They just kept coming. All right then, he thought. Not like you wanted this. He set his coffee in the sink and went to the door leading out to the porch and collected the shotgun kept there, racked a shell into the chamber, stepped outside.
>
> Streamers of cloud laced the sky, pale to the east, purplish dark to the west. A cold parched wind keened in the telephone wires. The landscape bristled with nopal, saguaro, cholla. Black ancient ironwood cropped up here and there among the mesquite and Joshua trees.

> He launched up and headed for the door, kicking several tea candles across the floor like little tin pucks. Wood-plank shelves faced each other down the dark hallway, stacked with unfired pots, bowls, vases: Mariko Detwiler, Fine Ceramics. The clay smelled cold and damp and it made him think of fresh graves and with that another song lyric teased its way up from memory: *The house is dark and my thoughts are cold.*
>
> He thumped down the porch steps, the fog cool on his skin, the air dank from the nearby wetlands. Lingering beneath the chinaberry tree in

the dark front yard, he watched as the hallway light came on and her silhouette materialized in the doorway. Timidly he ventured a farewell wave. She did not wave back.

The rabbit-eared TV flickered across the room. Nothing to watch at this hour, of course, just news any idiot could see through, no-name reruns. He'd squelched the sound, only to conjure not silence but the usual holocaust zoo tramping through his brain.

Focus on the physical, he reminded himself—the moment, as they say. The doughy mattress sighed beneath his weight. Armpit stench and foot funk added a manly tang. The rest of him was a wreck. He'd been hard and sleek after basic, plenty of PT, then hulking around the scalding desert with seventy pounds of gear, buffed and brutal. Now? A hundred-eighty pounds of discharge, a mess in the bed, a hash of scars weepy with some nagging infection.

The rancher speaks with the hard edges and clipped tempo of a man who's lived in the desert all his life. His attitude is observant, skeptical, and protective but not harsh or hateful. Roque betrays his coltish youth and rashness, and his rhythm is syncopated, underscoring his being a musician, but there is also a softness in the sounds near the end, to reflect his romantic sentimentality, his desire for Mariko to call him back. Godo jangles and crackles, and

more than either of the others his attitude jumps to the fore
to define him—bitter but not without humor, sad but smart,
a young warrior reduced to victimhood and hating it.

One of the main causes of inconsistent characterization is wanting to say something through a character for
whom it's ill-suited. The author's turned the character into
a puppet by being too wedded to a particular phrase, response, theme, or action. Such a writer thinks: But the
story requires it. That may well be true, but then it's necessary to reflect deeply on how and why this particular
character is the one who must say or do what's required, so
she can rise to the occasion. Ground yourself in the story
and see the problem through the characters' eyes.

In film and TV, you will have only actions and dialog
to define a specific character's distinctive voice, and so the
need for precision and economy is all the more enhanced.
You may need to draft scenes you don't use in the script, or
even sections of free-form prose, to gain a full feeling
for the character's voice so you can cherry-pick the best for
your screenplay, or use it as a springboard for a scene. Using the same three characters I've used as examples above,
you can tell from the way the rancher thinks how he'll talk.
Roque's storming out only to stop and wait to see if Mariko
calls him back goes to his essence as much as his thoughts
and impressions. And Godo's scarred face, his crumpling
beer cans and tossing them into a mounting pile while
watching mindless insomniac TV, the disdain and bitterness with which he regards his war-scarred body—all of this
informs us of his attitude, and how he'll sound and act once
his time to do so arrives.

Once you gain control of your own authorial voice, crafting the voices of characters will come naturally with practice. Using empathy, you'll slip into their personas, and just as the words came to you as author, they'll come to you as character.

Exercises

1. Who would you identify as your ideal reader if you were hoping to feel inspired to do your best work? Your father? Your favorite teacher? A friend you trust? A writer you admire? A statesman you revere? Christ? Satan?

2. What five works would you choose to copy if you were to follow James Frey's advice and copy out the text for a half hour each morning?

3. Review those five books for how voice is controlled to establish character. What distinguishes the voice of each character? The style of their word choice? The musicality and rhythm of their diction? The specific beliefs and fears that comprise their worldview? The snarl or song in their attitude?

4. Do the same for a piece you're currently working on. Assess your characters in terms of style, worldview, attitude. What could you do to enhance their characterization and to distinguish one from the other? How could you give them an "attitude adjustment" and enhance their distinctiveness?

Chapter Twenty-five
Word as Deed: Dialog

Dialog as Action

The screenwriter Waldo Salt wrote his dialog last, prefer-ring to lay out the dramatic movement and the key images in a scene before letting the characters speak. The playwright Harold Pinter remarked that his plays were invariably about silence, whether that silence took the form of no words at all, which he considered a kind of nakedness, or a self-concealing barrage of language. What both of these statements get at is the fundamental truth of dialog: There is something be-neath the words that is the real issue, and that subterranean something always reveals a push and pull of battling need.

Characters are not shooting the breeze in dialog, they're doing things to each other: persuading, teasing, mocking, challenging, probing, flattering, badgering, begging, deceiving, manipulating, pampering, scolding.

In every line, the characters are jockeying for status, trying to be seen and heard on their own terms. They're asserting or claiming or surrendering power. They're stumbling through a haze of misunderstanding. They're hiding from the truth. They're peeling back a deception. They're making sure, double-checking. They're confiding a terrible secret, or blowing smoke.

This is what is meant by *subtext*. To get dialog right you have to know what's going on beneath the words, beneath what's being said. The more you own what's stirring in the silence under the dialog—the respective rank of the speakers, their feelings about each other and where they are and what they're doing, the string of events that brought them here, where they hope to get to next—the more powerfully you can render what's happening between them in their actual dialog. And the words the characters use may contradict the subtext, they often do, but you'll show what's really at stake through their actions, or through unexpressed thoughts, incidentals, unconscious slips of the tongue, gestures, hints, contradictions.

Even monologues exhibit some sort of action—almost all of Shakespeare's end in a change of heart or a resolution to act.

And yet the action of dialog is verbal, and people do more than act when they speak. They reveal their background through regional dialect or idiom; educational level through syntax and grammar and word choice; mental or emotional state through urgency or reticence, as well as rhythm, fragmentation, coherence; inner life through slips of the tongue, mistakes, inadvertent admissions, and more. They reveal their comfort with aggression, their fondness for self-display, their prejudices, their shyness, their wit, their spite. The work you do in plumbing a character's physical, psychological, and sociological nature will all come to the fore in crafting her dialog. It's the principal way inner life escapes into the outer world.

But dialog doesn't just escape, it betrays what it left behind. We build up expectations concerning a character's mental or emotional disposition through the course of the action, but then suddenly she rejects that expectation and does or says something stunningly candid, even shamelessly wrong. Again, one of the best tools for revealing the unconscious is through contradiction, and dialog is a mean little tool for that.

Dialog must be rooted in character. It's not about what the writer believes ought to be said or the reader or audience needs to know or what the story seems to require at this particular juncture, but what the characters in the black recesses of their hearts want or need to say.

When going back to revise your dialog, it's crucial to dissect the underlying actions and determine what the characters are trying to do to each other, in order to weed out the inessential, strengthen what remains. And dialog is the one area of your writing that will require revision more than any other, because it has to accomplish so many things at once: Push the action, provide information, reveal character, echo previous revelations, foreshadow coming events. It's this multiplicity of functions that makes writing dialog so demanding—combined with the fact that it must sound natural, while not falling into the trap of mimicking actual speech.

Verisimilitude and Its Limits

No writer worthy of the name hasn't overheard a bit of talk between people out in the world and rushed to jot it down before he forgot it. And all too often, once he got to his desk and tried to work it into a scene, he found himself shoehorning it in, first one place then another, wondering why it seemed so hard to make fit.

Dialog is not speech. It needs to sound real without being real. It's more compressed and less repetitious, less circular, less banal than real speech. Tape a conversation between you and your friends and then transcribe it. As dialog, it's largely worthless, except as an object lesson in what not to do.

Dialog must capture in written words the brusque, canny, mellifluous inflections of real speech without its baggage. Ironically, the most effective way to do this is often to *leave things out*. Even at its punchiest, real speech is often needlessly repetitive. Dialog risks tedium by echoing this excess.

Dialog uses teasing, wit, insults, mockery, understatement, and exaggeration as forms of indirection, and indirection is valuable because of the crucial role of subtext. You're substituting one thing for another, and the result, by being unexpected, actually enhances the emotional impact. The surprise allows the reader to discover the emotion, rather than simply being told.

The power of Hemingway's "Hills Like White Elephants" is precisely in its use of indirection, the glancing blows both the man and woman make to the matter at hand—her pregnancy. Neither mentions it or the abortion the man is proposing, and they stake out their positions haltingly, provisionally, but with no lack of earnestness. He hides behind concern for her, and almost treats her as a kind of invalid or a truculent child. She sees right through him and resents his trumped-up solicitude but has not yet made a decision. They literally talk both right at and right past each other, and the reader suffers the same sense of commingled immediacy and distance as they struggle to reach some kind of truce.

But even though there are some aspects of actual speech that can lend realism to your dialog, you can only learn so much about crafting dialog from listening to people talk. The real study requires close attention to writers who do it well. This subtle, sneaky little truth lies at the heart of all dialog: To learn how to write it, one must read, not listen.

You need to glean from your own favorite authors how they manage the thing. There are no better teachers, in the end, than the writers you admire. Modern American authors known for their skill in dialog include Philip Roth, Joan Didion, Elmore Leonard, and Richard Price—to name a very selective few. As I remarked in the previous chapter, we learn from the writers we hold in high regard until our own voices gel.

Specific Techniques for Enhancing Realism

Where real speech can be most instructive, ironically, is in how it seems to break down.

Subtext forces us to look to the underlying motives, needs, wants, and actions swimming beneath the surface of the words. Although people often have hidden agendas in everyday speech, they're seldom as conscious of them as you will need to be in crafting your dialog.

And since the characters are contesting, blocking, countering each other's goals, there is often a halting, stop-and-start quality to dialog that beginners often miss. Remember

that each character has her own objective. Rather than respond to the first character, the second character may press
her own point, pursuing her own goal, and it may have little or nothing to do with what the first character tried to
get across.

A great deal of bad dialog is either dueling pronouncements or a kind of verbal tennis, in which each volley gets
answered by the next. This soon becomes labored and artificial, like the singsong back-and-forth between a teacher
and her star pupil. Characters must move the dialog forward, and this is often done by assuming the answer to the
preceding line and pushing on to the next point:

> "Why fight the will if there's a goddamn no-
> contest clause?"
> "This lawyer Johnny knows, he walks into
> court, the judge automatically figures the case is
> good. That's the rep he's got."

The second speaker blows past the question and the
first speaker's anger, assuming the answer—you can get
past a no-contest clause if a judge is willing to hear the
matter and not just toss it out—and moves on to the next
point: His friend Johnny knows a lawyer who can get the
judge to lean his way.

Sometimes a speaker rushes ahead of herself and skips
a section of what she meant to say. For example, instead of
saying, "Don't talk to me about spending myself into the
poorhouse. I won't take it, Jimmy, not from you," the speaker
might say (especially if upset), "Don't talk to me about
spending. No. Not from you." It seems angular, clipped,

even wrong, but it clues us in to the character in a way the full sentences don't.

Remember too that people cut each other off, they don't listen, they talk over each other. The result: truncated sentences, tangents, nonsequiturs. If used wisely, judiciously, and not too often, these tactics can provide a sense of realism. Used to excess, they quickly seem affected.

One common sentence fragment heard in real speech and increasingly seen in written dialog is the subjectless sentence, especially in questions: *Going over to the school tonight? Like me to take that for you?* This is informal and can be used to suggest familiarity, terseness, or limited schooling. It can also be used for contrast if the other character speaks more formally: *Are you going to the school tonight? Would you like me to take that for you?*

Other techniques that can enhance a sense of realism if not used to excess include:

Changing the subject: This is a principal way for one character to ignore what the other said, either because he's not interested, he has something more pressing he wants to talk about, or he's trying to avoid the implications of what the first speaker is saying. The new tack in the conversation becomes an obstacle the first speaker has to overcome to continue pursuing the conversational objective and not get sidetracked or stonewalled.

Giving unsolicited advice: When one character is trying to get a point across, having the other give him unwanted advice feels like being ignored, slathered with phony good intentions.

Topping the other person's story: Instead of just ignoring what the first speaker said, the second speaker minimizes it by going one better. "That's nothing, you should've seen what happened to me the other night." In one fell swoop, the second speaker has, perhaps inadvertently, invalidated and demeaned the first.

Finishing the other character's sentences: This again is a status play, demeaning the other character by subconsciously insinuating that what he has to say is obvious or unimportant.

Interpreting what the other character is saying: This often starts out as, "Are you trying to tell me . . ." or "Let me see if I've got this straight." This is different than paraphrasing the other character, which can be a way of trying to understand. This is a way for one character to say he knows what the other character was trying to say better than she does.

Fixing the other character's feelings: This comes out as: "It'll work out, you'll see . . . Why get so upset? . . . You're not crying are you?" This can seem like empathy, but it's a brush-off, a means of shutting down a troubling or revealing admission or turn in the conversation.

Asking a question, then not listening to the answer: If this has never happened to you, you're lucky indeed. It often comes across as a character wanting to seem interested when he really isn't. The question is a pose, not a real desire for information.

In the martial art known as dialog, all of these techniques are preemptive attacks, blocking maneuvers, dodges, or feints. Put to good use, they can add realism to dialog, but like anything else, they can also seem forced or overly clever if unmotivated.

Speech Tags

It is currently accepted practice that "reporting clauses" (as linguists call them) or "speech tags" (as editors typically refer to them) should be limited as much as possible to: he said, she said, Robert said, Rowena said, et cetera. The reason for this is because "said" is all but invisible on the page, barely registering in the mind, and thus does not stop the reader from following the flow of the dialog. If variety is needed, the words "replied" and "responded" are not too intrusive; "noted" gets close.

Inverting that order—for example, said he, said Mary—can be used for comic effect and at times for variety, but it quickly seems arched and false, very much so if overused.

Words that describe the volume of the words are often more necessary at the lower decibels—whisper, murmur, mutter—than at the higher. An exclamation point can automatically identify a scream or a shout, even a bellow, and distinguishing among them often amounts to oversalting the gravy.

Words such as "cried," "stated," "demanded," "snarled," "hissed," "retorted," "declared," "enjoined," "protested"—not to mention the infamous Ex Brothers: "exclaimed," "expostulated," "exhorted"—are considered archaic (they died with D. H. Lawrence) or the sign of a novice writer. They too can sometimes be used for comic or ironic effect, but sparing use even in these instances is wise.

Worse are words that slip an action into the mix— "jeered," "chuckled," "smiled," "sneered." Try chuckling and talking at the same time. There's a word for it: coughing.

American writers, working forevermore in the shadow of Hemingway, are also routinely advised to avoid the use of adverbs in speech tags: she said caringly, he said sardonically, Jane said earnestly, Sam said facetiously. They routinely draw too much attention to themselves and thus distract from the dialog itself, and are often unnecessary. Whatever freight the adverb is carrying, the dialog itself should bear.

That said, I have attended panels with British writer David Hewson and Scottish writer Denise Mina on which this American obsession has been belabored, and I've watched their jaws sag in disbelief. Mina, after enduring ten minutes of this harangue, finally took the microphone and quipped in her feathery brogue, "I'd like to stick up for adverbs."

Even wise rules are meant to be broken, but the infraction must be equally wise. Some adverbs work better than others, for they get at relatively subtle or conflicted states of mind—wryly, smartly, blandly, wickedly—but even then I often go back and find I can do without them. Where they work best is when they convey what the dialog itself does not:

"A perfect fit," she said wryly.
"You've never looked lovelier," he said wickedly.
"My dear drunk mother has arrived," she said blandly.
"I love you," he said bitterly.

Such adverbs will be necessary or not depending on how much context alone establishes the contradiction or irony. If so, cut. (My general rule: When in doubt, leave it out.)

A much better way to go about the whole business is to use beats—brief bits of action or setting or stage business—instead of attributions, as long as doing so doesn't become clumsy or labored. The advantage of this technique is that it roots the scene in its context—the time and place, the emotional and logistical background. It's amazing how often writers focus solely on talking heads, as though the room, the temperature, the time of day—even what the characters are wearing—all magically vanished. At best one or the other character sighs, looks off, meets the other's gaze, bites a lip, tucks a strand of hair behind an ear. This grows wearisome, like a litany of tics.

The propulsion of the dialog may carry the scene by itself, and where it can, let it. If one or the other character hesitates, reflects, or the rhythm of the scene for some other reason calls for a momentary pause, insert an action or a momentary notice of the surroundings by the character whose speech is being interrupted, or who is about to speak or has just spoken.

Note the use of context to identify the speakers and also to exploit setting in the following scene:

She stirred finally, burrowing her face into the pillow to stifle a yawn. Lifting her head, she whispered over her shoulder, eyes glistening with sleep: "It's you."

He took a moment to study her profile in the dim light, the distinctive shape of her eye, the girlish lashes, the pudgy nose. "You were expecting . . . ?"

She blinked herself further awake, moaned. "Hope springs eternal." She barked a raspy cough into her fist.

Roque waited. "Oh yeah?"

"Tell you what—do me a favor, before you go?" She wiggled her can.

The musk from their earlier lovemaking still lingered, mixed with the vaguely floral tang of cold wax from a dozen tea candles scattered across the hardwood floor, their flames spent. "Just go back to sleep," he said, recalling the scene from earlier, tiny tongues of fire all around as they thrashed and rocked and cried out, shadows quivering high up the bare white walls. Mariko, a Buddhist, had a flair for the ceremonial.

"No, I mean it." Her voice was fogged with drowsiness and she writhed luxuriously in a kind of half stretch, burying another yawn in the pillow. "It's okay."

"It feels, I dunno, wrong. You half asleep, I mean."

"For God's sake, Roque, it's all wrong. That's what makes it so delicious."

Sure, of course, that's what this is. Wrong. He shook it off. "You know what I'm saying."

She flipped over, blinking herself awake, finger-parting the tousled black hair framing her boxy face. "There. Awake. Better?"

"Don't be mad."

"Who says I'm mad?"

"I just—"

"Shush. Kiss me."

Another technique is to construct a subplot, some parallel event in the setting that somehow reflects on what is being said between the main characters, and have it run in the background so that one or both of the characters notice as the dialog proceeds.

For example, imagine a couple having an argument in a café, and the man is watching a lone young woman across the room. He thinks she's waiting for someone, a lover—her relationship is beginning while his is falling apart. But then she begins glancing at her watch, peering out the window. Her lover has stood her up. These observations affect the man's interaction with his own girlfriend—he chooses his words not just to reply to something she's said or to state his own mind, but as a reflection of what he's thinking about this stranger. They're in the same shoes. In that moment, he almost feels more for her than for the woman across the table, and not just because the latter so clearly finds him lacking. Finally the young stranger shoulders her bag, steps out onto the sidewalk, squints into the sun. She's been abandoned, he thinks, as I will be shortly.

THE ART OF CHARACTER

But then someone rushes up, breathless, apologetic: the young woman's mother, with dog in tow. He had it all wrong, a realization he makes just as his lover, once again, ridicules his narcissistic self-absorption.

Dialect, Obscenities, and Verbal Tics

Dialect is best used sparingly, with as few apostrophes as possible—for example, "runnin" instead of "runnin'." Double negatives ("He don't live nowhere round here") and the word "ain't" quickly lose effectiveness if used unwisely. Excess not just in words but in "expressiveness" often just focuses too much attention on stylization at the cost of meaning.

Obscenities wear thin on the page far more quickly than they do in real speech, even if uttered by a nun. As much as possible, try to make the dialog powerful without them, and if you use them, make them count.

As discussed in chapter 16, sometimes verbal tics—*Oh my God, Get outta town, Listen to this, Know what I mean?*—can help color a character's speech. Used judiciously, they identify the character and provide a gratifying echo for the reader. Again, however, like most bells and whistles, all too soon they begin to grate.

Creating Variety Among Characters

Especially in scenes with multiple characters, it's often necessary or desirable to create variety or contrast between speakers in dialog, something that can be difficult when the characters are of similar class, education, or experience—classmates or siblings, for example.

In orchestrating how the speakers will vie for space on the page, remember what it is they're trying to get in the scene, and let them loose. What they're after will often crystallize their manner, even if they're trying hard to conceal it. This can often even eliminate the need for speech tags, because the characters will be so readily identifiable by what they want and how they're going about it through their speech.

There is perhaps no better example of how to modulate and make unique a variety of voices, each singular in its own way while being part of a largely homogenous community—family and friends together for the Christmas holiday—than James Joyce's "The Dead." If "Hills Like White Elephants" can teach you everything you need to know about subtext, "The Dead" can teach you everything you need to know about orchestrating a large group of characters.

Basically, the key lies in each character's attitude, specifically the fears or needs or misgivings that define each one distinctly and that contrast with the general lightheartedness of the party—Gabriel with his desire not to seem pompous, Gretta with her sadly elegant confidence, Lily with her put-upon gruffness, Mr. Browne's earthy improprieties with the ladies, Aunt Kate's fretful dread that Freddy Malins will turn up "screwed" (drunk—which of course he does). Once they are introduced so vividly we have no problem picturing and hearing them as the festivities progress, and the emotions of the evening swell and recede.

Last, don't forget Sam Shepard's advice from the previous chapter, about thinking of the characters as various players in a duo, trio, quartet, quintet, each with his own sonic quality and tempo. Who's the piano in this scene, who's the bass, who gets to pound out the beat on the drums or add an accent on the snare?

Exercises

1. Take a section of dialog that you particularly admire from a book that has influenced you as a writer. Break down the scene in terms of each character's objective, obstacle, and the various adjustments he employs to circumvent or overcome the obstacle and continue pursuing his objective. How does the character's dialog reflect the objective, obstacle, and adjustments? How is his attitude reflected in the dialog? What elements of fear, joy, shame, guilt, pride, sorrow, or other emotional states come out during the scene? What elements of the character's backstory does the dialog reveal? How are his educational level, regional background, economic station, moral or political disposition, work or profession, community or church expressed in his dialog?

2. Do the same sort of breakdown analysis for a scene you're currently writing.

3. Take the same scene as in exercise 2 and use at least three of the techniques for enhancing realism in the dialog. How did you get the technique to conform to each character's objective? How did that change the dynamic of the scene or the portrayal of the characters?

4. Take a longer section of dialog you've written and re-move all the speech tags. Are the speakers still readily identifiable? If not, how could you use beats, setting, or description instead of speech tags to solve this problem?

5. Take a multicharacter dialog scene from a book or script and analyze what distinct vocal and attitude mannerisms are used to identify and render unique each individual.

EPILOGUE
The Examined Life Redux:
Our Characters, Our Selves

As I noted in our discussion of contradictions, Denis Diderot in his novel *Rameau's Nephew* disputed the notion of a distinct and singular human personality. He considered this a holdover from the days of superstition—it smacked of a soul and other discardable pieties. Using as a mouthpiece a fictionalized version of the composer Rameau—who was constantly obliged to curry favor with patrons, placate audiences, appease musicians, hold off creditors, sweet-talk paramours—Diderot argued that we assume a given role depending on the social circumstances we face, with completely contradictory roles required in different places at different times. Instead of being steadfast and certain—our "true nature," or the image of God—human character more resembles a swarm of bees, comprised of dozens, even hundreds of individual poses or personas swirling around a void.

This disturbing idea, that there is a strange insubstantiality, a kind of lack of gravity at the very heart of our lives, hardly vanished with Diderot. Nietzsche famously remarked: "The doer is just a fiction added to the deed—the deed is everything." Heidegger believed in a self but he argued it was an accomplishment, not a gift; it's something we do, not find. Sartre, with his famous dictum "existence precedes essence," dismissed any notion of a fundamental self, believing like Heidegger that we create our identities through the daily struggles of life. Only a pinhole of nothingness—consciousness, a kind of watchful disembodied "I"—resides at the center.

Sartre's nothingness resembles the Buddhist concept of No Self, which in its faceless, bodiless calm escapes the ravages of desire. In Buddhism the sense of inescapable need or want is referred to as *lack*—or, more colorfully, *feeding the hungry ghosts*. The lack is really caused by a desire to anchor consciousness in the physical world, which is impossible. And so we try to appease this hunger, this lack, through the usual worldly gratifications: power, wealth, love, sex, glory, pleasure. But this only exacerbates the appetite, like trying to quench one's thirst with salt water.

As my characters begin to feel more solid to me, more vivid and free and real, I sometimes experience that same sense of immateriality that Diderot and Sartre and the Buddhists describe. No matter how firm my grasp on who I think I am, another "me" hovers in the background, watching, appraising, keeping track.

Though this anchorless sense of self isn't so extreme I'm afraid I might wake up one day to discover I've turned into a cockroach, I do at times feel a little south of steadfast. Something's in play. If not my persona, my identity, my soul, then what? And yet who's asking this question if not "me"?

In one form or another this debate has gone on since the beginning of human time, and we've encountered it several times in several ways in this book. On the one hand, we feel committed to the moral gravity and claim to responsibility of a core human personality. On the other, there's this nagging sense that by and large we conform ourselves to whatever situation we face, knowingly or not. We're afflicted with unconscious impulses we barely understand and that all too often come out of nowhere. We contradict ourselves. We fall short of our hopes and expectations and even betray our better selves. Under scrutiny, the whole notion of a core personality begins to seem more like an ideal than a reality. Perhaps with focus and discipline we can move closer to that mirror image at the back of the mind, the idealized self. It's not an entirely misbegotten aspiration, unless it curdles into a need for perfection from ourselves and everyone around us.

Put another way: Do we discover ourselves or create ourselves? It's an issue we addressed in chapter 1, but with respect to the characters on the page, not our own personalities. What does it mean to ask the same question of oneself? Who's asking, and who gets to decide which answer is right?

Every notion of mankind that conjectures immutable laws of behavior—whether it comes from Platonic idealism, textual theology, scientific determinism, or your aunt Maude—stumbles over the idea of freedom. If everything is already predetermined—same as it ever was—how can our indecision, our anxiety, our planning, our choices be anything but illusion, the drama of our ignorance?

This tension between eternal truth and mortal freedom

has confounded minds great and small since the invention of the thinking cap. On the one hand, philosophers like Nietzsche, Heidegger, and Sartre argue that no man has access to a transcendental plane of unquestionable truth, and so life—and identity, character—is fundamentally an ongoing dress rehearsal. We can't discover ourselves, there's nothing there to discover. We create ourselves through the day-to-day invention of our lives.

But then how to account for conscience, that sense of shame at being inauthentic: Is this just one false persona calling another a liar? Would it be so devastating if that were true?

As a writer you shape a coherence of self through the establishment of your distinctive voice, but even that, I'm sure you'll find, will prove eerily fluid, and will require attention to control. There will be days when you write "off-key." Absent mindful concentration, the fluidity of character you'll feel, the dance of veils inside your psyche, can create an unsettling lack of gravity, a sense that you might be as beholden to folly as the Hollywood movie stars whom Jim Harrison mocks when he reminds us that we don't get to be anyone but ourselves.

But is that true, and if so, in what sense? Undeniably, I develop habits and history and the girl at the checkout counter recognizes me. I don't take a wrong turn off the freeway and discover I've just become Winston Churchill. But I'm not carved in stone, either. I remain a bit of a mystery, or at least a moving target, right up until the end.

Something wondrous and strange happens within our own hearts and minds as we push our characters to their unforeseen limits. As we test them, shake them, destroy and rejuvenate them, something similar takes place within ourselves. Our own understanding of risk, the stakes in our daily existence, the need for boldness and courage and skill, deepens. Imagined life is not life in the world but we can't imagine a hero's struggle without some understanding of what that means in our own lives. The unexamined life is not worth living, but the examined life must not just bear up under the scrutiny but be worthy of it. The writer's experience informs her characters but they in turn inform her. In a sneaky, subtle, important way, I become who I imagine.

Once again, it may sound like I'm proposing a kind of willful unhinging of your sanity. I'm not. I am suggesting, however, that though the anchor of the self can feel reassuring, like the solidity of the body or the certainty of your name, that doesn't make it real. Life is filled with reassuring fictions. And just as we saw how the Tyranny of Motive locks a character into a falsely limited set of behaviors, so the comforting notion of I Know Who I Am may serve cops and waitresses, politicians and panhandlers, cardiologists and fullbacks and airline pilots and second-story men, but for an artist it's shabby, lackluster, limiting. It suggests an end point, a triumphal self-definition prior to death, and as morally gratifying as that may seem, it's a fundamentally anticreative viewpoint.

Just as you must untether your characters from predictability by granting them the freedom to contradict themselves, to grow, to change, so you must grant yourself a similar freedom to play the trickster, shift at will, embrace the unexpected, be free. Your life is the palette for the canvas of your art. Be daring. Or be dull.

But if everything's an exploration, nothing's wrong. That swarm of bees still lacks a conscience, or need of one. How to reconcile this fancy-pants idea of the fundamentally creative life with rent due, a kid on the rug, a spouse waiting for an answer?

We do not live alone, and life among others requires responsibility. In fact, it's precisely the act of creating *among others* that alerts us to that curious truth we've touched on more than once: *We don't know ourselves by ourselves.* Identity is not just creative and provisional, it's communal, and that's what makes it honest. A writer who writes for himself is scribbling for a ghost. The reader anchors the writer to the reality they share, which lies on the page. Call it a contract, if that helps. But the reader keeps us honest, if we're aiming high enough. Conformity can kill, spiritually for sure, and yes, integrity matters. But there's always someone who taught you that. Write for them if no one else.

Just as our characters grow through conflict, through the tension of needing something, wanting something—encouraged by the lucky support of some, hounded by the relentless opposition of others—so we discover the limits of what we can and can't do through action and interaction, struggle and perseverance. Reflection and emotion provide guidance and context, but a direction is not a destination. We are what we do, and we're shaped not just by the effect of our actions on ourselves, but the effect of those actions on others. Part of that transformative action will be the words we write for others to read.

Morality, in other words, is inescapable, because choice and the society of others are inevitable. We can't possibly escape our connection to the people around us nor foresee the full consequence of anything we do. The ripples our actions cause branch outward into the known and unknown, the echoes we create reverberate through time and memory. And so for all the daring in our action there is the humility of the result.

As you launch your characters through the gauntlet of want and conflict, you will see this in your own life, suffer the scars, feel the tension of consequence like a wind humming through you. You will find yourself in your words if you work honestly and deeply.

Or, as I noted at the very beginning of this book, every work of fiction explores four key questions:

Who am I?
Where do I come from?
Where am I going?
What does it mean?

These questions apply not just to your characters. They apply to you. And the exploration is ongoing.

For me, this is the writer's journey. If there's anything universally true about the trip, I guess I'll know once they drop me off. Which applies to the creative life as well: Anyone who grabs you by the shirt and yodels into your face that there's one and only one true path—the way it must be done, the underlying structure to all dramatic narrative, the heart of every story, the journey every hero must undergo, the fundamental secret to every whatever—he's pointing you down a blind alley. Instead look to the writers you admire, study them, learn from them, obsess on their work like a jealous lover. Gain a sense for the relentless search for worth in their writing, the reckless adventure of a meaningful life, not just the thrills and giggles. Attend to detail and steal wisely. Beyond that, you're on your own.

And that's a sly, last, sneaky truth about the hero. And you. There comes that point where everything the hero knows proves lacking. At the decisive moment, she has to find the wildness within, get creative. To create is to change, and to that extent making art is a heroic act, an act of character. Every day with every word, chiseled from the wall of silence within, you rise up and stagger on, hoping to become just a little braver, wiser, more loving. You change. Before the demeaning blankness of the page, perched on the edge of the inscrutable future, you are the hero.

Don't let it go to your head. There's plenty more to come, and anything can happen.

BIBLIOGRAPHY

Addonizio, Kim. *Ordinary Genius: A Guide for the Poet Within.* W. W. Norton, 2009.

Auerbach, Erich. *Mimesis: The Representation of Reality in Western Literature.* Princeton University Press, 1974.

Baxter, Charles. *The Art of Subtext: Beyond Plot.* Graywolf Press, 2007.

Block, Lawrence. *Telling Lies for Fun and Profit: A Manual for Fiction Writers.* Quill, published by William Morrow, 1981.

Brooks, Peter. *Reading for Plot.* Harvard University Press. First Paperback Edition, 1992.

Browne, Renni, and Dave King. *Self-Editing for Fiction Writers: How to Edit Yourself into Print.* HarperPerennial, 1993.

Campbell, Joseph. *The Hero with a Thousand Faces.* Bollingen Series 17, Princeton University Press, 1968.

Camus, Albert. "On the Future of Tragedy," from *Lyrical and Critical Essays.* Vintage Books, 1970.

Chaikin, Joseph. *The Presence of the Actor.* Theatre Communications Group, 1993.

Chekhov, Michael. *To the Actor.* Harper & Row, 1953.

Damrosch, Leo. *The Enlightenment Invention of the Modern Self.* The Teaching Company, Great Courses Series, 2003.

Dillard, Annie. *The Writing Life.* Harper & Row, 1989.

Dobyns, Stephen. *Best Words, Best Order: Essays on Poetry*. Palgrave Macmillan, 1996.

Egri, Lajos. *The Art of Dramatic Writing: Its Basis in the Creative Interpretation of Human Motives*. A Touchstone Book, published by Simon & Schuster, 1960.

Forster, E. M. *Aspects of the Novel*. Mariner Books, 1956.

Frey, James N. *How to Write a Damn Good Novel*. St. Martin's Press, 1987.

George, Elizabeth. *Write Away: One Novelist's Approach to Fiction and the Writing Life*. Harper, 2004.

Goldberg, Lee, and William Rabkin. *Successful Television Writing*. John Wiley & Sons, 2003.

Hagen, Uta, with Haskel Frankel. *Respect for Acting*. Macmillan, 1973.

Hall, Oakley. *The Art and Craft of Novel Writing*. Writer's Digest Books, 1989.

Hemingway, Ernest. *Death in the Afternoon*. First Scribner Classics Edition, 1999.

Iyer, Pico. *The Man Within My Head*. Alfred A. Knopf, 2012.

James, William. *Principles of Psychology*. The Living Library/The World Publishing Company, 1948.

Kundera, Milan. *The Art of the Novel*. Grove Press, 1986.

Lakoff, George. *Moral Politics: How Liberals and Conservatives Think*. University of Chicago Press, 2002.

Mamet, David. *Three Uses of the Knife: On the Nature and Purpose of Drama*. Vintage Books, 2000.

———. *True and False: Heresy and Common Sense for the Actor*. Vintage Books, 1997.

McKee, Robert. *Story: Substance, Structure, Style, and the Principles of Screenwriting*. ItBooks, an imprint of HarperCollins, 1997.

Mullan, John. *How Novels Work*. Oxford University Press, 2006.

Nietzsche, Friedrich. *The Birth of Tragedy and the Geneology of Morals*. Doubleday Anchor Books, 1956.

Plutarch. *Lives—The Dryden Translation*. Modern Library, 2001.

Roderick, Rick. *The Self Under Siege: Philosophy in the Twentieth Century*. The Teaching Company, Great Courses Series, 1997.

Saccio, Peter. *Modern British Drama*. The Teaching Company, Great Courses Series, 1998.